Received 10-14-95 ($24.95)

HEROES OF OUR TIME
239 MEN OF THE VIETNAM WAR AWARDED THE
MEDAL OF HONOR

KENNETH N. JORDAN, SR.

239 MEN OF THE VIETNAM WAR
AWARDED THE
MEDAL OF HONOR

HEROES OF OUR TIME

KENNETH N. JORDAN, SR.

Schiffer Military/Aviation History
Atglen, PA

Acknowledgements

I would like to express my appreciation to all those who helped me with this book. My wife Louise, son Ken Jr., daughter Kathryn and a special thanks to my daughter Diane who spent many hours helping me with the research and typing of this book. To the VFW Vietnam Veterans Post in Wickliffe, Ohio. To my family and friends who helped along the way (it would take another book just to mention all their names). To the nice people at the Euclid, Beachwood and Willoughby, Ohio Libraries who helped me with my research. Last, but certainly not least, the 239 Medal of Honor recipients.

Sources

Get This

The Senate Committee on Veterans' Affairs. *Medal of Honor Recipients 1863-1978*. Washington, D.C.: U.S. Government Printing Office, 1979.
The New York Times, New York, NY.
The Cleveland Plain Dealer, Cleveland, OH.
The News Herald, Willoughby, Oh.

★ Dedication ★

This book is dedicated to the millions of men and women who served in Vietnam, with a special dedication to my brother James J. Jordan who served with the 4th Division at Dak To, Vietnam from September of 1967 to August of 1968. To me and to millions of other Americans, anyone who could face those incredible fears is a HERO.

HERO: A person admired for courage, nobility or exploits, especially in war. A person admired for qualities or achievements and regarded as an ideal or model.

Book Design by Robert Biondi.
Rear dust jacket photo courtesy of John Heyer.

Copyright © 1994 by Kenneth N. Jordan, Sr.
Library of Congress Catalog Number: 94-68857

Printed in the United States of America.
ISBN: 0-88740-741-2

We are interested in hearing from authors with book ideas on related topics.

Published by Schiffer Publishing Ltd.
77 Lower Valley Road
Atglen, PA 19310
Please write for a free catalog.
This book may be purchased from the publisher.
Please include $2.95 postage.
Try your bookstore first.

CONTENTS

2/

Dedication   4

Acknowledgements & Sources   4

Introduction   7

Chapter 1: 1964   8
Chapter 2: 1965   13
Chapter 3: 1966   33

Definition

Chapter 4: 1967   71
Chapter 5: 1968   147
Chapter 6: 1969   238
Chapter 7: 1970   303
Chapter 8: 1971   334
Chapter 9: 1972   343

Summary   348
Index   349

INTRODUCTION

The Medal of Honor is the highest military award for bravery that can be given to an individual in the United States of America. The president may award, and present in the name of congress, a Medal of Honor to a person who, while a member of the Armed Forces, distinguished himself conspicuously by gallantry and intrepidity at the risk of his life above and beyond the call of duty.

. . . firing his rifle as he advanced to neutralize the defenders. He dropped a grenade into the bunker and vaulted beyond. As the bunker blew up, he came under fire again. Rolling into a ditch to gain cover, he moved toward the new source of fire. Nearing the position, he leaped from the ditch and advanced with a grenade in one hand and firing his rifle with the other. He was gravely wounded just before he reached the bunker, but with a last valiant effort he staggered forward and destroyed the bunker, and its defenders with a grenade.

Fiction? Another "Rambo" story? No, this is an actual account of 1st Lt. James Gardner, one of the 239 men awarded the Medal of Honor in the Vietnam war.

From the first two men in 1964 to the last three in 1972, this book contains all 239 men who looked into the face of death and spit in its eye. You'll read their actual citations for gallantry above and beyond the call of duty. Interspersed are newspaper accounts of certain battles. Heroes Of Our Time is not about whether the war in Vietnam was right or wrong. It is simply a book honoring these 239 ordinary men who one day did something extraordinary and were awarded the Medal Of Honor. These men rose to the occasion, and along with the millions of others who served in Vietnam, never received their just recognition. They truly are the HEROES OF OUR TIME.

CHAPTER 1

1964

(† - Indicates Posthumous Award)

Note: The following newspaper article concerning Vietnam appeared on page 2 of *The New York Times*, January 1, 1964:

Johnson Promises Broadest Support To Saigon In 1964

TOKYO, Wed., Jan. 1 (AP) - President Johnson assured South Vietnam today that the United States would continue to offer that country "the fullest measure of support."

In a New Year's message to the head of South Vietnam's military regime, Maj. Gen. Goung Van Minh, Mr. Johnson pledged a flow of military aid and personnel "as needed to assist you in achieving victory" over Communist guerrillas.

The President's letter, distributed here by the Vietnamese press agency, also opposed neutralization of South Vietnam, an idea espoused by president de Gaulle of France.

"Neutralization of South Vietnam would only be another name for a Communist takeover," Mr. Johnson wrote. "Peace will return to your country just as soon as the authorities in Hanoi (capital of Communist North Vietnam) Cease and desist from their terrorist aggression."

"Our aims, I know, identical with yours: To enable your Government to protect its people from the acts of terror perpetrated by Communist insurgents from the north," Mr. Johnson went on. "As the forces of your Government become increasingly capable of dealing with this aggression, American military personnel in South Vietnam can be progressively withdrawn."

"Thus, your Government and mine are in complete agreement on the political aspects of your war against the forces of enslavement, brutality and material misery. Within this framework of political agreement we can confidently continue and improve our cooperation."

DONLON, ROGER HUGH C.
Rank and Organization: Captain, U.S. Army.
Born: January 30, 1934, Saugerties, New York
Entered Service At: Fort Chaffee, Arkansas
Place and Date: Near Nam Dong, Republic of Vietnam, July 6, 1964.
Citation: For conspicuous gallantry and intrepidity at the risk of his life above and beyond the call of duty while defending a U.S. military installation against a fierce attack by hostile forces. Capt. Donlon was serving as the commanding officer of the U.S. Army Special Forces Detachment A-726 at Camp Nam Dong when a reinforced Viet Cong battalion suddenly launched a full scale, predawn attack on the camp. During the violent battle that ensued, lasting five hours and resulting in heavy casualties on both sides, Capt. Donlon directed the defense operations in the midst of an enemy barrage of mortar shells, falling grenades, and extremely heavy gun fire. Upon the initial onslaught, he swiftly marshaled his forces and ordered the removal of the needed ammunition from a blazing building. He then dashed through a hail of small arms and exploding hand grenades to abort a breach of the main gate. Enroute to this position he detected an enemy demolition team of three in the proximity of the main gate and quickly annihilated them. Although exposed to the intense grenade attack, he then succeeded in reaching a 60mm mortar position despite sustaining a severe stomach wound as he was within five yards of the gunpit. When he discovered that most of the men in this gunpit were also wounded, he completely disregarded his own injury, directed their withdrawal to a location 30 meters away, and again risked his life by remaining behind and covering the movement with the utmost effectiveness. Noticing that his team sergeant was unable to evacuate the gunpit he crawled toward him and, while dragging the fallen soldier out of the gunpit, an enemy mortar exploded and inflicted a wound in Capt. Donlon's left shoulder. Although suffering from multiple wounds, he carried the abandoned 60mm mortar weapon to a new location 30 meters away where he found three wounded defenders. After administering first aid and encouragement to these men, he left the weapon with them, headed toward another position, and retrieved a 57mm recoilless rifle. Then with great courage and coolness under fire, he returned to the abandoned gunpit, evacuated ammunition for the two weapons, and while crawling and dragging the urgently needed ammunition, received a third wound in

his leg from an enemy hand grenade. Despite his critical physical condition, he again crawled 175 meters to an 81mm position and directed firing operations which protected the seriously threatened east sector of the camp. He then moved to an eastern 60mm mortar position and upon determining that the vicious enemy assault had weakened, crawled back to the gunpit with the 60mm mortar, set it up for defensive operations, and turned it over to two defenders with minor wounds. Without hesitation, he left his sheltered position, and moved from position to position around the beleaguered perimeter while hurling hand grenades at the enemy and inspiring his men to superhuman effort. As he bravely continued to move around the perimeter, a mortar shell exploded, wounding him in the face and the body. As the long awaited daylight brought defeat to the enemy forces and their retreat back to the jungle leaving behind 54 of their dead, many weapons, and grenades, Capt. Donlon immediately reorganized his defenses and administered first aid to the wounded. His dynamic leadership, fortitude, and valiant efforts inspired not only the American personnel but the friendly Vietnamese defenders as well and resulted in the successful defense of the camp. Capt. Donlon's extraordinary heroism, at the risk of his life above and beyond the call of duty are in the highest traditions of the U.S. Army and reflect great credit upon himself and the Armed Forces of his country.

Note: The Viet Cong assault against the Special Forces camp at Nam Dong was the first major attack against an American base in South Vietnam.

†COOK, DONALD GILBERT

Rank and Organization: Colonel, U.S. Marine Corps, Prisoner of War.

Born: August 9, 1934, Brooklyn, New York

Entered Service At: Brooklyn, New York

Place and Date: Vietnam, December 31, 1964 to December 8, 1964.

Citation: For conspicuous gallantry and intrepidity at the risk of his life above and beyond the call of duty while interned as a Prisoner of War. Despite the fact that by doing so he would bring about harsher treatment for himself, Colonel (then Captain) Cook established himself as a senior prisoner, even though in actuality he was not. Repeatedly assuming more than his share of their health, Colonel Cook willingly and unselfishly put the interest of his comrades before that of his own well-being and, eventually, his life. Giving more needy men his medicine and drug allowance while constantly nursing them, he risked infection from contagious diseases while in a rapidly deteriorating state of health. This unselfish and exemplary conduct, coupled with his refusal to stray even the slightest from the Code of Conduct, earned him the deepest respect from not only his fellow prisoners, but his captors as well. Rather than negotiate for his own release or better treatment, he steadfastly frustrated attempts by the Viet Cong to break his indomitable spirit, and passed this same resolve on to the men whose well-being he so closely associated himself. Knowing his refusal would prevent his release prior to the end of the war, and also knowing his chances for prolonged survival would be small in the event of continued refusal, he chose nevertheless to adhere to a Code of Conduct far above that which could be expected. His personal valor and exceptional spirit of loyalty in the face of almost certain death reflected the highest credit upon Colonel Cook, the Marine Corps, and the United States Naval Service.

CHAPTER 2

1965

(† - Indicates Posthumous Award)

Note: The following newspaper article concerning Vietnam appeared on the front page of *The New York Times* on January 1, 1965:

Saigon Leaders Meet Amid Signs Crisis Is Ending

SAIGON, South Vietnam, Dec. 31 - Lieut. Gen. Nguyen Khanh, commander in chief of South Vietnam's armed forces, met with civilian leaders here today amid indications that a compromise solution to the political crisis in Saigon had been reached.

He conferred with Phan Khac Suu, the chief of state, and Premier Tran Van Houng for two hours after he had flown in from two days of talks with other generals in the beach resort of Vung Tau, 50 miles southeast of Saigon.

After the meeting a spokesman for Mr. Suu said the chief of state wanted a committee set up as soon as possible to speed arrangements for convening a National Congress, which would be South Vietnam's permanent legislature.

The spokesman did not say whether Mr. Suu and Gen. Khanh had reached complete agreement.

6 Members Envisioned

He declared that the committee envisioned by Mr. Suu would have six members, which would make it less than half the size of the High National Council, the provisional legislature that was dissolved by the generals 11 days ago.

The United States has made it clear that it regards political unity in South Vietnam and a civilian government free of military interference as vital to sustain an effective war effort against the Viet Cong guerrilla forces.

The generals' action started the present crisis, which put a severe strain on relations with the United States.

Washington wants a restoration of the High National Council in some form and the release of its arrested members.

WILLIAMS, CHARLES Q.

Rank and Organization: First Lieutenant (then 2d Lt.), U.S. Army, 5th Special Forces Group.
Born: September 17, 1933, Charleston, South Carolina
Entered Service At: Fort Jackson, South Carolina
Place and Date: Dong Xoai, Republic of Vietnam, June 9 & 10, 1965.
Citation: First Lt. Williams distinguished himself by conspicuous gallantry and intrepidity at the risk of his life above and beyond the call of duty while defending the Special Forces Camp against a violent attack by hostile forces that lasted 14 hours. 1st Lt. Williams was serving as executive officer of a Special Forces Detachment when an estimated Viet Cong reinforced regiment struck the camp and threatened to overrun it and the adjacent district headquarters. He awoke personnel, organized them, determined the source of the insurgents' main effort and led the troops to their defensive positions on the south and west walls. Then, after running to the District Headquarters to establish communications, he found that there was no radio operational with which to communicate with his commanding officer in the other compound. To reach the other compound, he traveled through darkness but was halted in this effort by a combination of shrapnel in his right leg and the increase of Viet Cong gunfire. Ignoring his wound, he returned to the district headquarters to direct the defense against the first assault. As the insurgents attempted to scale the walls and as some of the Vietnamese defenders began to retreat, he dashed through a barrage of gunfire, succeeded in rallying these defenders, and led them back to their positions. Although wounded in the thigh and left leg during this gallant action, he returned to his position and, upon being told that communications were reestablished and that his commanding officer was seriously wounded, Lt. Williams took charge of actions in both compounds. Then, in an attempt to reach the communications bunker, he sustained wounds in the stomach and right arm from grenade fragments. As the defensive positions on the walls had been held for hours and casualties were mounting, he ordered the consolidation of the American personnel from both compounds to establish a defense in the district building. After radio contact was made with a friendly air controller, he disregarded his wounds and directed the defense from the district building, using descending flares as reference points to adjust air

strikes. By his courage, he inspired his team to hold out against the insurgent force that was closing in on them and throwing grenades into the windows of the building. As daylight arrived and the Viet Cong continued to besiege the stronghold, firing a machine-gun directly south of the district building, he was determined to eliminate this menace that threatened the lives of his men. Taking a 3.5 rocket launcher and a volunteer to load it, he worked his way across open terrain, reached the berm south of the district headquarters, and took aim at the Viet Cong machine-gun 150 meters away. Although the sight was faulty, he succeeded in hitting the machine-gun. While he and the loader were trying to return to the district headquarters, they were both wounded. With a fourth wound, this time in the right arm and leg, and realizing he was unable to carry his wounded comrade back to the district building, Lt. Williams pulled him to a covered position and made his way back to the district building where he sought the help of others who went out and evacuated the injured soldier. Although seriously wounded and tired, he continued to direct the air strikes closer to the defensive position. As morning turned to afternoon and the Viet Cong pressed their effort with direct recoilless rifle fire into the building, he ordered the evacuation of the seriously wounded to the safety of the communications bunker. When informed that helicopters would attempt to land as the hostile gunfire had abated, he led his team from the building to the artillery position, making certain of the timely evacuation of the wounded from the communications area, and then on to the pickup point. Despite resurgent Viet Cong gunfire, he directed the rapid evacuation of all personnel. Throughout the long battle, he was undaunted by the vicious Viet Cong assault and inspired the defenders in decimating the determined insurgents. 1st Lt. Williams extraordinary heroism, are in the highest traditions of the U.S. Army and reflect great credit upon himself and the Armed Forces of his country.

†SHIELDS, MARVIN G.
Rank and Organization: Construction Mechanic Third Class, U.S. Navy, Seabee Team 1104.
Born: December 30, 1939, Port Townsend, Washington
Entered Service At: Seattle, Washington
Place and Date: Dong Xoai, Republic of Vietnam, June 10, 1965
Citation: For conspicuous gallantry and intrepidity at the risk of his life above and beyond the call of duty. Although wounded when the compound of Detachment A-342, 5th Special Forces Group (Airborne), 1st Special Forces, came under intense fire from an estimated reinforced Viet Cong regiment employing machine-guns, heavy weapons and small arms, Shields continued to resupply his fellow Americans who needed ammunition and to return the enemy fire for a period of approximately three hours, at which time the Viet Cong launched a massive attack at close range with flame-throwers, hand grenades and small-arms fire. Wounded a second time during this attack, Shields nevertheless assisted in carrying a more critically wounded man to safety, and then resumed firing at the enemy for four more hours. When the commander asked for a volunteer to accompany him in an attempt to knock out an enemy machine-gun emplacement which was endangering the lives of all the personnel in the compound because of the accuracy of its fire, Shields unhesitatingly volunteered for this extremely hazardous mission. Proceeding toward their objective with a 3.5 inch rocket launcher, they succeeded in destroying the enemy machine-gun emplacement, thus undoubtedly saving the lives of many of their fellow servicemen in the compound. Shields was mortally wounded by hostile fire while returning to his defensive position. His heroic initiative and great personal valor in the face of intense enemy fire sustain and enhance the finest traditions of the U.S. Naval Service.

Note: The following is a newspaper account of the preceding battle in which both Lt. Williams and Navy Seabee Shields were involved:

21 Yanks Vietnam Victims

SAIGON, Vietnam (AP)-A curtain of machine-gun fire cut down Vietnamese reinforcements today as they jumped from helicop-

ters at Dong Xoai, a district capital overrun by 1,500 Viet Cong. All the 21 Americans at a nearby special forces camp were listed as dead, missing or wounded.

A U.S. military spokesman said the losses at Dong Xoai, 60 miles north of Saigon, were the heaviest suffered by the United States in any single engagement of the Vietnam war.

The casualty reports varied. Official reports said at least 1 of the Americans was definitely killed, 6 and possibly 7 were missing and 13 wounded.

But at Phuoc Vinh, an advance command post from which reinforcements were being dispatched by helicopters, officers said all living Americans - only nine wounded - had been evacuated.

†REASONER, FRANK S.

Rank and Organization: First Lieutenant, U.S. Marine Corps, Company A, 3d Recon. Bat., 3d Marine Division.
Born: September 16, 1937, Spokane, Washington
Entered Service At: Kellogg, Idaho
Place and Date: Near Da Nang, Republic of Vietnam, July 12, 1965.
Citation: For conspicuous gallantry and intrepidity at the risk of his life above and beyond the call of duty. The reconnaissance patrol led by 1st Lt. Reasoner had deeply penetrated heavily controlled enemy territory when it came under extremely heavy fire from an estimated 50 to 100 Viet Cong insurgents. Accompanying the advance and the point that consisted of five men, he immediately deployed his men for an assault after the Viet Cong had opened fire from numerous concealed positions. Boldly shouting encouragement, and virtually isolated from the main body, he organized a base of fire for an assault on the enemy positions. The slashing fury of the Viet Cong machine-gun and automatic weapons fire made it impossible for the main body to move forward. Repeatedly exposing himself to the devastating attack he skillfully provided covering fire, killing at least two Viet Cong and effectively silencing an automatic weapons position in a valiant attempt to effect evacuation of a wounded man. As casualties began to mount his radio operator was wounded and 1st Lt. Reasoner immediately moved to his side and tended his wounds. When the radio operator was hit a second time while attempting to reach a covered position, 1st Lt. Reasoner courageously running to his aid through the grazing machine-gun fire fell mortally wounded. His indomitable fighting spirit, valiant leadership and unflinching devotion to duty provided the inspiration that was to enable the patrol to complete its mission without further casualties. In the face of almost certain death he gallantly gave his life in the service of his country. His actions upheld the highest traditions of the Marine Corps and the U.S. Naval Service.

O'MALLEY, ROBERT E.
Rank and Organization: Sergeant (then Cpl.), U.S. Marine Corps, Company I, 3d Bat., 3d Marine Regiment, 3d Marine Division.
Born: June 3, 1943, New York, New York
Entered Service At: New York, New York
Place and Date: Near An Cu'ong 2, South Vietnam, August 18, 1965.
Citation: For conspicuous gallantry and intrepidity in action against the communist (Viet Cong) forces at the risk of his life above and beyond the call of duty. While leading his squad in the assault against a strongly entrenched enemy force, his unit came under intense small-arms fire. With complete disregard for his personal safety, Sgt. O'Malley raced across an open rice paddy to a trench line where the enemy forces were located. Jumping into the trench, he attacked the Viet Cong with his rifle and grenades, and single handedly killed 8 of the enemy. He then led his squad to the assistance of an adjacent Marine unit which was suffering heavy casualties. Continuing to press forward, he reloaded his weapon and fired with telling effect into the enemy emplacement. He personally assisted in the evacuation of several wounded Marines, and again regrouping the remnants of his squad, he returned to the point of the heaviest fighting. Ordered to an evacuation point by an officer, Sgt. O'Malley gathered his besieged and badly wounded squad, and boldly led them under fire to a helicopter for withdrawal. Although three times wounded in this encounter, and facing imminent death from a fanatic and determined enemy, he steadfastly refused evacuation and continued to cover his squad's boarding of the helicopters while, from an exposed position, he delivered fire against the enemy until his wounded men were evacuated. Only then, with his last mission accomplished, did he permit himself to be removed from the battlefield. By his valor, leadership, and courageous efforts in behalf of his comrades, he served as an inspiration to all who observed him, and reflected the highest credit upon the Marine Corps and the U.S. Naval Service.

†**PAUL, JOE C.**
Rank and Organization: Lance Cpl., U.S. Marine Corps, Company H, 2d Bat., 4th Marine Regiment, 3d Marine Division.
Born: April 23, 1946, Williamsburg, Kentucky
Entered Service At: Dayton, Ohio
Place and Date: Near Chu Lai, Republic of Vietnam, August 18, 1965.
Citation: For conspicuous gallantry and intrepidity at the risk of his life above and beyond the call of duty. In violent battle, L/Cpl. Paul's platoon sustained five casualties as it was temporarily pinned down, by devastating mortar, recoilless rifle, automatic weapons, and rifle fire delivered by insurgent communist (Viet Cong) forces in well entrenched positions. The wounded Marines were unable to move from their perilously exposed positions forward of the remainder of their platoon, and were suddenly subjected to a barrage of white phosphorous rifle grenades. L/Cpl. Paul, fully aware that his tactics would almost certainly result in serious injury or death to himself, chose to disregard his safety and boldly dashed across the fire-swept rice paddies, placed himself between his wounded comrades and the enemy, and delivered effective suppressive fire with his automatic weapon in order to divert the attack long enough to allow the casualties to be evacuated. Although critically wounded during the course of the battle, he resolutely remained in his exposed position and continued to fire his rifle until he collapsed and was evacuated. By his fortitude and gallant spirit of self-sacrifice in the face of almost certain death, he saved the lives of several of his fellow Marines. His heroic action served to inspire all who observed him and reflect the highest credit upon himself, the Marine Corps and the U.S. Naval Service. He gallantly gave his life in the cause of freedom.

Note: The following is a newspaper account of the preceding battle in which both Sgt. O'Malley and L/Cpl. Paul earned the Medal of Honor:

U.S. MARINES TRAP 2,000 OF VIETCONG, KILL "HUNDREDS"

Ships and Planes Aid Drive
— Reds Strike at Mountain Camp

SAIGON, South Vietnam, Thursday, Aug. 19 — United States marines have trapped about 2,000 Vietcong guerrillas with their backs to the sea and killed "hundreds" of them in the first major battle involving American troops in Vietnam, a military spokesman reported yesterday.

But as the successful attack near Chulai continued this morning, other vietcong troops were attacking and threatening to overrun a Special Forces camp at Daksut, manned by 12 United States defenders and mountain tribesmen they have armed and trained.

Daksut is an isolated mountain post 300 miles north of Saigon and about 90 miles southwest of the scene of the Marine battle.

Marine casualties were described officially as "light," but it appeared they were the highest ever suffered by an American unit in one battle in Vietnam. Communist mortar fire did most of the damage, Marine sources indicated.

Landing by Air and Sea

The marines landed yesterday morning and throughout the day by helicopter and from the sea by landing craft in the area of Vantuong, a village 315 miles northeast of Saigon.

By late last night they reported that they had surrounded the guerrillas and "continued to grind" them toward the South China Sea. The enemy had been reported as being "heavily entrenched" and armed with such weapons as recoilless rifles.

[A Marine Corps spokesman said the bodies of 552 Vietcong had been counted at the end of the first day's fighting on Vantuong peninsula. The Associated Press reported.]

The area of the fighting, which is 16 miles south of the United States air base at Chulai, has been controlled and held by the Vietcong for two years, the spokesman said.

500 to 600 in Force

The force that attacked at Daksut was estimated at a battalion, or 500 to 600 men.

By early this morning, the Vietcong guerrillas were reported to have occupied about half of the 400-man Vietnamese sector of the camp and to have penetrated the American Special Forces compound.

Communications with the camp were cut off about dawn. A radio report shortly before midnight said that the camp was afire in several places and that ammunition bunkers were exploding.

The operation by the marines near Chulai was given the code name Starlight. It began with elements of the Third and Fourth Marine Regiments landing in helicopters near Vantuong while other marines made the first combat amphibious landing of the war. Part of the Third Regiment was placed by helicopter as a blocking force across the arms of a small peninsula north of the two landings.

A spokesman said that by noon the troops landed by helicopter linked up with those landed by sea "to close the trap completely around three sides of the enemy forces."

About noon the marines came under fire from 57-mm recoilless rifles.

In addition to the assault by Marine rifle companies, the Vietcong force was high by artillery, naval gunfire and air strikes, the military spokesman said.

The marines used reserves during the battle. By early afternoon yesterday, elements of the Seventh Regiment landing team were brought into play and landed from the aircraft carrier Iwo Jima, the spokesman said. By 4:30 P.M., more marines from the attack transport Tandaga went ashore to join the fight.

It was reported that marine helicopters had flown nearly 1,000 sorties, ferrying troops, giving fire support and resupplying infantry forces. Unofficially, it was said there were many medical evacuation flights, indicating marine casualties.

In Saigon, the United States Military Command issued a summary of military activities for last week reporting that 1,330 Vietcong were killed in comparison with eight Americans and 215 South Vietnamese soldiers. Twenty-four Americans were wounded and one was listed as missing.

Battle On in Quangtri

A sizable battle was continuing in Quangtri Province near the 17th parallel, forming the border with North Vietnam. It was reported that a large South Vietnamese force probing into the Vietcong-controlled Balong Valley had killed 39 Vietcong adding to the 32 killed since the operation began Saturday.

It was noticed in the daily summary of air actions over North Vietnam that an item said that United States Marine Phantom jets had encountered light antiaircraft fire while flying a "support" mission about 65 miles northeast of the port city of Haiphong, one of the urban areas exempted from air attack.

Spokesmen said they could not say what the Phantoms had been supporting and that they had no report of an air strike in the area. One spokesman said he could not remember any earlier strikes in the area or so close to Haiphong.

†PIERCE, LARRY S.

Rank and Organization: Sergeant, U.S. Army, Headquarters Company, 1st Bat. (Airborne), 503d Infantry, 173d Airborne Brigade.
Born: July 6, 1941, Wewoka, Oklahoma
Entered Service At: Fresno, California
Place and Date: Near Ben Cat, Republic of Vietnam, September 20, 1965.
Citation: For conspicuous gallantry and intrepidity at the risk of his life above and beyond the call of duty. Sgt. Pierce was serving as squad leader in a reconnaissance platoon when his patrol was ambushed by hostile forces. Through his inspiring leadership and personal courage, the squad succeeded in eliminating an enemy machine-gun and routing the opposing force. While pursuing the fleeing enemy, the squad came upon a dirt road and, as the main body of his men entered the road, Sgt. Pierce discovered an antipersonnel mine emplaced in the road bed. Realizing that the mine could destroy the majority of his squad, Sgt. Pierce saved the lives of his men at the sacrifice of his own life by throwing himself directly onto the mine as it exploded. Through his indomitable courage, complete disregard for his safety, and profound concern for his fellow soldiers, he averted loss of life and injury to the members of his squad. Sgt. Pierce's extraordinary heroism, at the cost of his life, are in the highest traditions of the U.S. Army and reflect great credit upon himself and the Armed Forces of his country.

†OLIVE, MILTON L. III
Rank and Organization: Private First Class, U.S. Army, Company B, 2d Battalion (Airborne), 503d Infantry, 173d Airborne Brigade.
Born: November 7, 1946, Chicago, Illinois
Entered Service At: Chicago, Illinois
Place and Date: Phu Coung, Republic of Vietnam, October 22, 1965.
Citation: For conspicuous gallantry and intrepidity at the risk of his life above and beyond the call of duty. Pfc. Olive was a member of the 3d Platoon of Company B, as it moved through the jungle to find the Viet Cong operating in the area. Although the platoon was subjected to a heavy volume of enemy gunfire and pinned down temporarily, it retaliated by assaulting the Viet Cong positions, causing the enemy to flee. As the platoon pursued the insurgents, Pfc. Olive and four other soldiers were moving through the jungle together when a grenade was thrown into their midst. Pfc. Olive saw the grenade, and saved the lives of his fellow soldiers at the sacrifice of his by grabbing the grenade in his hand and falling on it to absorb the blast with his body. Through his bravery, unhesitating actions, and complete disregard for his safety, he prevented additional loss of life or injury to the members of his platoon. Pfc. Olive's extraordinary heroism, at the risk of his life above and beyond the call of duty are in the highest traditions of the U.S. Army and reflect great credit upon himself and the Armed Forces of his country.

JOEL, LAWRENCE
Rank and Organization: Specialist Sixth Class (then Sp5c), U.S. Army, Headquarters Company, 1st Battalion (Airborne), 503d Infantry, 173d Airborne Brigade.
Born: February 22, 1928, Winston-Salem, North Carolina
Entered Service At: New York, New York
Place and Date: Republic of Vietnam, November 8, 1965.
Citation: For conspicuous gallantry and intrepidity at the risk of his life above and beyond the call of duty. Sp6c. Joel demonstrated indomitable courage, and professional skill when a numerically superior and well-concealed Viet Cong element launched a vicious attack that wounded or killed nearly every man in the lead squad of the company. After treating the men wounded by the initial burst of gunfire, he bravely moved forward to assist others who were wounded while proceeding to their objective. While moving from man to man, he was struck in the right leg by machine-gun fire. Although painfully wounded his desire to aid his fellow soldiers transcended all personal feeling. He bandaged his own wound and self-administered morphine to deaden the pain enabling him to continue his dangerous undertaking. Through this period of time, he constantly shouted words of encouragement to all around him. Then, completely ignoring the warnings of others, and his pain, he continued his search for wounded, exposing himself to hostile fire; and, as bullets dug up the dirt around him, he held plasma bottles high while kneeling completely engrossed in his life saving mission. Then, after being struck a second time and with a bullet lodged in his thigh, he dragged himself over the battlefield and succeeded in treating 13 more men before his medical supplies ran out. Displaying resourcefulness, he saved the life of one man by placing a plastic bag over a severe chest wound to congeal the blood. As one of the platoons pursued the Viet Cong, an insurgent force in concealed positions opened fire on the platoon and wounded many more soldiers. With a new stock of medical supplies, Sp6c. Joel again shouted words of encouragement as he crawled through an intense hail of gunfire to the wounded men. After the 24 hour battle subsided and the Viet Cong dead numbered 410, snipers continued to harass the company. Throughout the long battle, Sp6c. Joel never lost sight of his mission as a medical aidman and continued to comfort and treat the wounded until his own evacuation was ordered. His meticulous attention to duty saved a large number of

lives and his unselfish, daring example under most adverse conditions was an inspiration to all. Sp6c. Joel's profound concern for his fellow soldiers, at the risk of his life above and beyond the call of duty are in the highest traditions of the U.S. Army and reflect great credit upon himself and the Armed Forces of his country.

MARM, WALTER JOSEPH, JR.

Rank and Organization: First Lt. (then 2d Lt.), U.S. Army, Company A, 1st Battalion, 7th Cavalry, 1st Cavalry Division (Airmobile).

Born: November 20, 1941, Washington, Pennsylvania

Entered Service At: Pittsburgh, Pennsylvania

Place and Date: Vicinity of Ia Drang Valley, Republic of Vietnam, November 14, 1965.

Citation: For conspicuous gallantry and intrepidity at the risk of his life above and beyond the call of duty. As a platoon leader in the 1st Cavalry Division, 1st Lt. Marm demonstrated indomitable courage during a combat operation. His company was moving through the valley to relieve a friendly unit surrounded by an enemy force of estimated regimental size. 1st Lt. Marm led his platoon through withering fire until they were finally forced to take cover. Realizing that his platoon could not hold very long, and seeing four enemy soldiers moving into his position, he moved quickly under heavy fire and annihilated all four. Then, seeing that his platoon was receiving intense fire from a concealed machine-gun, he deliberately exposed himself to draw its fire. Thus locating its position, he attempted to destroy it with an antitank weapon. Although he inflicted casualties, the weapon did not silence the enemy fire. Quickly, disregarding the intense fire directed at him and his platoon, he charged 30 meters across open ground, and hurled grenades into the enemy position, killing some of the eight insurgents manning it. Although severely wounded, when his grenades were expended, armed with only a rifle, he continued the momentum of his assault on the position and killed the remainder of the enemy. 1st Lt. Marm's selfless actions reduced the fire on his platoon, broke the enemy assault, and rallied his unit to continue toward the accomplishment of this mission. 1st Lt. Marm's gallantry on the battlefield and his extraordinary intrepidity at the risk of his life are in the highest traditions of the U.S. Army and reflect great credit upon himself and the Armed Forces of his country.

Note: The following is a newspaper account of the preceding battle in which Lt. Marm earned the Medal of Honor:

G.I.'s Fight Heavy Battle
In Foothills Near Pleime

PLEIKU, South Vietnam, Monday, Nov. 15 - United States troops fought a sharp four-hour battle yesterday and today with a battalion of North Vietnamese regulars dug into a series of jungle ridges between Pleime and the Cambodian border.

The battle involved units of the First Cavalry Division (Airmobile).

Although the action slackened late in the afternoon, Airmobile officers here said it continued during the night and began building up at dawn toward what could develop into another sizable engagement.

The Airmobile men formed a defensive perimeter for the night around a helicopter landing zone in foothills of the small Iadrang River Valley and traded shots and automatic-weapons fire with the North Vietnamese above them.

U.S. Casualties Light

The Airmobile units were reported to have light casualties.

Yesterday afternoon, a United States Air Force Skyraider fighter-bomber was shot down while strafing and bombing the North Vietnamese positions. The aircraft exploded and burned on impact, and the pilot was presumed dead.

At 10 A.M. yesterday, three companies of Airmobile troops, totaling about 450 men, were carried in helicopters to the narrow Iadrang Valley, about 38 miles southwest of Pleiku and seven miles from the Cambodian border.

Since a brigade of the Airmobile Division was moved here from Ankhe two and a half weeks ago to help relieve the American Special Forces camp at Pleime, the Americans have been searching the jungles and mountains of this area to destroy the North Vietnamese units. The latest battle was their fourth serious contact with the enemy.

So far the Airmobile men have counted the bodies of at least 20 North Vietnamese killed in the fighting yesterday afternoon. Commanders at the battlefield estimate that 50 more enemy troops were cut down by the small-arms fire of the infantrymen or the inferno of the artillery shells, bombs and napalm from nearby 105mm howitzer batteries and planes.

The enemy troops were identified as North Vietnamese regulars initially by the fact that the dead were found wearing green combat fatigues and steel helmets unlike the makeshift Viet Cong guerrilla uniforms. A prisoner captured in the fighting was reported to have told interrogators that he belonged to a battalion from the North Vietnamese 304th Army Division.

This was believed to be the first time the Airmobile Division had encountered the 304th. United States intelligence officers have suspected for some time that a regiment of the 304th has infiltrated the Central Highlands.

By 4 P.M. the fire power of the ground troops, the planes and artillery had driven the North Vietnamese to their main defensive positions within the ridge lines, and Communist fire directly into the valley had slackened enough for other helicopters to land with two companies of reinforcements.

BARNUM, HARVEY C., JR.

Rank and Organization: Captain (then Lt.), U.S. Marine Corps, Company H, 2d Battalion, 9th Marines, 3d Marine Division.
Born: July 21, 1940, Cheshire, Connecticut
Entered Service At: Cheshire, Connecticut
Place and Date: Ky Phu in Quang Tin Province, Republic of Vietnam, December 18, 1965.
Citation: For conspicuous gallantry and intrepidity at the risk of his life above and beyond the call of duty. When the company was suddenly pinned down by a hail of extremely accurate enemy fire and was quickly separated from the remainder of the battalion by over 500 meters of open and fire-swept ground, and casualties mounted rapidly. Lt. Barnum quickly made a hazardous reconnaissance of the area, seeking targets for his artillery. Finding the rifle company commander mortally wounded and the radio operator killed, he, with complete disregard for his safety, gave aid to the dying commander, then removed the radio from the dead operator and strapped it to himself. He immediately assumed command of the rifle company, and moving at once into the midst of the heavy fire, rallying and giving encouragement to all units, reorganized them to replace the loss of key personnel and led their attack on enemy positions from which deadly fire continued to come. His sound and swift decisions and his obvious calm served to stabilize the badly decimated units and his gallant example as he stood exposed repeatedly to point out targets served as an inspiration to all. Provided with two armed helicopters, he moved fearlessly through enemy fire to control the air attack against the firmly entrenched enemy while skillfully directing one platoon in a successful counterattack on the key enemy positions. Having thus cleared a small area, he requested and directed the landing of two transport helicopters for the evacuation of the dead and wounded. He then assisted in the mopping up and final seizure of the battalion's objective. His gallant initiative and heroic conduct reflected great credit upon himself and were in keeping with the highest traditions of the Marine Corps and the U.S. Naval Service.

CHAPTER 3

1966

(† - Indicates Posthumous Award)

Note: The following newspaper article concerning Vietnam appeared on page 2 of *The New York Times* Jan. 1, 1966:

President Gives Urgency To Drive Peace Campaign Pressed In Context Of Bombing Lull

WASHINGTON, Dec. 31 - President Johnson is making no new offers to North Vietnam in his "peace offensive" but is attempting to give added urgency and sincerity to the call for "unconditional negotiations" that he has been making since April 7.

The offer is being pressed home in major world capitals in a new context. When Mr. Johnson first urged "unconditional negotiations" in a speech at The Johns Hopkins University in Baltimore, it was only weeks after the bombing of North Vietnam started.

Now, in a world-wide diplomatic effort, he is reiterating the message in the context of a cessation of the bombing, which as yet has no time limit.

This was indicated today by high authorities as the "peace offensive" moved into its third day and the bombing pause into its eighth.

No Positive Response
So far, no positive response from the North Vietnamese or from

informed Communist leaders anywhere has been received in Washington. Administration officials see no significance in this, since they believe any significant response would take some time to develop.

Administration sources said that unpublicized channels, as well as the missions of W. Averell Harriman, Arthur J. Goldberg, and McGeorge Bundy were being used to emphasize the President's wish for unconditional negotiations.

American envoys are not, however, directly approaching representatives of the National Liberation Front, the political organization behind the Communist Viet Cong in South Vietnam.

Representatives of the Liberation Front are available in Paris, Algiers, Moscow and several other capitals.

Informed sources said it was likely that third parties were presenting the President's message to the Liberation Front representatives.

†GARDNER, JAMES A.

Rank and Organization: First Lieutenant, U.S. Army, Headquarters Company, 1st Battalion (Airborne), 327th Infantry, 1st Brigade, 101st Airborne Division.
Born: February 7, 1943, Dyersburg, Tennessee
Entered Service At: Memphis, Tennessee
Place and Date: My Canh, Vietnam, February 7, 1966.
Citation: For conspicuous gallantry and intrepidity in action at the risk of his life above and beyond the call of duty. 1st Lt. Gardner's platoon was advancing to relieve a company of the 1st Battalion that had been pinned down for several hours by a numerically superior enemy force in the village of My Canh, Vietnam. The enemy occupied a series of strongly fortified bunker positions which were mutually supporting and expertly concealed. Approaches to the position were well covered by an integrated pattern of fire including automatic weapons, machine-guns and mortars. Air strikes and artillery placed on the fortifications had little effect. 1st Lt. Gardner's platoon was to relieve the friendly company by encircling and destroying the enemy force. Even as it moved to begin the attack, the platoon was under heavy enemy fire. During the attack the enemy fire intensified. Leading the assault and disregarding his own safety, 1st Lt. Gardner charged through a withering hail of gun fire across an open rice paddy. Upon reaching the first bunker he destroyed it with a grenade and without hesitation dashed to the second bunker and eliminated it by tossing a grenade inside. Then, crawling swiftly along the dike of the rice paddy, he reached the third bunker. Before he could arm the grenade, the enemy gunner leaped forth, firing at him. 1st Lt. Gardner instantly returned the fire and killed the enemy gunner at a distance of six feet. Following the seizure of the main enemy position, he reorganized the platoon to continue the attack. Advancing to the new assault position, the platoon was pinned down by an enemy machine gun emplaced in a fortified bunker. 1st Lt. Gardner immediately collected several grenades and charged the enemy position, firing his rifle as he advanced to neutralize the defenders. He dropped the grenade into the bunker and vaulted beyond. As the bunker blew up, he came under fire again. Rolling into a ditch to gain cover, he moved toward the source of the fire. Nearing the position, he leaped from the ditch and advanced with a grenade in one hand and firing his rifle with the other. He was gravely wounded just before he reached

the bunker, but with a last valiant effort he staggered forward and destroyed the bunker and its defenders with a grenade. Although he fell dead on the rim of the bunker, his extraordinary actions so inspired the men of his platoon that they resumed the attack and completely routed the enemy. 1st Lt. Gardner's conspicuous gallantry was in the highest traditions of the U.S. Army and reflect great credit upon himself and the Armed Forces of his country.

†FERNANDEZ, DANIEL

Rank and Organization: Specialist Fourth Class, U.S. Army, Company C, 1st Battalion, 5th Infantry (Mechanized), 25th Infantry Division.

Born: June 30, 1944, Albuquerque, New Mexico

Entered Service At: Albuquerque, New Mexico

Place and Date: Cu Chi, Hau Nghia Province, Republic of Vietnam, February 18, 1966.

Citation: For conspicuous gallantry and intrepidity at the risk of his life above and beyond the call of duty. Sp4c. Fernandez demonstrated indomitable courage when the patrol was ambushed by a Viet Cong rifle company and driven back by the intense enemy automatic weapons fire before it could evacuate an American soldier who had been wounded in the Viet Cong attack. Sp4c. Fernandez, a sergeant and two other volunteers immediately fought their way through devastating fire and exploding grenades to reach the fallen soldier. Upon reaching their fallen comrade the sergeant was struck in the knee by machine-gun fire and immobilized. Sp4c. Fernandez took charge, rallied the left flank of his patrol and began to assist in the recovery of the wounded sergeant. While first aid was being administered to the wounded man, a sudden increase in the accuracy and the intensity of enemy fire forced the volunteer group to take cover. As they did, an enemy grenade landed in the midst of the group, although some men did not see it. Realizing there was no time for the wounded sergeant or the other men to protect themselves from the grenade blast, Sp4c. Fernandez vaulted over the wounded sergeant and threw himself on the grenade as it exploded, saving the lives of his four comrades at the sacrifice of his own life. Sp4c. Fernandez' profound concern for his fellow soldiers, at the risk of his life above and beyond the call of duty are in the highest traditions of the U.S. Army and reflect great credit upon himself and the Armed Forces of his country.

†CONNER, PETER S.

Rank and Organization: Staff Sergeant, U.S. Marine Corps, Company F, 2d Battalion, 3d Marines, 1st Marine Division.
Born: September 4, 1932, Orange, New Jersey
Entered Service At: South Orange, New Jersey
Place and Date: Quang Ngai Province, Republic of Vietnam, February 25, 1966.
Citation: For conspicuous gallantry and intrepidity in action against Viet Cong forces at the risk of his life above and beyond the call of duty. Leading his platoon on a search and destroy operation in an area made particularly hazardous by extensive cave and tunnel complexes, Sgt. Conner maneuvered his unit aggressively forward under intermittent enemy small-arms fire. Exhibiting particular alertness and keen observation, he spotted an enemy spider hole emplacement approximately 15 meters to his front. He pulled the pin from a fragmentation grenade intending to charge the hole boldly and drop the grenade into its depths. Upon pulling the pin he realized that the firing mechanism was faulty, and that even as he held the safety device firmly in place, the fuse charge was already activated. With only precious seconds to decide, he further realized that he could not cover the distance to the small opening of the spider hole in sufficient time, and that to hurl the deadly grenade in any direction would result in death or injury to some of his comrades tactically deployed near him. Manifesting extraordinary gallantry and with utter disregard for his personal safety, he chose to hold the grenade against his body in order to absorb the terrific explosion and spare his comrades. His act of extreme valor and selflessness in the face of virtually certain death, although leaving him mortally wounded, spared many of his fellow Marines from death or injury. His gallant action in giving his life in the cause of freedom, reflected great credit upon himself, the Marine Corps and the Armed Forces of the United States.

†**HIBBS, ROBERT JOHN**
Rank and Organization: Second Lieutenant, U.S. Army, Company B, 2d Battalion, 28th Infantry, 1st Infantry Division.
Born: April 21, 1943, Omaha, Nebraska
Entered Service At: Des Moines, Iowa
Place and Date: Don Dien Lo Ke, Republic of Vietnam, March 5, 1966.
Citation: For conspicuous gallantry and intrepidity at the risk of his life above and beyond the call of duty. 2d Lt. Hibbs was in command of a 15 man ambush patrol of the 2d Battalion, when his unit observed a company of Viet Cong advancing along the road toward the 2d Battalion's position. Informing his command post by radio of the impending attack, he prepared his men for the oncoming Viet Cong, emplaced two mines in their path and, when the insurgents were within 20 feet of the patrol's position, he fired the two antipersonnel mines, wounding or killing half of the enemy company. Then, to cover the withdrawal of his patrol, he threw hand-grenades, stepped onto the open road, and opened fire on the remainder of the Viet Cong force of approximately 50 men. Having rejoined his men, he was leading them toward the battalion perimeter when the patrol encountered the rear elements of another Viet Cong company deployed to attack the battalion. With the advantage of surprise, he directed a charge against the Viet Cong, which carried the patrol through the insurgent force, completely disrupting its attack. Learning that a wounded patrol member was wandering in the area between the two opposing forces and although moments from safety and wounded in the leg himself, he and a sergeant went back to the battlefield to recover the stricken man. After they maneuvered through the withering fire of two Viet Cong machine-guns, the sergeant grabbed the dazed soldier and dragged him back toward the friendly lines while 2d Lt. Hibbs remained behind to provide covering fire. Armed with only an M-16 and a pistol, but determined to destroy the enemy positions, he then charged the two machine-gun emplacements and was struck down. Before succumbing to his mortal wounds, he destroyed the starlight telescope sight attached to his rifle to prevent its capture and use by the Viet Cong. 2d Lt. Hibbs' profound concern for his fellow soldiers, and his intrepidity at the risk of his life above and beyond the call of duty are in the highest traditions of the U.S. Army and reflect great credit upon himself and the Armed Forces of his country.

FISHER, BERNARD FRANCIS
Rank and Organization: Major, U.S. Air Force, 1st Air Commandos.
Born: January 11, 1927, San Bernardino, California
Entered Service At: Kuna, Idaho
Place and Date: Bien Hoa and Pleiku, Vietnam, March 10, 1966.
Citation: For conspicuous gallantry and intrepidity at the risk of his life above and beyond the call of duty. On that date the special forces camp at A Shau was under attack by 2,000 North Vietnamese Army regulars. Hostile troops had positioned themselves between the airstrip and the camp. Other hostile troops had surrounded the camp and were continuously raking it with automatic weapons fire from the surrounding hills. The tops of the 1,500 foot hills were obscured by an 800 foot ceiling, limiting aircraft maneuverability and forcing pilots to operate within range of hostile gun positions, which often were able to fire down on the attacking aircraft. During the battle, Maj. Fisher observed a fellow airman crash land on the battle-torn airstrip. In the belief that the downed pilot was seriously injured and in imminent danger of capture, Maj. Fisher announced his intention to land on the airstrip to effect a rescue. Although aware of the extreme danger and likely failure of such an attempt, he elected to continue. Directing his own air cover, he landed his aircraft and taxied almost the full length of the runway, which was littered with battle debris and parts of an exploded aircraft. While effecting a successful rescue of the downed pilot, heavy ground fire was observed, with 19 bullets striking his aircraft. In the face of the withering gunfire, he applied power and gained enough speed to lift-off at the overrun of the airstrip. Maj. Fisher's profound concern for his fellow airman, and at the risk of his life above and beyond the call of duty are in the highest traditions of the U.S. Air Force and reflect great credit upon himself and the Armed Forces of his country.

†ROBINSON, JAMES W., JR.

Rank and Organization: Sergeant, U.S. Army, Company D, 2d Battalion, 16th Infantry, 1st Infantry Division.
Born: August 30, 1940, Hinsdale, Illinois
Entered Service At: Chicago, Illinois
Place and Date: Republic of Vietnam, April 11, 1966.
Citation: For conspicuous gallantry and intrepidity in action at the risk of his life above and beyond the call of duty. Company C was engaged in fierce combat with a Viet Cong battalion. Despite the heavy fire, Sgt. Robinson moved among the men of his fire team, instructing and inspiring them, and placing them in advantageous positions. Enemy snipers located in nearby trees were inflicting heavy casualties on forward elements of Sgt. Robinson's unit. Upon locating the enemy sniper whose fire was taking the heaviest toll, he took a grenade launcher and eliminated the sniper. Seeing a medic hit while administering aid to a wounded sergeant in front of his position and aware that now the two wounded men were at the mercy of the enemy, he charged through a withering hail of fire and dragged his comrades to safety, where he rendered first aid and saved their lives. As the battle continued and casualties mounted, Sgt. Robinson moved about under intense fire to collect from the wounded their weapons and ammunition and redistribute them to able-bodied soldiers. Adding his fire to that of his men, he assisted in eliminating a major enemy threat. Seeing another wounded comrade in front of his position, Sgt. Robinson again defied the enemy's fire to effect a rescue. In so doing he was himself wounded in the shoulder and leg. Despite his painful wounds, he dragged the soldier to shelter and saved his life by administering first aid. While patching his own wounds, he spotted an enemy machine-gun that had inflicted a number of casualties on the American force. His rifle ammunition expended, he seized two grenades and, in an act of unsurpassed heroism, charged toward the entrenched enemy weapon. Hit again in the leg, this time with a tracer round that set fire to his clothing, Sgt. Robinson ripped the burning clothing from his body and staggered through the enemy fire, now concentrated solely on him, to within grenade range of the enemy machine-gun position. Sustaining two additional chest wounds, he marshaled his fleeting physical strength and hurled the two grenades, thus destroying the enemy gun position, as he fell dead upon the battlefield. His magnificent display of leadership and bravery

saved several lives and inspired his soldiers to defeat the numerically superior enemy force. Sgt. Robinson's conspicuous gallantry and intrepidity, at the cost of his life, are in keeping with the finest traditions of the U.S. Army and reflect great credit himself, the 1st Infantry Division and the U.S. Armed Forces.

†STEWART, JIMMY G.

Rank and Organization: Staff Sergeant, U.S. Army, Company B, 2d Battalion, 12th Cavalry, 1st Cavalry Division (Airmobile).
Born: December 25, 1942, West Columbia, West Virginia
Entered Service At: Ashland, Kentucky
Place and Date: Republic of Vietnam, May 18, 1966.
Citation: For conspicuous gallantry and intrepidity in action at the risk of his life above and beyond the call of duty. Early in the morning a reinforced North Vietnamese company attacked Company B, which was manning a defensive perimeter in Vietnam. The surprise onslaught wounded five members of a six-man squad caught in the direct path of the enemy's thrust. S/Sgt Stewart became a lone defender of vital terrain, virtually one man against a hostile platoon. Refusing to take advantage of a lull in the firing that would have permitted him to withdraw, S/Sgt. Stewart elected to hold his ground to protect his fallen comrades and prevent an enemy penetration of the company perimeter. As the full force of the platoon-sized man attack struck his lone position, he fought like a man possessed; emptying magazine after magazine at the determined, on-charging enemy. The enemy drove almost to his position and hurled grenades, but S/Sgt. Stewart decimated them by retrieving and throwing the grenades back. Exhausting his ammunition, he crawled under intense fire to his wounded team members and collected ammunition that they were unable to use. Far past the normal point of exhaustion, he held his position for four harrowing hours and through three assaults, annihilating the enemy as they approached and before they could get a foothold. As a result of his defense, the company position held until the arrival of a reinforcing platoon which counterattacked the enemy, now occupying foxholes to the left of S/Sgt. Stewart's position. After the counterattack, his body was found in a shallow enemy hole where he had advanced in order to add his fire to that of the counterattacking platoon. Eight enemy dead were found around his immediate position, with evidence that 15 others had been dragged away. The wounded whom he gave his life to protect, were recovered and evacuated. S/Sgt. Stewart's indomitable courage, in the face of overwhelming odds, stands as a tribute to himself and an inspiration to all the men of his unit. His actions were in the highest traditions of the U.S. Army and the Armed Forces of his country.

DOLBY, DAVID CHARLES

Rank and Organization: Sergeant (then Sp4c.), U.S. Army, Company B, 1st Battalion (Airborne), 8th Cavalry, 1st Cavalry Division (Airmobile).

Born: May 14, 1946, Norristown, Pa.

Entered Service At: Philadelphia, Pa.

Place and Date: Republic of Vietnam, May 21, 1966

Citation: For conspicuous gallantry and intrepidity at the risk of his life above and beyond the call of duty. Sgt. Dolby's platoon, while advancing tactically, suddenly came under intense fire from the enemy located on a ridge immediately to the front. Six members of the platoon were killed instantly and a number were wounded, including the platoon leader. Sgt. Dolby's every move brought fire from the enemy. However, aware that the platoon leader was critically wounded, and that the platoon was in a precarious situation, Sgt. Dolby moved the wounded men to safety and deployed the remainder of the platoon to engage the enemy. Subsequently, his dying platoon leader ordered Sgt. Dolby to withdraw the forward elements to rejoin the platoon. Despite the continuing intense enemy fire and with utter disregard for his own safety, Sgt. Dolby positioned able-bodied men to cover the withdrawal of the forward elements, assisted the wounded to the new position, and he, alone, attacked enemy positions until his ammunition was expended. Replenishing his ammunition, he returned to the area of most intense action, singlehandedly killed three enemy machine-gunners and neutralized the enemy fire, thus enabling friendly elements on the flank to advance on the enemy redoubt. He defied the enemy fire to personally carry a seriously wounded soldier to safety where he could be treated and, returning to the forward area, he crawled through withering fire to within 50 meters of the enemy bunkers and threw smoke grenades to mark them for air strikes. Although repeatedly under fire at close range by enemy snipers and automatic weapons, Sgt. Dolby directed artillery fire on the enemy and succeeded in silencing several enemy weapons. He remained in his exposed location until his comrades had displaced to more secure positions. His actions of unsurpassed valor during four hours of intense combat were a source of inspiration to his entire company, contributed significantly to the success of the overall assault on the enemy position, and were directly responsible for saving the lives of a number of his fellow soldiers. Sgt.

Dolby's heroism was in the highest tradition of the U.S. Army and reflect great credit upon himself and the Armed Forces of his country.

HOWARD, JIMMIE E.

Rank and Organization: Gunnery Sergeant (then S/Sgt.), U.S. Marine Corps, Company C, 1st Reconnaissance Battalion, 1st Marine Division.
Born: July 27, 1929, Burlington, Iowa
Entered Service At: Burlington, Iowa
Place and Date: Republic of Vietnam, June 16, 1966
Citation: For conspicuous gallantry and intrepidity at the risk of his own life above and beyond the call of duty. G/Sgt. Howard and his 18 man platoon were occupying an observation post deep within enemy-controlled territory. Shortly after midnight a Viet Cong force, of estimated battalion size, approached the marines' position and launched a vicious attack with small arms fire, automatic weapons and mortar fire. Reacting swiftly and fearlessly in the face of the overwhelming odds, G/Sgt. Howard skillfully organized his small but determined force into a tight perimeter defense and calmly moved from position to position to direct his men's fire. Throughout the night, during assault after assault, his courageous example and firm leadership inspired and motivated his men to withstand the unrelenting fury of the hostile fire in the seemingly hopeless situation. He constantly shouted encouragement to his men and exhibited imagination and resourcefulness in directing their return fire. When fragments of an exploding enemy grenade wounded him severely and prevented him from moving his legs, he distributed his ammunition to the remaining members of his platoon and proceeded to maintain radio communications and direct air strikes on the enemy with uncanny accuracy. At dawn, despite the fact that five men were killed and all but one wounded, his beleaguered platoon was still in command of its position. When evacuation helicopters approached his position, G/Sgt. Howard warned them away and called for additional air strikes and directed devastating small-arms and air strikes against enemy automatic weapons positions in order to make the landing zone as secure as possible. Through his extraordinary courage and resolute fighting spirit, G/Sgt. Howard was largely responsible for preventing the loss of his entire platoon. His valiant leadership and courageous fighting spirit served to inspire the men of his platoon to heroic endeavor in the face of overwhelming odds, and reflect the highest credit upon G/Sgt. Howard, the Marine Corps and the U.S. Naval Service.

Note: Of the 18 men in the platoon, besides the Purple Heart and the Medal of Honor awarded to Sgt. Howard, 15 received the Silver Star and 2 received the Navy Cross. The following is a newspaper article describing this battle:

20 Marines Thwart A Six-Hour Attack By 400 Against Hill

SAIGON, South Vietnam, June 16 - About 20 U.S. Marines held a barren, rocky hill for almost six hours today against repeated attacks by a Vietcong force estimated at 400.

By the end of the battle only two of the marines had not been wounded or killed. [Five marines died fighting the force, which was about the size of a battalion, The Associated Press reported.]

Thirty two enemy bodies were counted around the marines' position, a hill that was used as an observation point, a military spokesman said. The position is situated 12 miles northwest of the Marine Corps base at Chu Lai, which is 350 miles northeast of Saigon.

Attacked From All Sides

"Within minutes the Vietcong began an intense automatic-weapons and small-arms barrage on the post and launched assaults from all sides," a military statement said.

The reconnaissance platoon fired so much ammunition that only eight rounds remained when it was relieved by about 200 marines.

The surrounded and out numbered marines used bayonets, grenades and even hurled rocks against the enemy force.

RAY, RONALD ERIC

Rank and Organization: Captain (then 1st Lt.), U.S. Army, Company A, 2d Battalion, 35th Infantry, 25th Infantry Division.
Born: December 7, 1941, Cordelle, Georgia
Entered Service At: Atlanta, Georgia
Place and Date: Ia Drang Valley, Republic of Vietnam, June 19, 1966.
Citation: For conspicuous gallantry and intrepidity in action at the risk of his life above and beyond the call of duty. Capt. Ray distinguished himself while serving as platoon leader of Company A. When one of his ambush patrols was attack by an estimated reinforced Viet Cong company, Capt. Ray organized a reaction force and quickly moved through two kilometers of mountainous jungle terrain to the contact area. After breaking through the hostile lines to reach the beleaguered patrol, Capt. Ray began directing the reinforcement of the site. When an enemy position pinned down three of his men with a heavy volume of automatic weapons fire, he silenced the emplacement with a grenade and killed four Viet Cong with his rifle fire. As medics were moving a casualty toward a sheltered position, they began receiving intense hostile fire. While directing suppressive fire on the enemy position, Capt. Ray moved close enough to silence the enemy with a grenade. A few moments later Capt. Ray saw an enemy grenade land, unnoticed, near two of his men. Without hesitation or regard for his safety he dove between the grenade and his men, thus shielding them from the explosion while receiving wounds in his exposed feet and legs. He immediately sustained additional wounds in his legs from an enemy machine-gun, but nevertheless he silenced the emplacement with another grenade. Although suffering great pains from his wounds, Capt. Ray continued to direct his men, providing the outstanding courage and leadership they vitally needed, and prevented their annihilation by successfully leading them from their surrounded position. Only after assuring that his platoon was no longer in immediate danger did he allow himself to be evacuated for medical treatment. By his gallantry at the risk of his life, in the highest traditions of the military service, Capt. Ray has reflected great credit on himself, his unit and the U.S. Army.

MORRIS, CHARLES B.

Rank and Organization: Staff Sergeant (then Sgt.), U.S. Army, Company A, 2d Battalion (airborne), 503d Infantry, 173d Airborne Brigade.
Born: December 29, 1931, Carrol County, Virginia
Entered Service At: Roanoke, Virginia
Place and Date: Republic of Vietnam, June 29, 1966.
Citation: For conspicuous gallantry and intrepidity at the risk of his life above and beyond the call of duty. Seeing indications of the enemy's presence in the area, S/Sgt. Morris deployed his squad and continued forward alone to make a reconnaissance. He unknowingly crawled within 20 meters of an enemy machine-gun, whereupon the machine-gunner fired, wounding him in the chest. S/Sgt. Morris instantly returned the fire and killed the gunner. Continuing to crawl within a few feet of the gun, he hurled a grenade and killed the remainder of the enemy crew. Although in pain and bleeding profusely, S/Sgt. Morris continued his reconnaissance. Returning to the platoon area, he reported the results of his reconnaissance to the platoon leader. As he spoke, the platoon came under heavy fire. Refusing medical attention for himself, he deployed his men in better firing positions confronting the entrenched enemy to his front. Then for eight hours the platoon engaged the numerically superior enemy force. Withdrawal was impossible without abandoning many wounded and dead. Finding the platoon medic dead, S/Sgt. Morris administered first aid to himself and was returning to treat the wounded members of his squad with the medics first aid kit when he was again wounded. Knocked down and stunned, he regained consciousness and continued to treat the wounded, reposition his men, and inspire and encourage their efforts. Wounded again when an enemy grenade shattered his left hand, nonetheless he personally took up the fight and armed and threw several grenades which killed a number of enemy soldiers. Seeing that an enemy machine-gun had maneuvered behind his platoon and was delivering fire upon his men, S/Sgt. Morris and another man crawled toward the gun to knock it out. His comrade was killed and S/Sgt. Morris sustained another wound but, firing his rifle with one hand, he silenced the enemy machine-gun. Returning to the platoon, he courageously exposed himself to the devastating enemy fire to drag the wounded to a protected area, and with utter disregard for his personal safety and the pain he suffered, he contin-

ued to lead and direct the efforts of his men until relief arrived. Upon termination of the battle, important documents were found among the enemy dead revealing a planned ambush of a Republic of Vietnam battalion. Use of this information prevented the ambush and saved many lives. S/Sgt. Morris' gallantry was instrumental in the successful defeat of the enemy, saved many lives and was in the highest traditions of the U.S. Army.

†LONG, DONALD RUSSELL

Rank and Organization: Sergeant, U.S. Army, Troop C, 1st Squadron, 4th Cavalry, 1st Infantry Division.
Born: August 27, 1939, Blackfork, Ohio
Entered Service At: Ashland, Kentucky
Place and Date: Republic of Vietnam, June 30, 1966.
Citation: For conspicuous gallantry and intrepidity in action at the risk of his life above and beyond the call of duty. Troops B and C, while conducting a reconnaissance mission along a road were suddenly attacked by a Viet Cong regiment, supported by mortars, recoilless rifles and machine-guns, from concealed positions astride the road. Sgt. Long abandoned the relative safety of his armored personnel carrier and braved a withering hail of enemy fire to carry wounded men to evacuation helicopters. As the platoon fought its way forward to resupply advanced elements, Sgt. Long repeatedly exposed himself to enemy fire at point blank range to provide the needed supplies. While assaulting the Viet Cong position, Sgt. Long inspired his comrades by fearlessly standing unprotected to repel the enemy with rifle fire and grenades as they tempted to mount his carrier. When the enemy threatened to overrun a disabled carrier nearby, Sgt. Long again disregarded his own safety to help the severely wounded crew to safety. As he was handing arms to the less seriously wounded and reorganizing them to press the attack, an enemy grenade was hurled onto the carrier deck. Immediately recognizing the imminent danger, he instinctively shouted a warning to the crew and pushed to safety one man who had not heard his warning over the roar of the battle. Realizing that these actions would not fully protect the exposed crewmen from the deadly explosion, he threw himself over the grenade to absorb the blast and thereby saved the lives of eight of his comrades at the expense of his life. Throughout the battle, Sgt. Long's extraordinary heroism, courage and supreme devotion to his men were in the finest traditions of the military service, and reflect great credit upon himself and the U.S. Army.

MODRZEJEWSKI, ROBERT J.

Rank and Organization: Major (then Capt.), U.S. Marine Corps, Company K, 3d Battalion, 4th Marines, 3d Marine Division, FMF.
Born: July 3, 1934, Milwaukee, Wisconsin
Entered Service At: Milwaukee, Wisconsin
Place and Date: Republic of Vietnam, July 15 to 18, 1966.
Citation: For conspicuous gallantry and intrepidity at the risk of his life above and beyond the call of duty. On 15 July, during Operation HASTINGS, Company K was landed in an enemy-infested jungle area to establish a blocking position at a major enemy trail network. Shortly after landing, the company encountered a reinforced enemy platoon in a well organized, defensive position. Major Modrzejewski led his men in the successful seizure of the enemy stronghold, which contained large quantities of ammunition and supplies. That evening, a numerically superior enemy force counterattacked in an effort to retake the vital supply area, thus setting the pattern of activity for the next 2 1/2 days. In the first series of attacks, the enemy assaulted repeatedly in overwhelming numbers but each time was repulsed by the gallant marines. The second night, the enemy struck in battalion strength, and Maj. Modrzejewski was wounded in this intensive action which was fought at close quarters. Although exposed to enemy fire, and despite his painful wounds, he crawled 200 meters to provide critically needed ammunition to an exposed element of his command and was constantly present wherever the fighting was heaviest, despite numerous casualties, a dwindling supply of ammunition and the knowledge that they were surrounded, he skillfully directed artillery fire to within a few meters of his position and courageously inspired the efforts of his company in repelling the aggressive enemy attack. On 18 July, Company K was attacked by a regimental-sized enemy force. Although his unit was vastly outnumbered and weakened by the previous fighting, Maj. Modrzejewski reorganized his men and calmly moved among them to encourage and direct their efforts to heroic limits as they fought to overcome the vicious enemy onslaught. Again he called in air and artillery strikes at close range with devastating effect on the enemy, which together with the bold and determined fighting of the men of Company K, repulsed the fanatical attack of the larger North Vietnamese force. His unparalleled personal heroism and indomitable leadership inspired his men to a significant victory over the enemy force and reflected great credit upon himself, the Marine Corps and the U.S. Naval Service.

Note: The following is a newspaper account of the preceding battle for which Maj. Modrzejewski received the Medal of Honor:

118 Of Enemy Slain

Troops have killed 118 North Vietnamese and captured two since Operation HASTINGS was officially announced. Thirteen others were killed earlier.

Two Marine companies, dug in near a suspected North Vietnamese army headquarters encampment within two miles of the demilitarized zone, fought off two attacks last night. No significant ground action was reported after that.

One of the Marine units, K Company of the Third Battalion, Fourth Marines, accounted for nearly half of the enemy dead.

McGINTY, JOHN J. III

Rank and Organization: Second Lieutenant (then S/Sgt.), U.S. Marine Corps, Company K, 3d Battalion, 4th Marines, 3d Marine Division, Fleet Marine Force.

Born: January 21, 1940, Boston, Massachusetts

Entered Service At: Laurel Bay, South Carolina

Place and Date: Republic of Vietnam, July 18, 1966.

Citation: For conspicuous gallantry and intrepidity at the risk of his life above and beyond the call of duty. 2d Lt. McGinty's platoon, which was providing rear security to protect the withdrawal of the battalion from a position which had been under attack for 3 days, came under heavy small arms, automatic weapons and mortar fire from an estimated enemy regiment. With each successive human wave that assaulted his 32 man platoon during the four hour battle, 2d Lt. McGinty rallied his men to beat off the enemy. In one bitter assault, two of the squads became separated from the remainder of the platoon. With complete disregard for his safety, 2d Lt. McGinty charged through intense automatic weapons and mortar fire to their position. Finding 20 men wounded and the medical corpsman killed, he quickly reloaded ammunition magazines and weapons for the wounded men and directed their fire upon the enemy. Although he was painfully wounded as he moved to care for the disabled men, he continued to shout encouragement to his troops and direct their fire so effectively that the attacking hoards were beaten off. When the enemy tried to out-flank his position, he killed five of them at point-blank range with his pistol. When they again seemed on the verge of overrunning the small force, he skillfully adjusted artillery and air strikes within 50 yards of his position. This destructive firepower routed the enemy, who left an estimated 500 bodies on the battlefield. 2d Lt. McGinty's personal heroism, indomitable leadership, selfless devotion to duty and bold fighting spirit inspired his men to resist the repeated attacks by a fanatical enemy, reflected great credit upon himself, and upheld the highest traditions of the Marine Corps and the U.S. Naval Service.

PITTMAN, RICHARD A.

Rank and Organization: Sergeant (then L/Cpl.), U.S. Marine Corps, Company I, 3d Battalion, 5th Marines, 1st Marine Division.
Born: May 26, 1945, French Camp, San Joaquin, California
Entered Service At: Stockton, California
Place and Date: Near the Demilitarized Zone, Republic of Vietnam, July 24, 1966.
Citation: For conspicuous gallantry and intrepidity at the risk of his life above and beyond the call of duty. While Company I was conducting an operation along the axis of a narrow jungle trail, the leading company elements suffered numerous casualties when they suddenly came under heavy fire from a well concealed and numerically superior enemy force. Hearing the engaged marines' calls for more firepower, Sgt. Pittman quickly exchanged his rifle for a machinegun and several belts of ammunition, left the relative safety of his platoon, and unhesitatingly rushed forward to aid his comrades. Taken under intense enemy small-arms fire at point blank range during his advance, he returned the fire, silencing the enemy position. As Sgt. Pittman continued to forge forward to aid members of his leading platoon, he again came under heavy fire from two automatic weapons which he promptly destroyed. Learning that there were additional wounded marines 50 yards further along the trail, he braved a withering hail of enemy mortar and small-arms fire to continue onward. As he reached the position where the leading marines had fallen, he was suddenly confronted with a bold frontal attack by 30 to 40 enemy. Totally disregarding his safety, he calmly established a position in the middle of the trail and raked the advancing enemy with devastating machine-gun fire. His weapon rendered ineffective, he picked up an enemy submachinegun and, together with a pistol seized from a fallen comrade, continued his lethal fire until the enemy had withdrawn. Having exhausted his ammunition except for a grenade which he hurled at the enemy, he then rejoined his platoon. Sgt. Pittman's daring initiative, bold fighting spirit and selfless devotion to duty inflicted many enemy casualties, disrupted the enemy attack and saved the lives of many of his wounded comrades. His personal valor at personal risk to himself reflects the highest credit upon himself, the Marine Corps, and the U.S. Naval Service.

LEE, HOWARD V.

Rank and Organization: Major (then Capt.), U.S. Marine Corps, Company E, 2d Battalion, 4th Marines, 3d Marine Division.
Born: August 1, 1933, New York, New York
Entered Service At: Dumfries, Virginia
Place and Date: Near Cam Lo, Republic of Vietnam, August 8 and 9, 1966.
Citation: For conspicuous gallantry and intrepidity at the risk of his life above and beyond the call of duty. A platoon of Maj. Lee's company, while on an operation deep in enemy territory, was attacked and surrounded by a large enemy force. Realizing that the unit had suffered numerous casualties, depriving it of effective leadership, and fully aware that the platoon even then was under heavy attack by the enemy, Maj. Lee took seven men and proceeded by helicopter to reinforce the beleaguered platoon. Maj. Lee disembarked from the helicopter with two of his men and, braving withering enemy fire, led them into the perimeter, where he fearlessly moved from position to position, directing and encouraging the overtaxed troops. The enemy then launched a massive attack with the full might of their forces. Although painfully wounded by fragments from an enemy grenade, including his eye, Maj. Lee continued undauntedly throughout the night to direct the valiant defense, coordinating supporting fire, and apprise higher headquarters of the plight of the platoon. The next morning he collapsed from his wounds and was forced to relinquish his command. However the small band of marines had held their position and repeatedly fought off many vicious enemy attacks for a grueling six hours until their evacuation was effected the following morning. Maj. Lee's actions saved his men from capture, minimized the loss of lives, and dealt the enemy a severe defeat. His indomitable fighting spirit, superb leadership, and great personal valor in the face of tremendous odds, reflect great credit upon himself and are in keeping with the highest traditions of the Marine Corps and the U.S. Naval Service.

†LAUFFER, BILLY LANE
Rank and Organization: Private First Class, U.S. Army, Company C, 2d Battalion, 5th Cavalry, 1st Air Cavalry Division.
Born: October 20, 1945, Murray, Kentucky
Entered Servive At: Phoenix, Arizona
Place and Date: Near Bon Son in Binh Dinh Province, Republic of Vietnam, September 21, 1966.
Citation: For conspicuous gallantry and intrepidity in action at the risk of his life above and beyond the call of duty. Pfc. Lauffer's squad, a part of Company C, was suddenly struck at close range by an intense machine-gun crossfire from two concealed bunkers astride the squad's route. Pfc. Lauffer, the second man in the column, saw the leadman fall and noted that the remainder of the squad was unable to move. Two comrades, previously wounded and being carried on litters, were lying helpless in the beaten zone of the enemy fire. Reacting instinctively, Pfc. Lauffer quickly engaged both bunkers with fire from his rifle, but when the other squad members attempted to maneuver under his covering fire, the enemy fusillade increased in volume and thwarted every attempt to move. Seeing this and his wounded comrades helpless in the open, Pfc. Lauffer rose to his feet and charged the enemy machine-gun positions, firing his weapon and drawing the enemy's attention. Keeping the enemy confused and off balance, his one-man assault provided the crucial moments for the wounded point man to crawl to a covered position, the squad to move the exposed litter patients to safety, and his comrades to gain more advantageous positions. Pfc. Lauffer was fatally wounded during his selfless act of courage and devotion to his fellow soldiers. His gallantry at the cost of his life served as an inspiration to his comrades and saved the lives of an untold number of his companions. His actions are in keeping with the highest traditions of military service and reflect great credit upon himself, his unit, and the U.S. Army.

WILLIAMS, JAMES E.

Rank and Organization: Boatswain's Mate First Class (PO1c.), U.S. Navy, River Section 531, My Tho, RVN.

Born: June 13, 1930, Rock Hill, South Carolina

Entered Service At: Columbia, South Carolina

Place and Date: Mekong River, Republic of Vietnam, October 13, 1966

Citation: For conspicuous gallantry and intrepidity at the risk of his life above and beyond the call of duty. PO1c. Williams was serving as Boat Captain and Patrol Officer aboard River Patrol Boat (PBR) 105 accompanied by another patrol boat when the patrol was suddenly taken under fire by two enemy sampans. PO1c. Williams immediately ordered the fire returned, killing the crew of one enemy boat and causing the other sampan to take refuge in a nearby river inlet. Pursuing the fleeing sampan, the U.S. patrol encountered a heavy volume of small-arms fire from enemy forces, at close range, occupying well-concealed positions along the river bank. Maneuvering through this fire, the patrol confronted a numerically superior enemy force aboard two enemy junks and eight sampans augmented by heavy automatic weapons fire from ashore. In the savage battle that ensued, PO1c. Williams, with utter disregard for his safety exposed himself to the withering hail of enemy fire to direct counter-fire and inspire the actions of his patrol. Recognizing the overwhelming strength of the enemy force, PO1c. Williams deployed his patrol to await the arrival of armed helicopters. In the course of his movement he discovered an even larger concentration of enemy boats. Not waiting for the arrival of the armed helicopters, he displayed great initiative and boldly led the patrol through the intense enemy fire and damaged or destroyed 50 enemy sampans and seven junks. This phase of the action completed, and with arrival of the armed helicopters, PO1c. Williams directed the attack on the remaining enemy force. Now virtually dark, and although PO1c. Williams was aware that his boats would become even better targets, he ordered the patrol boats' search lights turned on to better illuminate the area and moved the patrol perilously close to shore to press the attack. Despite the waning supply of ammunition the patrol successfully engaged the enemy ashore and completed the rout of the enemy force. Under the leadership of PO1c. Williams, who demonstrated unusual professional skill and indomitable courage throughout the three hour battle, the patrol accounted for the destruction or loss of 65 enemy boats and inflicted numerous casualties on the enemy personnel. His extraordinary heroism and exemplary fighting spirit in the face of grave risks inspired the efforts of his men to defeat the larger enemy force, and are in keeping with the finest traditions of the U.S. Naval Service.

BAKER, JOHN F., JR.

Rank and Organization: Sergeant (then Pfc.), U.S. Army, Company A, 2d Battalion, 27th Infantry, 25th Infantry Division.
Born: October 30, 1945, Davenport, Iowa
Entered Service At: Moline, Illinois
Place and Date: Near Quan Dau Tieng, Republic of Vietnam, November 5, 1966.
Citation: For conspicuous gallantry and intrepidity in action at the risk of his life above and beyond the call of duty. Enroute to assist another unit that was engaged with the enemy, Company A came under intense enemy fire and the lead man was killed instantly. Sgt. Baker immediately moved to the head of the column and together with another soldier knocked out two enemy bunkers. When his comrade was mortally wounded, Sgt. Baker, spotting four Viet Cong snipers, killed all of them, evacuated the fallen soldier and returned to lead repeated assaults against the enemy positions, killing several more Viet Cong. Moving to attack two additional enemy bunkers, he and another soldier drew intense enemy fire and Sgt. Baker was blown from his feet by an enemy grenade. He quickly recovered and single-handedly destroyed one bunker before the other soldier was wounded. Seizing his fallen comrade's machine-gun, Sgt. Baker charged through the deadly fusillade to silence the other bunker. He evacuated his comrade, replenished his ammunition and returned to the forefront to brave the enemy fire and continue the fight. When the forward element was ordered to withdraw, he carried one wounded man to the rear. As he returned to evacuate another soldier, he was taken under fire by snipers, but raced beyond the friendly troops to attack and kill the snipers. After evacuating the wounded man, he returned to cover the deployment of the unit. His ammunition now exhausted, he dragged two more of his fallen comrades to the rear. Sgt. Baker's selfless heroism, indomitable fighting spirit, and extraordinary gallantry were directly responsible for saving the lives of several of his comrades, and inflicting serious damage on the enemy. His acts were in keeping with the highest traditions of the U.S. Army and reflect great credit upon himself and the Armed Forces of his country.

FOLEY, ROBERT F.

Rank and Organization: Captain, U.S. Army, Company A, 2d Battalion, 27th Infantry, 25th Infantry Division.
Born: May 30, 1941, Newton, Massachusetts
Entered Service At: Newton, Massachusetts
Place and Date: Near Quan Dau Tieng, Republic of Vietnam, November 5, 1966
Citation: For conspicuous gallantry and intrepidity in action at the risk of his life above and beyond the call of duty. Capt. Foley's company was ordered to extricate another company of the battalion. Moving through the dense jungle to aid the besieged unit, Company A encountered a strong enemy force occupying well concealed, defensive positions, and the company's leading element quickly sustained several casualties. Capt. Foley immediately ran forward to the scene of the most intense action to direct the company's efforts. Deploying one platoon on the flank, he led the other two platoons in an attack on the enemy in the face of intense fire. During this action both radio operators accompanying him were wounded. At grave risk to himself he defied the enemy's murderous fire, and helped the wounded operators to a position where they could receive medical care. As he moved forward again, one of his machine-gun crews was wounded. Seizing the weapon, he charged forward firing the machine-gun, shouting orders and rallying his men, thus maintaining the momentum of the attack. Under increasingly heavy enemy fire he ordered his assistant to take cover and, alone, Capt. Foley continued to advance firing the machine-gun until the wounded had been evacuated and the attack in this area could be resumed. When movement on the other flank was halted by the enemy's fanatical defense, Capt. Foley moved to personally direct this critical phase of the battle. Leading the renewed effort he was blown off his feet and wounded by an enemy grenade. Despite his painful wounds, he refused medical aid and persevered in the forefront of the attack on the enemy redoubt. He led the assault on several enemy gun emplacements and, single-handedly, destroyed three such positions. His outstanding personal leadership under intense enemy fire during the fierce battle which lasted for several hours, inspired his men to heroic efforts and was instrumental in the ultimate success of the operation. Capt. Foley's magnificent courage, selfless concern for his men and professional skill reflect the utmost credit upon himself and the U.S. Army.

Note: The following is a newspaper account of the preceding battle for which both Pfc. Baker and Capt. Foley were awarded the Medal Of Honor:

Company Is Rescued

SAIGON, Nov. 5 (UPI) - U.S. infantrymen hurled back six Vietcong attacks today and rescued a company of troops cut off overnight in the War Zone C stronghold.

The company was pinned down by heavy machine-gun fire from what was described as a" fortified Vietcong village".

The unit spent the night in the open in the field of fire of four Vietcong machine-guns. A relief force reached it early this afternoon after battling its way through heavy jungle and withering fire.

†RUBIO, EURIPIDES

Rank and Organization: Captain, U.S. Army, Headquarters Company, 1st Battalion, 28th Infantry, 1st Infantry Division.
Born: March 1, 1938, Ponce, Puerto Rico
Entered Service At: Fort Buchanan, Puerto Rico
Place and Date: Tay Ninh Province, Republic of Vietnam, November 8, 1966.
Citation: For conspicuous gallantry and intrepidity in action at the risk of his life above and beyond the call of duty. Capt. Rubio was serving as communications officer when a numerically superior enemy force launched a massive attack against the battalion defensive position. Intense enemy machine-gun fire raked the area while mortar rounds and rifle grenades exploded within the perimeter. Leaving the relative safety of his post, Capt. Rubio received two serious wounds as he braved the withering fire to go to the area of most intense action where he distributed ammunition, re-established positions and rendered aid to the wounded. Disregarding the painful wounds, he unhesitatingly assumed command when a rifle company commander was medically evacuated. Capt. Rubio was wounded a third time as he selflessly exposed himself to the devastating enemy fire to move among his men and encourage them to fight with renewed effort. While aiding in the evacuation of wounded personnel, he noted that a smoke grenade which was intended to mark the Viet Cong position for air strikes had fallen dangerously close to the friendly lines. Capt. Rubio ran to reposition the grenade but was immediately struck to his knees by enemy fire. Despite his several wounds, Capt. Rubio scooped up the grenade, ran through the deadly hail of fire to within 20 meters of the enemy position and hurled the already smoking grenade into the midst of the enemy before he fell for the final time. Using the repositioned grenade as a marker, friendly air strikes were directed to destroy the hostile positions. Capt. Rubio's singularly heroic act turned the tide of battle, and his extraordinary leadership and valor were a magnificent inspiration to his men. His remarkable bravery and selfless concern for his men are in keeping with the highest traditions of the military service and reflect great credit on himself and the U.S. Army.

Note: The following is a newspaper account of the preceding battle in which Capt. Rubio earned the Medal of Honor:

BATTLE IN JUNGLE BREAKS OUT AGAIN

Fighting Follows Day's Lull
Toll of Vietcong Put at Over 300 in 6 Days

SAIGON, South Vietnam, Tuesday, Nov. 8 — A battalion of about 500 United States infantrymen was reported engaged in renewed fighting this morning in the jungle northwest of Saigon.

After four days of battling, in which more than 300 Vietcong guerrillas were killed, the Americans fired only a few scattered shots yesterday.

As they combed the thick underbrush, however, they continued to find the bodies of enemy soldiers. This morning a spokesman put the enemy death toll in the operation at 433.

The operation in Tayninh Province began Oct. 15, but until Thursday there was no significant action.

Most of the guerrillas killed between Thursday and Sunday fell while facing as many as 11 American rifle companies of about 200 men each under the command of Maj. Guy S. Meloy 3d of San Antonio, Tex.

Major Meloy touched off 30 hours of intense fighting when he walked into the jungle in Tayninh Province with two companies Friday afternoon.

Three of the 11 companies that eventually came under his command suffered heavy casualties and three others took moderate casualties, but the spokesman said that casualties among the more than 7,000 troops committed to the operation were light.

After taking heavy loses a unit is no longer considered an effective fighting force according to American military terminology in use here. Moderate losses impair effectiveness somewhat and light losses only slightly.

The spokesman said 175 planes had strafed and bombed the region, 30 to 50 miles northwest of Saigon in the last three days.

Yesterday, the infantrymen found two base camps and several enemy bunkers, but only a few enemy soldiers had been left behind as a rear guard and there was little fighting.

Intelligence sources said they believed the Americans had been fighting major elements of the 272d Vietcong Regiment, one of the three main components of the 9th Vietcong Division, the best trained and equipped enemy unit in South Vietnam.

The division has for years made its headquarters in the dense undergrowth of War Zone C, just north of where most of the recent action has been taking place.

American troops were engaged in little ground action elsewhere, but 308 miles northeast of Saigon, two companies of about 300 South Vietnamese militiamen repulsed a Vietcong battalion of 300 to 500 men this morning, killing 300.

A Government spokesman said the guerrillas attacked at about 9:30 A.M. and that quick reaction by artillerymen nearby saved the outpost from being overrun.

Government troops also killed 42 guerrillas Sunday in an operation about 34 miles northeast of the outpost, a South Vietnamese spokesman said.

†GRANT, JOSEPH XAVIER

Rank and Organization: Captain (then 1st Lt.), U.S. Army, Company A, 1st Battalion, 14th Infantry, 25th Infantry Division.
Born: March 28, 1940, Cambridge, Massachusetts
Entered Service At: Boston, Massachusetts
Place and Date: Republic of Vietnam, November 13, 1966
Citation: For conspicuous gallantry and intrepidity in action at the risk of his life above and beyond the call of duty. Company A was participating in a search and destroy operation when the leading platoon made contact with the enemy and a fierce fire-fight ensued. Capt. Grant was ordered to disengage the two remaining platoons and to maneuver them to envelop and destroy the enemy. After beginning their movement, the platoons encountered intense enemy automatic weapons and mortar fire from the front and flank. Capt. Grant was ordered to deploy the platoons in a defensive position. As this action was underway, the enemy attacked, using "human wave" assaults, In an attempt to literally overwhelm Capt. Grant's force. In a magnificent display of courage and leadership, Capt. Grant moved under intense fire along the hastily formed defensive line repositioning soldiers to fill gaps created by the mounting casualties and inspiring and directing the efforts of his men to successfully repel the determined enemy onslaught. Seeing the platoon leader wounded, Capt. Grant hastened to his aid, in the face of the mass of fire of the entire enemy force, and moved him to a more secure position. During this action, Capt. Grant was wounded in the shoulder. Refusing medical treatment, he returned to the forward part of the perimeter, where he continued to lead and to inspire his men by his own indomitable example. While attempting to evacuate a wounded soldier, he was pinned down by fire from an enemy machinegun. With a supply of hand grenades, he crawled forward under a withering hail of fire and knocked out the machinegun, killing the crew, after which he moved the wounded man to safety. Learning that several other wounded men were pinned down by enemy fire forward of his position, Capt. Grant disregarded his painful wound and lead five men across the fire-swept open ground to effect a rescue. Following the return of the wounded men to the perimeter, a concentration of mortar fire landed in their midst and Capt. Grant was killed instantly. His heroic actions saved the lives of a number of his comrades and en-

abled the task force to repulse the vicious assaults and defeat the enemy. Capt. Grant's actions reflect great credit upon himself and were in keeping with the finest traditions of the U.S. Army.

†BELCHER, TED

Rank and Organization: Sergeant, U.S. Army, Company C, 1st Battalion, 14th Infantry, 25th Infantry Division.
Born: July 21, 1924, Accoville, West Virginia.
Entered Service At: Huntington, West Virginia
Place and Date: Plei Djerang, Republic of Vietnam, November 19, 1966.
Citation: For conspicuous gallantry and intrepidity in action at the risk of his life above and beyond the call of duty. Sgt. Belcher's unit was engaged in a search and destroy mission with Company B, 1st Battalion, the Battalion Reconnaissance Platoon and a special forces company of civilian irregular defense group personnel. As a squad leader of the 2d Platoon of Company C, Sgt. Belcher was leading his men when they encountered a bunker complex. The reconnaissance platoon, located a few hundred meters northwest of Company C, received a heavy volume of fire from well camouflaged snipers. As the 2d Platoon moved forward to assist the unit under attack, Sgt. Belcher and his squad, advancing only a short distance through the dense jungle terrain, met heavy and accurate automatic weapons and sniper fire. Sgt. Belcher and his squad were momentarily stopped by the deadly volume of enemy fire. He quickly gave the order to return fire and resume the advance toward the enemy. As he moved up with his men, a hand grenade landed in the midst of the sergeant's squad. Instantly realizing the immediate danger to his men, Sgt. Belcher, unhesitatingly and with complete disregard for his safety, lunged forward, covering the grenade with his body. Absorbing the grenade blast at the cost of his life, he saved his comrades from becoming casualties. Sgt. Belcher's profound concern for his fellow soldiers, at the risk of his life above and beyond the call of duty are in keeping with the highest traditions of the U.S. Army and reflect great credit upon himself and the Armed Forces of his country.

†ALBANESE, LEWIS
Rank and Organization: Private First Class, U.S. Army, Company B, 5th Battalion (Airmobile), 7th Cavalry, 1st Cavalry Division.
Born: April 27, 1946, Venice, Italy
Entered Service At: Seattle, Washington
Place and Date: Republic of Vietnam, December 1, 1966
Citation: For conspicuous gallantry and intrepidity in action at the risk of his life above and beyond the call of duty. Pfc. Albanese's platoon, while advancing through densely covered terrain to establish a blocking position, received intense automatic weapons fire from close range. As other members maneuvered to assault the enemy position, Pfc. Albanese was ordered to provide security for the left flank of the platoon. Suddenly, the left flank received fire from enemy located in a well-concealed ditch. Realizing the imminent danger to his comrades from this fire, Pfc. Albanese fixed his bayonet and moved aggressively into the ditch. His action silenced the sniper fire, enabling the platoon to resume movement toward the main enemy position. As the platoon continued to advance, the sound of heavy firing emanated from the left flank from a pitched battle that ensued in the ditch which Pfc. Albanese had entered. The ditch was actually a well-organized complex of enemy defenses designed to bring devastating flanking fire on the forces attacking the main enemy position. Pfc. Albanese, disregarding the danger to himself, advanced 100 meters along the trench and killed six of the snipers, who were armed with automatic weapons. Having exhausted his ammunition, Pfc. Albanese was mortally wounded when he engaged and killed two more enemy soldiers in fierce hand-to-hand combat. His unparalleled action saved the lives of many members of his platoon who otherwise would have fallen to the sniper fire from the ditch, and enabled his platoon to successfully advance against an enemy force of overwhelming numerical superiority. Pfc. Albanese's extraordinary heroism and supreme dedication to his comrades were commensurate with finest traditions of the military service and remain a tribute to himself, his unit, and the U.S. Army.

JENNINGS, DELBERT O.

Rank and Organization: Staff Sergeant, U.S. Army, Company C, 1st Battalion (Airborne), 12th Cavalry, 1st Air Cavalry Division.
Born: July 23, 1936, Silver City, New Mexico
Entered Service At: San Francisco, California
Place and Date: Kim Song Valley, Republic of Vietnam, December 27, 1966.
Citation: For conspicuous gallantry and intrepidity at the risk of his life above and beyond the call of duty. Part of Company C was defending an artillery position when attacked by a North Vietnamese Army regiment supported by mortar, recoilless-rifle, and machinegun fire. At the outset, S/Sgt. Jennings sprang to his bunker, astride the main attack route, and slowed the on-coming enemy wave with highly effective machinegun fire. Despite a tenacious defense in which he killed at least 12 of the enemy, his squad was forced to the rear. After covering the withdrawal of the squad, he rejoined his men, destroyed an enemy demolition crew about to blow up a nearby howitzer, and killed three enemy soldiers at his initial bunker position. Ordering his men back into a secondary position, he again covered their withdrawal, killing one enemy with the butt of his weapon. Observing that some of the defenders were unaware of an enemy force to their rear, he raced through a fire-swept area to warn the men, turn their fire on the enemy, and lead them into the secondary perimeter. Assisting in the defense of the new position, he aided the air-landing of reinforcements by throwing white phosphorous grenades on the landing zone despite dangerously silhouetting himself with the light. After helping to repulse the final enemy assaults, he led a group of volunteers well beyond friendly lines to an area where eight seriously wounded men lay. Braving enemy sniper fire and ignoring the presence of boobytraps in the area, they recovered the eight men who would have probably perished without early medical treatment. S/Sgt. Jennings' extraordinary heroism and inspirational leadership saved the lives of many of his comrades and contributed greatly to the defeat of a numerically superior enemy force. His actions stand with the highest traditions of the military profession and reflect great credit upon himself, his unit, and the U.S. Army.

CHAPTER 4

1967

(† - Indicates Posthumous Award)

Note: The following newspaper article concerning Vietnam appeared on the front page of *The New York Times* on Jan. 1, 1967:

President Makes New Bid To Hanoi On Truce Or Talks

JOHNSON CITY, Tex. Dec. 31 - President Johnson said that he would be "very glad to do more than our part in meeting Hanoi halfway in any possible cease-fire, truce or peace conference negotiations."

The President, at a news conference, described himself as very interested in the response of North Vietnam to this offer and to appeals by Britain and others. But he had to know that response, he added, before irrevocably committing the United States to unilateral reductions in the fighting or in the bombing of North Vietnam.

Commenting on the bombing, the President said that "inevitably and almost invariably" there were casualties and losses of life among civilians. He insisted that raids had been authorized only on military targets, that there had been no change in his orders and that the available evidence indicated that no mistakes had been made in their execution.

Mr. Johnson said the United States did everything possible to minimize civilian casualties. He added that he wished that everyone was equally concerned about the deaths of thousands of civilians caused in South Vietnam this year by grenades and bombs. Presumably he meant deaths by Viet Cong terrorists and by American attacks on villages occupied by the Viet Cong.

He regrets every casualty, North and South, Mr. Johnson said.

†EVANS, DONALD W., JR.

Rank and Organization: Specialist Fourth Class, U.S. Army, Company A, 2d Battalion, 12th Infantry, 4th Infantry Division.
Born: July 23, 1943, Covina, California
Entered Service At: Covina, California
Place and Date: Tri Tam, Republic of Vietnam, January 27, 1967.
Citation: For conspicuous gallantry and intrepidity in action at the risk of his life above and beyond the call of duty. Sp4c. Evans left his position of relative safety with his platoon, which had not yet been committed to the battle, to answer the calls for medical aid from the wounded men of another platoon that was heavily engaged with the enemy force. Dashing across 100 meters of open area through a withering hail of enemy fire and exploding grenades, he administered lifesaving treatment to one individual and continued to expose himself to the deadly enemy fire as he moved to treat each of the other wounded men and to offer them encouragement. Realizing that the wounds of one man required immediate attention, Sp4c. Evans dragged the injured soldier back across the dangerous fire-swept area, to a secure position from which he could be further evacuated. Miraculously escaping the enemy fusillade, Sp4c. Evans returned to the forward location. As he continued the treatment of the wounded, he was struck by fragments from an enemy grenade. Despite his serious and painful injury, he succeeded in evacuating another wounded comrade, rejoined his platoon as it was committed to battle and was soon treating other wounded soldiers. As he evacuated another wounded man across the fire covered field, he was severely wounded. Continuing to refuse medical attention and ignoring advice to remain behind, he managed with his waning strength to move yet another wounded comrade across the dangerous open area to safety. Disregarding his painful wounds and seriously weakened from profuse bleeding, he continued his lifesaving medical aid and was killed while treating another wounded comrade. Sp4c. Evans' extraordinary valor, dedication, and indomitable spirit saved the lives of several of his fellow soldiers, served as an inspiration to the men of company, was instrumental in the success of their mission, and reflect great credit upon himself and the Armed Forces of his country.

†SISLER, GEORGE K.

Rank and Organization: First Lieutenant, U.S. Army, Headquarters Company, 5th Special Forces Group (Airborne), 1st Special Forces.
Born: September 19, 1937, Dexter, Mo.
Entered Service At: Dexter, Mo.
Place and Date: Republic of Vietnam, February 7, 1967.
Citation: For conspicuous gallantry and intrepidity at the risk of his life above and beyond the call of duty. 1st Lt. Sisler was the platoon leader/adviser to a Special United States/Vietnam force. While on patrol deep within enemy dominated territory, 1st Lt. Sisler's platoon was attacked from three sides by a company sized enemy force. 1st Lt. Sisler quickly rallied his men, deployed them to a better defensive position, called for air strikes, and moved among his men to encourage and direct their efforts. Learning that two men were wounded and unable to pull back to the perimeter, 1st Lt. Sisler charged from the position through the intense enemy fire to assist them. He reached the men and began carrying one of them back to the perimeter, when he was taken under more intensive weapons fire by the enemy. Laying down his wounded comrade, he killed three onrushing enemy soldiers by firing his rifle and silenced the enemy machinegun with a grenade. As he returned the wounded man to the perimeter, the left flank of the position came under extremely heavy attack by the superior enemy force and several additional men of his platoon were quickly wounded. Realizing the need for instant action to prevent his position from being overrun, 1st Lt. Sisler picked up some grenades and charged singlehandedly into the enemy onslaught, firing his weapon and throwing grenades. This singularly heroic action broke up the vicious assault and forced the enemy to begin withdrawing. His extraordinary leadership, infinite courage, and selfless concern for his men saved the lives of a number of his comrades. His actions reflect great credit upon himself and uphold the highest traditions of the military service.

†WILLETT, LOUIS E.

Rank and Organization: Private First Class, U.S. Army, Company C, 1st Battalion, 12th Infantry, 4th Infantry Division.

Born: June 19, 1945, Brooklyn, New York

Entered Service At: Brooklyn, New York

Place and Date: Kontum Province, Republic of Vietnam, February 15, 1967.

Citation: For conspicuous gallantry and intrepidity at the risk of his life above and beyond the call of duty. Pfc. Willett distinguished himself while serving as a rifleman in Company C, during combat operations. His squad was conducting a security sweep when it made contact with a large enemy force. The squad was immediately engaged with a heavy volume of automatic weapons fire and pinned to the ground. Despite the deadly fusillade, Pfc. Willett rose to his feet firing rapid bursts from his weapon and moved to a position from which he placed highly effective fire on the enemy. His action allowed the remainder of his squad to begin to withdraw from superior enemy force toward the company perimeter. Pfc. Willett covered the squad's withdrawal, but his position drew heavy enemy machinegun fire, and he received multiple wounds enabling the enemy to again pin down the remainder of the squad. Pfc. Willett struggled to an upright position, and, disregarding his painful wounds, he again engaged the enemy with his rifle to allow his squad to continue its movement and to evacuate several of his comrades who were by now wounded. Moving from position to position, he engaged the enemy at close range until he was mortally wounded. By his unselfish acts of bravery, Pfc. Willett insured the withdrawal of his comrades to the company position, saving their lives at the cost of his. Pfc. Willett's valorous actions were in keeping with the highest traditions of the U.S. Army and reflect great credit upon himself and the Armed Forces of his country.

†MONROE, JAMES H.

Rank and Organization: Private First Class, U.S. Army, Headquarters Company, 1st Battalion, 8th Cavalry, 1st Cavalry Division (Airmobile).

Born: October 17, 1944, Aurora, Ill.

Entered Service At: Chicago, Ill.

Place and Date: Bong Son, Hoai Nhon Province, Republic of Vietnam, February 16, 1967.

Citation: For conspicuous gallantry and intrepidity in action at the risk of his life above and beyond the call of duty. His platoon was deployed in a night ambush when the position was suddenly subjected to an intense and accurate grenade attack, and one foxhole was hit immediately. Responding without hesitation to the calls for help from the wounded men, Pfc. Monroe moved forward through heavy small-arms fire to the foxhole but found that all of the men had expired. He turned immediately and crawled back through the deadly hail of fire toward other calls for aid. He moved to the platoon sergeant's position where he found the radio operator bleeding profusely from fragmentation and bullet wounds. Ignoring the continuing enemy attack, Pfc. Monroe began treating the wounded man when he saw a live grenade fall directly in front of the position. He shouted a warning to all those nearby, pushed the wounded radio operator and the platoon sergeant to one side, and lunged forward to smother the grenade's blast with his body. Through his valorous actions, performed in a flash of inspired selflessness, Pfc. Monroe saved the lives of two of his comrades and prevented the probable injury of several others. His gallantry and intrepidity were in the highest traditions of the U.S. Army, and reflect great credit upon himself and the Armed Forces of his country.

†SMITH, ELMELINDO R.

Rank and Organization: Platoon Sergeant (then S/Sgt.), U.S. Army, 1st Platoon, Company C, 2d Battalion, 8th Infantry, 4th Infantry Division.

Born: July 27, 1935, Honolulu, Hawaii

Entered Service At: Honolulu, Hawaii

Place and Date: Republic of Vietnam, February 16, 1967

Citation: For conspicuous gallantry and intrepidity at the risk of his life above and beyond the call of duty. During a reconnaissance patrol, his platoon was suddenly engaged by intense machinegun fire hemming in the platoon on three sides. A defensive perimeter was hastily established, but the enemy added mortar and rocket fire to the deadly fusillade and assaulted the position from several directions. With complete disregard for his safety, P/Sgt. Smith moved through the deadly fire along the defensive line, positioning soldiers, distributing ammunition and encouraging his men to repel the enemy attack. Struck to the ground by enemy fire that caused a severe shoulder wound, he regained his feet, killed the enemy soldier and continued to move about the perimeter. He was again wounded in the shoulder and stomach but continued moving on his knees to assist in the defense. Noting the enemy massing at a weakened point on the perimeter, he crawled into the open and poured deadly fire into the enemy ranks. As he crawled on he was struck by a rocket. Moments later, he regained consciousness, and drawing on his fast dwindling strength, continued to crawl from man to man. When he could move no farther, he chose to remain in the open where he could alert the perimeter to the approaching enemy. P/Sgt. Smith perished, never relenting in his determined effort against the enemy. The valorous acts and heroic leadership of this outstanding soldier inspired those remaining members of his platoon to beat back the enemy assaults. P/Sgt. Smith's gallant actions were in keeping with the highest traditions of the U.S. Army and reflect great credit upon himself and the Armed Forces of his country.

†WILBANKS, HILLIARD A.

Rank and Organization: Captain, U.S. Air Force, 21st Tactical Air Support Squadron, Nha Trang AFB, RVN.
Born: July 26, 1933, Cornelia, Georgia
Entered Service At: Atlanta, Georgia
Place and Date: Near Dalat, Republic of Vietnam, February 24, 1967.
Citation: For conspicuous gallantry and intrepidity in action at the risk of his life above and beyond the call of duty. As a forward air controller Capt. Wilbanks was pilot of an unarmed, light aircraft flying visual reconnaissance ahead of a South Vietnamese Army Ranger Battalion. His intensive search revealed a well-concealed and numerically superior hostile force poised to ambush the advancing rangers. The Viet Cong, realizing that Capt. Wilbanks' discovery had compromised their position and ability to launch a surprise attack, immediately fired on the small aircraft with all available firepower. The enemy then began advancing against the exposed forward elements of the ranger force which were pinned down by devastating fire. Capt. Wilbanks recognized that close support aircraft could not arrive in time to enable the rangers to withstand the advancing enemy onslaught. With full knowledge of the limitations of his unarmed, unarmored, light reconnaissance aircraft, and the great danger imposed by the enemy's vast firepower, he unhesitatingly assumed a covering , close support role. Flying through a hail of withering fire at treetop level, Capt. Wilbanks passed directly over the advancing enemy and inflicted many casualties by firing his rifle out of the side window of his aircraft. Despite increasingly intense antiaircraft fire, Capt. Wilbanks continued to completely disregard his own safety and made repeated low passes over the enemy to divert their fire away from the rangers. His daring tactics successfully interrupted the enemy advance, allowing the rangers to withdraw to safety from their perilous position. During his final courageous attack to protect the withdrawing forces, Capt. Wilbanks was mortally wounded and his bullet-riddled aircraft crashed between the opposing forces. Capt. Wilbanks' magnificent action saved numerous friendly personnel from certain injury or death. His unparalleled concern for his fellow man and his extraordinary heroism were in the highest traditions of the military service, and reflect great credit upon himself and the U.S. Air Force.

†YABES, MAXIMO

Rank and Organization: First sergeant, U.S. Army, Company A, 4th Battalion, 9th Infantry, 25th Infantry Division.
Born: January 29, 1932, Lodi, California.
Entered Service At: Eugene, Oregon
Place and Date: Near Phu Hoa Dong, Republic of Vietnam, February 26, 1967.
Citation: For conspicuous gallantry and intrepidity at the risk of his life above and beyond the call of duty. 1st Sergeant Yabes distinguished himself with Company A, which was providing security for a land clearing operation. Early in the morning the company suddenly came under intense automatic weapons and mortar fire followed by a battalion sized assault from three sides. Penetrating the defensive perimeter the enemy advanced on the company command post bunker. The command post received increasingly heavy fire and was in danger of being overwhelmed. When several enemy grenades landed within the command post, 1st Sgt. Yabes shouted a warning and used his body as shield to protect others in the bunker. Although painfully wounded by numerous grenade fragments, and despite the vicious enemy fire on the bunker, he remained there to provide covering fire and enable others in the command group to relocate. When the command group had reached a new position, 1st Sgt. Yabes moved through a withering hail of enemy fire to another bunker 50 meters away. There he secured a grenade launcher from a fallen comrade and fired point blank into the attacking Viet Cong stopping further penetration of the perimeter. Noting wounded men helpless in the fire swept area, he moved them to a safer position where they could be given medical treatment. He resumed his accurate and effective fire killing several enemy soldiers and forcing others to withdraw from the vicinity of the command post. As the battle continued, he observed an enemy machinegun within the perimeter that threatened the whole position. On his own, he dashed across the exposed area, assaulted the machinegun, killed the crew, destroyed the weapon, and fell mortally wounded. 1st Sgt. Yabes' valiant and selfless actions saved the lives of many of his fellow soldiers and inspired his comrades to effectively repel the enemy assault. His indomitable fighting spirit, extraordinary courage and intrepidity at the cost of his life are in the highest military traditions and reflect great credit upon himself and the Armed Forces of his country.

†ANDERSON, JAMES JR.

Rank and Organization: Private First Class, U.S. Marine Corps, 2d Platoon, Company F, 2d Battalion, 3d Marines, 3d Marine Division.
Born: January 22, 1947, Los Angeles, California
Entered Service At: Los Angeles, California
Place and Date: Republic of Vietnam, February 28, 1967
Citation: For conspicuous gallantry and intrepidity at the risk of his life above and beyond the call of duty. Company F was advancing in dense jungle northwest of Cam Lo in an effort to extract a heavily besieged reconnaissance patrol. Pfc. Anderson's platoon was the lead element and had advanced only about 200 meters when they were brought under extremely intense enemy small-arms and automatic weapons fire. The platoon reacted swiftly, getting on the line as best they could in the thick terrain, and began returning fire. Pfc. Anderson found himself tightly bunched together with the other members of his platoon only 20 meters from the enemy positions. As the fire fight continued several of the men were wounded by the deadly enemy assault. Suddenly, an enemy grenade landed in the midst of the marines and rolled alongside Pfc. Anderson's head. Unhesitatingly and with complete disregard for his personal safety, he reached out, grasped the grenade, pulled it to his chest and curled around it as it went off. Although several marines received shrapnel from the grenade, his body absorbed the major force of the explosion. In this singularly heroic act, Pfc. Anderson saved his comrades from serious injury and possible death. His personal heroism, extraordinary valor, and inspirational supreme self-sacrifice reflected great credit upon himself and the U.S. Marine Corps and upheld the highest traditions of the U.S. Naval Service. He gallantly gave his life for his country.

†LEONARD, MATTHEW

Rank and Organization: Platoon Sergeant, U.S. Army, Company B, 1st Battalion, 16th Infantry, 1st Infantry Division.
Born: November 26, 1929, Eutaw, Alabama
Entered Service At: Birmingham, Alabama
Place and Date: Near Suoi Da, Republic of Vietnam, February 28, 1967.
Citation: For conspicuous gallantry and intrepidity in action at the risk of his life above and beyond the call of duty. P/Sgt. Leonard's platoon was suddenly attacked by a large enemy force employing small arms, automatic weapons, and hand grenades. Although the platoon leader and several other key leaders were among the first wounded, P/Sgt. Leonard quickly rallied his men to throw back the initial enemy assaults. During the short pause that followed, he organized a defensive perimeter, re distributed ammunition, and inspired his comrades through his forceful leadership and words of encouragement. Noticing a wounded companion outside the perimeter, he dragged the man to safety but was struck by a sniper's bullet that shattered his left hand. Refusing medical attention and continuously exposing himself to the increasing fire as the enemy again assaulted the perimeter, P/Sgt. Leonard moved from position to position to direct the fire of his men against the well camouflaged foe. Under the cover of the main attack, the enemy moved a machinegun into a location where it could sweep the entire perimeter. This threat was magnified when the platoon machinegun in this area malfunctioned. P/Sgt. Leonard quickly crawled to the gun position and was helping to clear the malfunction when the gunner and the other men in the vicinity were wounded by fire from the enemy machinegun. P/Sgt. Leonard rose to his feet, charged the enemy gun, and destroyed the hostile crew despite being hit several times by enemy fire. He moved to a tree, propped himself against it, and continued to engage the enemy until he succumbed to his many wounds. His fighting spirit, heroic leadership, and valiant acts inspired the remaining members of his platoon to hold back the enemy until assistance arrived. P/Sgt. Leonard's profound courage and devotion to his men are in keeping with the highest traditions of the military service, and his gallant actions reflect great credit upon himself and the U.S. Army.

†OUELLET, DAVID G.
Rank and Organization: Seaman, U.S. Navy, River Squadron 5, My Tho Detachment 532.
Born: June 13, 1944, Newton, Mass.
Entered Service At: Boston, Mass.
Place and Date: Mekong River, Republic of Vietnam, March 6, 1967.
Citation: For conspicuous gallantry and intrepidity at the risk of his life above and beyond the call of duty. As the forward machine gunner on River Patrol Boat (PBR) 124, that was on patrol during the evening hours, Seaman Ouellet observed suspicious activity near the river bank, alerted his captain, and recommended movement of the boat to the area to investigate. While the PBR was making a high-speed run along the river bank, Seaman Ouellet spotted an incoming enemy grenade falling toward the boat. He immediately left the protected position of his gun mount and ran aft for the full length of the speeding boat, shouting to his fellow crew members to take cover. Observing the boat captain standing unprotected, Seaman Ouellet bounded onto the engine compartment cover, and pushed the boat captain down to safety. In the split second that followed the grenade's landing, and in the face of certain death, Seaman Ouellet fearlessly placed himself between the deadly missile and his shipmates, courageously absorbing most of the blast fragments with his body in order to protect his shipmates from injury and death. His extraordinary heroism and his selfless and courageous actions on behalf of his comrades at the expense of his life were in the finest traditions of the U.S. Naval Service.

DETHLEFSEN, MERLYN HANS

Rank and Organization: Major (then Captain), U.S. Air Force.
Born: June 29, 1934, Greenville, Iowa.
Entered Service At: Royal, Iowa
Place and Date: In the air over North Vietnam, March 10, 1967.
Citation: For conspicuous gallantry and intrepidity at the risk of his life above and beyond the call of duty. Maj. Dethlefsen was one of a flight of F-105 aircraft engaged in a fire suppression mission designed to destroy a key antiaircraft defensive complex containing surface-to-air missiles (SAM), an exceptionally heavy concentration of antiaircraft artillery, and other automatic weapons. The defensive network was situated to dominate the approach and provide protection to an important North Vietnam industrial center that was scheduled to be attacked by fighter bombers immediately after the strike by Maj. Dethlefsen's flight. In the initial attack on the defensive complex the lead aircraft was crippled, and Maj. Dethlefsen's aircraft was extensively damaged by the intense enemy fire. Realizing that the success of the impending fighter bomber attack on the center now depended on his ability to effectively suppress the defensive fire, Maj. Dethlefsen ignored the enemy's overwhelming firepower and the damage to his aircraft and pressed his attack. Despite a continuing hail of antiaircraft fire, deadly surface-to-air missiles, and counterattacks by MIG interceptors, Maj. Dethlefsen flew repeated close range strikes to silence the enemy defensive positions with bombs and cannon fire. His action in rendering ineffective the defensive SAM and antiaircraft artillery sites enabled the ensuing fighter bombers to strike successfully the important industrial target without loss or damage to their aircraft, thereby appreciably reducing the enemy's ability to provide essential war material. Maj. Dethlefsen's consummate skill and selfless dedication to this significant mission were in keeping with the highest traditions of the U.S. Air Force and reflect great credit upon himself and the Armed Forces of his country.

†KAROPCZYC, STEPHEN EDWARD

Rank and Organization: First Lieutenant, U.S. Army, Company A, 2d Battalion, 35th Infantry, 25th Infantry Division.
Born: March 5, 1944, New York, NY
Entered Service At: Bethpage, NY
Place and Date: Kontum Province, Republic of Vietnam, March 12, 1967.
Citation: For conspicuous gallantry and intrepidity in action at the risk of his life above and beyond the call of duty. While leading the 3d Platoon, Company A, on a flanking maneuver against a superior enemy force. 1st Lt. Karopczyc observed that his lead element was engaged with a small enemy unit along his route. Aware of the importance of quickly pushing through to the main enemy force in order to provide relief for a hard-pressed friendly platoon, he dashed through the intense enemy fire into the open and hurled colored smoke grenades to designate the foe for attack by helicopter gunships. He moved among his men to embolden their advance, and he guided their attack by marking enemy locations with bursts of fire from his own weapon. His forceful leadership quickened the advance, forced the enemy to retreat, and allowed his unit to close with the main hostile force. Continuing the deployment of his platoon, he constantly exposed himself as he ran from man to man to give encouragement and to direct their efforts. A shot from an enemy sniper struck him above the heart but he refused aid for his serious injury, plugging the bleeding wound with his finger until it could be properly dressed. As the enemy strength mounted, he ordered his men to organize a defensive position in and around some abandoned bunkers where he conducted a defense against the increasingly strong enemy attacks. After several hours, a North Vietnamese soldier hurled a hand grenade to within a few feet of 1st Lt. Karopczyc and two other wounded men. Although his position protected him, he leaped up to cover the grenade with a steel helmet. It exploded to drive fragments into 1st Lt. Karopczyc's legs, but his action prevented further injury to the two wounded men. Severely weakened by his multiple wounds, he continued to direct the actions of his men until he succumbed two hours later. 1st Lt. Karopczyc's heroic leadership, unyielding perseverance, and selfless devotion to his men were directly responsible for the successful and spirited action of his platoon throughout the battle and are in keeping with the highest traditions of the U.S. Army and reflect great credit upon himself and the Armed Forces of his country.

†SARGENT, RUPPERT L.

Rank and Organization: First Lieutenant, U.S. Army, Company B, 4th Battalion, 9th Infantry, 25th Infantry Division.
Born: January 6, 1938, Hampton, Va.
Entered Service At: Richmond, Va.
Place and Date: Hau Nghia Province, Republic of Vietnam, March 15, 1967.
Citation: For conspicuous gallantry and intrepidity in action at the risk of his life above and beyond the call of duty. While leading a platoon of Company B, 1st Lt. Sargent was investigating a reported Viet Cong meeting house and weapons cache. A tunnel entrance which 1st Lt. Sargent observed was boobytrapped. He tried to destroy the boobytrap and blow the cover from the tunnel using hand grenades, but this attempt was not successful. He and his demolition man moved in to destroy the boobytrap and cover which flushed a Viet Cong soldier from the tunnel, who was immediately killed by a nearby platoon sergeant. 1st Lt. Sargent, the platoon sergeant, and a forward observer moved toward the tunnel entrance. As they approached, another Viet Cong soldier emerged and threw two hand grenades that landed in the midst of the group. 1st Lt. Sargent fired three shots at the enemy then turned and unhesitatingly threw himself over the two grenades. He was mortally wounded, and his two companions were lightly wounded when the grenades exploded. By his courageous and selfless act of exceptional heroism, he saved the lives of the platoon sergeant and the forward observer and prevented the injury or death of several nearby comrades. 1st Lt. Sargent's actions were in keeping with the highest traditions of the military services and reflect great credit upon himself and the U.S. Army.

HAGEMEISTER, CHARLES CRIS

Rank and Organization: Specialist Fifth Class (then Sp4c.), U.S. Army, Headquarters Company, 1st Battalion, 5th Cavalry, 1st Cavalry Division (Airmobile).
Born: August 21, 1946, Lincoln, Nebraska
Entered Service At: Lincoln, Nebraska
Place and Date: Binh Dinh Province, Republic of Vietnam, March 20, 1967.
Citation: For conspicuous gallantry and intrepidity in action at the risk of his life above and beyond the call of duty. While conducting combat operations against a hostile force, Sp5c. Hagemeister's platoon suddenly came under heavy attack on three sides by an enemy force occupying well concealed, fortified positions and supported by machineguns and mortars. Seeing two of his comrades seriously wounded in the initial action, Sp5c. Hagemeister unhesitatingly and with total disregard for his safety, raced through the deadly hail of enemy fire to provide them medical aid. Upon learning that the platoon leader and several other soldiers had also been wounded, Sp5c. Hagemeister continued to brave the withering enemy fire and crawled forward to render lifesaving treatment and to offer words of encouragement. Attempting to evacuate the seriously wounded soldiers, Sp5c. Hagemeister was taken under fire at close range by an enemy sniper. Realizing that the lives of his fellow soldiers depended on his actions, Sp5c. Hagemeister seized a rifle from a fallen comrade, killed the sniper, three other enemy soldiers that were attempting to encircle his position and silenced an enemy machinegun that covered the area with deadly fire. Unable to remove the wounded to a less exposed location and aware of the enemy's efforts to isolate his unit, he dashed through a fusillade of fire to secure help from a nearby platoon. Returning with help, he placed men in positions to cover his advance as he moved to evacuate the wounded forward of his location. These efforts successfully completed, he then moved to the other flank and evacuated additional wounded men despite the fact that his every move drew fire from the enemy. Sp5c. Hagemeister's repeated heroic and selfless actions at the risk of his life saved the lives of many of his comrades and inspired their actions in repelling the enemy assault. Sp5c. Hagemeister's indomitable courage was in the highest traditions of the U.S. Army and reflect great credit upon himself and the Armed Forces of his country.

†HOSKING, CHARLES ERNEST JR.

Rank and Organization: Master Sergeant, U.S. Army, Company A, 5th Special Forces Group (Airborne), 1st special Forces.
Born: May 12, 1924, Ramsey, New Jersey.
Entered Service At: Fort Dix, New Jersey
Place and Date: Phuoc Long Province, Republic of Vietnam, March 21, 1967.
Citation: For gallantry and intrepidity in action at the risk of his life above and beyond the call of duty. M/Sgt. Hosking (then Sgt. First Class), Detachment A-302, Company A, greatly distinguished himself while serving as company advisor in the III Corps Civilian Irregular Defense Group Reaction Battalion during combat operations in Don Luan District. A Viet Cong suspect was apprehended and subsequently identified as a Viet Cong sniper. While M/Sgt. Hosking was preparing the enemy for movement back to the base camp, the prisoner suddenly grabbed a hand grenade from M/Sgt. Hosking's belt, armed the grenade, and started running towards the company command group which consisted two Americans and two Vietnamese who were standing a few feet away. Instantly realizing that the enemy intended to kill the other men, M/Sgt. Hosking immediately leaped upon the Viet Cong's back. With utter disregard for his personal safety, he grasped the Viet Cong in a "bear hug" forcing the grenade against the enemy soldier's chest. He then wrestled the Viet Cong to the ground and covered the enemy's body with his body until the grenade detonated. The blast instantly killed both M/Sgt. Hosking and the Viet Cong. By absorbing the full force of the exploding grenade with his body and that of the enemy, he saved the other members of his command group from death or serious injury. M/Sgt. Hosking's risk of his life above and beyond the call of duty are in the highest traditions of the U.S. Army and reflect great credit upon himself and the Armed Forces of his country.

McNERNEY, DAVID H.

Rank and Organization: First Sergeant, U.S. Army, Company A, 1st Battalion, 8th Infantry, 4th Infantry Division.
Born: June 2, 1931, Lowell, Mass.
Entered Service At: Fort Bliss, Texas
Place and Date: Polei Doc, Republic of Vietnam, March 22, 1967.
Citation: For conspicuous gallantry and intrepidity in action at the risk of his life above and beyond the call of duty. 1st Sgt. McNerney distinguished himself when his unit was attacked by a North Vietnamese battalion near Polei Doc. Running through the hail of enemy fire to the area of heaviest contact, he was assisting in the development of a defensive perimeter when he encountered several enemy at close range. He killed the enemy but was painfully injured when blown from his feet by a grenade. In spite of this injury, he assaulted and destroyed an enemy machinegun position that had pinned down five of his comrades beyond the defensive line. Upon learning his commander and artillery forward observer had been killed, he assumed command of the company. He adjusted artillery fire to within 20 meters of the position in a daring measure to repulse enemy assaults. When the smoke grenades used to mark the position were gone, he moved into a nearby clearing to designate the location to friendly aircraft. In spite of enemy fire he remained exposed until he was certain the position was spotted and then climbed into a tree and tied the identification panel to its highest branches. Then he moved among his men readjusting their position, encouraging the defenders and checking the wounded. As the hostile assaults slackened, he began clearing a helicopter landing sight to evacuate the wounded. When explosives were needed to remove large trees, 1st Sgt. McNerney crawled outside the relative safety of his perimeter to collect demolition material from abandoned rucksacks. Moving through a fusillade of fire he returned with the explosives that were vital to clearing the landing zone. Disregarding the pain of his injury and refusing medical evacuation, 1st Sgt. McNerney remained with his unit until the next day when the new commander arrived. First Sgt. McNerney's outstanding heroism and leadership were inspirational to his comrades. His actions were in keeping with the highest traditions of the U.S. Army and reflect great credit upon himself and the Armed Forces of his country.

Note: The following is a newspaper account of the preceding battle in which Sgt. McNerney earned the Medal of Honor:

Outnumbered G.I.'s Rout
Foe In Jungle, Killing 423

SAIGON, South Vietnam - Overwhelmingly outnumbered artillerymen and infantrymen today turned an enemy attack into one of the major American victories of the war.

A United States military spokesman said 423 enemy soldiers were killed and six captured in six hours of jungle fighting about 70 miles northwest of Saigon. The losses were among the highest taken by the enemy in a single battle.

American casualties were reported as 30 dead, 109 wounded and 3 missing.

The enemy attack near Saigon began about 6 A.M. with a mortar barrage on a position of the United States' Fourth Infantry Division. About 300 troops manned the 18 howitzers there, and about 300 riflemen of two companies waited around them in foxholes.

Shortly after the mortar fire began, some 2,000 soldiers - the bulk of the 272nd Viet Cong Regiment - charged toward the guns.

According to sources in the field, the American infantrymen were driven back toward the howitzers. But the artillerymen lowered the barrels of their guns, striking the Viet Cong point-blank with volley after volley of shotgun-like 105mm shells.

"The guns shot out a shower of shrapnel with each blast and just cleared a path right through the Viet Cong" a soldier said. "The VC got within 25 yards of the guns, but the men stayed right there. Eventually they had to use small arms.

"When a mechanized battalion of reinforcements rolled in-and armored personnel carriers-the guys started jumping up and down," the soldier added.

Capt. George Shoemaker, commander of one of the infantry companies assigned to protect the artillerymen, said: "The first thing I saw was two M-48 tanks, and I wanted to kiss them."

Lt. Col. John A. Bender of Bremerton, Wash., commander of all of the infantrymen assigned to the artillery post, said the attack was "worse than anything I've seen in World War II or Korea."

Enemy soldiers destroyed four howitzers, the sources in the field said.

"They were so intent on getting at the guns that a whole pack of them ran right past me and Specialist Edward Ziegler," said Sgt. Milburn Van Meter. "We just turned and picked them off as fast as we could shoot."

When the tanks and armored cars arrived at about 10:30 with their heavy machineguns blasting, most enemy soldiers fell away. But as late as noon, guerrilla bands rallied against the Americans, the field spokesman said.

In the evening, the military spokesman in Saigon said the armored force was pursuing the enemy soldiers to the northeast and southeast rather than toward Cambodia, where the enemy has often fled.

†SINGLETON, WALTER K.

Rank and Organization: Sergeant, U.S. Marine Corps, Company A, 1st Battalion, 9th Marines, 3d Marine Division.
Born: December 7, 1944, Memphis, Tenn.
Entered Service At: Memphis, Tenn.
Place and Date: Gio Linh District, Quang Tri Province, Republic of Vietnam, March 24, 1967.
Citation: For conspicuous gallantry and intrepidity in action at the risk of his life above and beyond the call of duty. Sgt. Singleton's company was conducting combat operations when the lead platoon received intense small arms, automatic weapons, rocket, and mortar fire from a well entrenched enemy force. As the company fought its way forward, the extremely heavy enemy fire caused numerous friendly casualties. Sensing the need for early treatment of the wounded, Sgt. Singleton quickly moved from his relatively safe position in the rear of the foremost point of the advance and made numerous trips through the enemy killing zone to move the injured men out of the danger area. Noting that a large part of the enemy fire was coming from a hedgerow, he seized a machinegun and assaulted the key enemy location, delivering devastating fire as he advanced. He forced his way through the hedgerow directly into the enemy strong point. Although he was mortally wounded, his fearless attack killed eight of the enemy and drove the remainder from the hedgerow. Sgt. Singleton's bold actions completely disorganized the enemy defense and saved the lives of many of his comrades. His daring initiative, selfless devotion to duty and indomitable fighting spirit reflect great credit upon himself and the U.S. Marine Corps, and his performance upheld the highest traditions of the U.S. Naval Service.

†DICKEY, DOUGLAS E.

Rank and Organization: Private First Class, U.S. Marine Corps, Company C, 1st Battalion, 4th Marines, 9th Marine Amphibious Brigade, 3d Marine Division.

Born: December 24, 1946, Greenville, Darke, Ohio

Entered Service At: Cincinnati, Ohio

Place and Date: Republic of Vietnam, March 26, 1967.

Citation: For conspicuous gallantry and intrepidity at the risk of his life above and beyond the call of duty. While participating in Operation Beacon Hill 1, the 2d Platoon was engaged in a fierce battle with the Viet Cong at close range in dense jungle foliage. Pfc. Dickey had come forward to replace a radio operator who had been wounded in this intense action and was being treated by a medical corpsman. Suddenly an enemy grenade landed in the midst of a group of marines, which included the wounded radio operator who was immobilized. Fully realizing the inevitable result of his actions, Pfc. Dickey, in a final valiant act, quickly and unhesitating threw himself upon the deadly grenade, absorbing with his body the full and complete force of the explosion. Pfc. Dickey's personal heroism, extraordinary valor and selfless courage saved a number of his comrades from certain injury and possible death at the cost of his life. His actions reflect great credit upon himself , the Marine Corps and the U.S. Naval Service. He gallantly gave his life for his country.

†BOBO, JOHN P.

Rank and Organization: Second Lieutenant, U.S. Marine Corps Reserve, Company I, 3d Battalion, 9th Marines, 3d Marine Division, FMF.

Born: February 14, 1943, Niagara Falls, New York

Entered Service At: Buffalo, New York

Place and Date: Quang Tri Province, Republic of Vietnam, March 30, 1967.

Citation: For conspicuous gallantry and intrepidity at the risk of his life above and beyond the call of duty. Company I was establishing night ambush sights when the command group was attacked by a reinforced North Vietnamese company supported by heavy automatic weapons and mortar fire. 2d Lt. Bobo immediately organized a hasty defense and moved from position to position encouraging the outnumbered marines despite the murderous enemy fire. Recovering a rocket launcher from among the friendly casualties, he organized a new launcher team and directed its fire into the enemy machinegun positions. When an exploding enemy mortar round severed 2d Lt. Bobo's right leg below the knee, he refused to be evacuated and insisted upon being placed in a firing position to cover the movement of the command group to a better location. With a web belt around his leg serving as a tourniquet and with his leg jammed into the dirt to curtain the bleeding, he remained in this position and delivered devastating fire into the ranks of the enemy attempting to overrun the marines. 2d Lt. Bobo was mortally wounded while firing his weapon into the mainpoint of the enemy attack but his valiant spirit inspired his men to heroic efforts, and his tenacious stand enabled the command group to gain a protective position where it repulsed the enemy onslaught. 2d LT. Bobo's superb leadership, dauntless courage, and bold initiative reflect great credit upon himself and upheld the highest traditions of the U.S. Marine Corps and the U.S. Naval Service. He gallantly gave his life for his country.

†MICHAEL, DON LESLIE
Rank and Organization: Specialist Fourth Class, U.S. Army, Company C, 4th Battalion, 503d Infantry, 173d Airborne Brigade.
Born: July 31, 1947, Florence, Alabama
Entered Service At: Montgomery, Alabama
Place and Date: Republic of Vietnam, April 8, 1967
Citation: For conspicuous gallantry and intrepidity at the risk of his life above and beyond the call of duty. Sp4c. Michael, U.S. Army, distinguished himself while serving with Company C. Sp4c. Michael was part of a platoon that was moving through an area of suspected enemy activity. While the rest of the platoon stopped to provide security, the squad to which Sp4c. Michael was assigned moved forward to investigate signs of recent enemy activity. After moving approximately 125 meters, the squad encountered a single Viet Cong soldier. When he was fired upon by the squad's machine gunner, other Viet Cong opened fire with automatic weapons from a well concealed bunker to the squad's right front. The volume of enemy fire was so withering as to pin down the entire squad and halt all forward movement. Realizing the gravity of the situation, Sp4c. Michael exposed himself to throw two grenades, but failed to eliminate the enemy position. From his position on the left flank, Sp4c. Michael maneuvered forward with two more grenades until he was within 20 meters of the enemy bunkers, when he again exposed himself to throw two grenades, which failed to detonate. Undaunted, Sp4c. Michael made his way back to the friendly positions to obtain more grenades. With two grenades in hand, he again started his perilous move towards the enemy bunker, which by this time was under intense artillery fire from friendly positions. As he neared the bunker, an enemy soldier attacked him from a concealed position. Sp4c. Michael killed him with his rifle and, in spite of the enemy fire and the exploding artillery rounds, was successful in destroying the enemy positions. Sp4c. Michael took up the pursuit of the remnants of the retreating enemy. When his comrades reached Sp4c. Michael, he had been mortally wounded. His inspiring display of determination and courage saved the lives of many of his comrades and successfully eliminated a destructive enemy force. Sp4c. Michael's actions were in keeping with the highest traditions of the military service and reflect utmost credit upon himself and the U.S. Army.

†INGALLS, GEORGE ALAN

Rank and Organization: Specialist Fourth Class, U.S. Army, Company A, 2d Battalion, 5th Cavalry, 1st Cavalry Division (Airmobile).
Born: March 9, 1946, Hanford, California
Entered Service At: Los Angeles, California
Place and Date: Near Duc Pho, Republic of Vietnam, April 16, 1967.
Citation: For conspicuous gallantry and intrepidity in action at the risk of his life above and beyond the call of duty. Sp4c. Ingalls, a member of Company A, accompanied his squad on a night ambush mission. Shortly after the ambush was established, an enemy soldier entered the killing zone and was shot when he tried to evade capture. Other enemy soldiers were expected to enter the area, and the ambush was maintained in the same location. Two quiet hours passed without incident, then suddenly a hand grenade was thrown from the nearby dense undergrowth into the center of the squad's position. The grenade did not explode, but shortly thereafter a second grenade landed directly between Sp4c. Ingalls and a nearby comrade. Although he could have jumped to a safe position, Sp4c. Ingalls, in a spontaneous act of great courage, threw himself on the grenade and absorbed the full blast. The explosion mortally wounded Sp4c. Ingalls, but his heroic action saved the lives of the remaining members of his squad. His gallantry and selfless devotion to his comrades are in keeping with the highest traditions of the military service and reflects great credit upon Sp4c. Ingalls, his unit, and the U.S. Army.

THORSNESS, LEO K.

Rank and Organization: Lieutenant Colonel (then Major), U.S. Air Force, 357th Tactical Fighter Squadron.
Born: February 14, 1932, Walnut Grove, Minn.
Entered Service At: Walnut Grove Minn.
Place and Date: Over North Vietnam, April 19, 1967.
Citation: For conspicuous gallantry and intrepidity in action at the risk of his life above and beyond the call of duty. As a pilot of an F-105 aircraft, Lt. Col. Thorsness was on a surface-to-air missile suppression mission over North Vietnam. Lt. Col. Thorsness and his wingman attacked and silenced a surface-to-air missile site with air-to-ground missiles, and then destroyed a second surface-to-air missile site with bombs. In the attack on the second missile site, Lt. Col. Thorsness' wingman was shot down by intensive antiaircraft fire, and the two crew members abandoned their aircraft. Lt. Col. Thorsness circled the descending parachutes to keep the crew members in sight and relay their position to the Search and Rescue Center. During this maneuver, a MIG-17 was sighted in the area. Lt. Col. Thorsness immediately initiated an attack and destroyed the MIG. Because his aircraft was low on fuel, he was forced to depart the area in search of a tanker. Upon being advised that two helicopters were orbiting over the downed crew's position and that there were hostile MIGs in the area posing a serious threat to the helicopters, Lt. Col. Thorsness, despite his low fuel condition, decided to return alone through a hostile environment of surface-to-air missiles and antiaircraft defenses to the downed crew's position. As he approached the area, he spotted four MIG-17 aircraft and immediately initiated an attack on the MIGs, damaging one and driving the others from the rescue scene. When it became apparent that an aircraft in the area was critically low on fuel and the crew would have to abandon the aircraft unless they could reach a tanker, Lt. Col. Thorsness, although critically low on fuel himself, helped to avert further loss of life and a friendly aircraft by recovering at a forward operating base, thus allowing the aircraft in emergency fuel condition to refuel safely. Lt Col. Thorsness' extraordinary heroism, self-sacrifice, and personal bravery involving conspicuous risk of life were in the highest tradition of the military service and reflect great credit upon himself and the U.S. Air Force.

†ESTOCIN, MICHAEL J.

Rank and Organization: Captain (then Lt. Cmdr.), U.S. Navy, Attack Squadron 192, USS Ticonderoga (CVA-14).
Born: April 27, 1931, Turtle Creek, Pa.
Entered Service At: Akron, Ohio
Place and Date: Haiphong, North Vietnam, April 20 and 26, 1967.
Citation: For conspicuous gallantry and intrepidity at the risk of his life above and beyond the call of duty on 20 and 26 April 1967 as a pilot in Attack Squadron 192, embarked in USS Ticonderoga. Leading a three plane group of aircraft in support of a coordinated strike against two thermal powerplants in Haiphong, North Vietnam, on April 20, 1967, Capt. Estocin provided continuous warnings to the strike group leaders of the surface-to-air missile (SAM) threats, and personally neutralized three SAM sites. Although his aircraft was severely damaged by an exploding missile, he reentered the target area and relentlessly prosecuted a SHRIKE attack in the face of intense antiaircraft fire. With less then five minutes of fuel remaining he departed the target area and commenced inflight refueling which continued for over 100 miles. Three miles aft of Ticonderoga, and without enough fuel for a second approach, he disengaged from the tanker and executed a precise approach to a fiery arrested landing. On April 26, 1967, in support of a coordinated strike against the vital fuel facilities in Haiphong, he led an attack on a threatening SAM site, during which his aircraft was seriously damaged by an exploding SAM; nevertheless, he regained control of his burning aircraft and courageously launched his SHRIKE missiles before departing the area. By his inspiring courage and unswerving devotion to duty in the face of great personal danger, Capt. Estocin upheld the highest traditions of the U.S. Naval Service.

†MARTINI, GARY W.

Rank and Organization: Private First Class, U.S. Marine Corps, Company F, 2d Battalion, 1st Marines, 1st Marine Division.
Born: September 21, 1948, Lexington, Virginia
Entered Service At: Portland, Oregon
Place and Date: Binh Son, Republic of Vietnam, April 21, 1967.
Citation: For conspicuous gallantry and intrepidity at the risk of his life above and beyond the call of duty. On April 21, 1967, during operation UNION, elements of Company F, conducting offensive operations at Binh Son, encountered a firmly entrenched enemy force and immediately deployed to engage them. The marines in Pfc. Martini's platoon assaulted across an open rice paddy to within 20 meters of the enemy trench line where they were suddenly struck by hand grenades, intense small-arms, automatic weapons, and mortar fire. The enemy onslaught killed 14 and wounded 18 marines, pinning the remainder of the platoon down behind a low paddy dike. In the face of imminent danger, Pfc. Martini immediately crawled over the dike to a forward open area within 15 meters of the enemy position where, continuously exposed to the hostile fire, he hurled hand grenades, killing several of the enemy. Crawling back through the intense fire, he rejoined his platoon which had moved to the relative safety of a trench line. From this position he observed several of his wounded comrades lying helpless in the fire-swept paddy. Although he knew that one man had been killed attempting to assist the wounded, Pfc. Martini raced through the open area and dragged a comrade back to a friendly position. In spite of a serious wound received during this first daring rescue, he again braved the unrelenting fury of the enemy fire to aid another companion lying wounded only 20 meters in front of the enemy trench line. As he reached the fallen marine, he received a mortal wound, but disregarding his own condition, he began to drag the marine toward his platoon's position. Observing men from his unit attempting to leave the security of their position to aid him, concerned only for their safety, he called to them to remain under cover, and through a final supreme effort, moved his injured comrade to where he could be pulled to safety, before he fell, succumbing to his wounds. Stout hearted and indomitable, Pfc. Martini unhesitating yielded his life to save two of his comrades and insure the safety of the remainder of his platoon. His outstanding

courage, valiant fighting spirit and selfless devotion to duty reflected the highest credit upon himself, the Marine Corps, and the U.S. Naval Service. He gallantly gave his life for his country.

STUMPF, KENNETH E.

Rank and Organization: Staff Sergeant (then Sp4c.), U.S. Army, Company C, 1st Battalion, 35th Infantry, 25th Infantry Division.
Born: September 28, 1944, Neenah, Wis.
Entered Service At: Milwaukee, Wis.
Place and Date: Near Duc Pho, Republic of Vietnam, April 25, 1967.
Citation: For conspicuous gallantry and intrepidity in action at the risk of his life above and beyond the call of duty. S/Sgt. Stumpf distinguished himself while serving as a squad leader of the 3d Platoon, Company C, on a search and destroy mission. As S/Sgt. Stumpf's company approached a village, it encountered a North Vietnamese rifle company occupying a well fortified bunker complex. During the initial contact, three men from his squad fell wounded in front of a hostile machinegun emplacement. The enemy's heavy volume of fire prevented the unit from moving to the aid of the injured men,but S/Sgt. Stumpf left his secure position in a deep trench and ran through the barrage of incoming rounds to reach his wounded comrades. He picked up one of the men and carried him back to the safety of the trench. Twice more S/Sgt. Stumpf dashed forward while the enemy turned automatic weapons and machineguns upon him, yet he managed to rescue the remaining two squad members. He then organized his squad and led an assault against several enemy bunkers from which continuously heavy fire was being received. He and his squad successfully eliminated two of the bunker positions, but one to the front of the advancing platoon remained a serious threat. Arming himself with extra hand grenades, S/Sgt. Stumpf ran over open ground, through a volley of fire directed at him by a determined enemy, toward the machinegun position. As he reached the bunker, he threw a hand grenade through the aperture. It was immediately returned by the occupants, forcing S/Sgt. Stumpf to take cover. Undaunted he pulled the pins on two more grenades, held them for a few seconds after activation, then hurled them into the position, this time successfully destroying the emplacement. With the elimination of this key position, his unit was able to assault and overrun the enemy. S/Sgt. Stumpf's relentless spirit of aggressiveness, intrepidity, and ultimate concern for the lives of his men, are in the highest traditions of the military service and reflect great credit upon himself and the U.S. Army.

KELLER, LEONARD B.

Rank and Organization: Sergeant, U.S. Army, Company A, 3d Battalion, 60th Infantry, 9th Infantry Division.
Born: February 25, 1947, Rockford, Ill.
Entered Service At: Chicago, Ill.
Place and Date: Ap Bac Zone, Republic of Vietnam, May 2, 1967.
Citation: For conspicuous gallantry and intrepidity in action at the risk of his life above and beyond the call of duty. Sweeping through an area where an enemy ambush had occurred earlier, Sgt. Keller's unit suddenly came under intense automatic weapons and small-arms fire from a number of enemy bunkers and numerous snipers in nearby trees. Sgt. Keller quickly moved to a position where he could fire at a bunker from which automatic fire was received, killing one Viet Cong who attempted to escape. Leaping to the top of a dike, he and a comrade charged the enemy bunkers, dangerously exposing themselves to the enemy fire. Armed with a light machinegun, Sgt. Keller and his comrade began a systematic assault on the enemy bunkers. While Sgt. Keller neutralized the fire from the first bunker with his machinegun, the other soldier threw in a hand grenade killing its occupant. Then he and the other soldier charged a second bunker, killing its occupant. A third bunker contained an automatic rifleman who had pinned down much of the friendly platoon. Again, with utter disregard for the fire directed to them, the two men charged, killing the enemy within. Continuing their attack, Sgt. Keller and his comrade assaulted four more bunkers, killing the enemy within. During their furious assault, Sgt. Keller and his comrade had been almost continuously exposed to intense sniper fire as the enemy desperately sought to stop their attack. The ferocity of their assault had carried the soldiers beyond the line of bunkers into the tree line, forcing the snipers to flee. The two men gave immediate chase, driving the enemy away from the friendly unit. When his ammunition was exhausted, Sgt. Keller returned to the platoon to assist in the evacuation of the wounded. The two man assault had driven an enemy platoon from a well prepared position, accounted for numerous enemy dead, and prevented further friendly casualties. Sgt. Keller's selfless heroism and indomitable fighting spirit saved the lives of many of his comrades and inflicted serious damage to the enemy. His acts were in keeping with the highest traditions of the military service and reflect great credit upon himself and the U.S. Army.

WRIGHT, RAYMOND R.
Rank and Organization: Specialist Fourth Class, U.S. Army, Company A, 3d Battalion, 60th Infantry, 9th Infantry Division.
Born: December 5, 1945, Moriah, New York
Entered Service At: Moriah, New York
Place and Date: Ap Bac Zone, Republic of Vietnam, May 2, 1967.
Citation: For conspicuous gallantry and intrepidity in action at the risk of his life above and beyond the call of duty. While serving as a rifleman with Company A, Sp4c. Wright distinguished himself during a combat patrol in an area where an enemy ambush had occurred earlier. Sp4c. Wright's unit suddenly came under intense automatic weapons and small-arms fire from an enemy bunker system protected by numerous snipers in nearby trees. Despite the heavy enemy fire, Sp4c. Wright and another soldier leaped to the top of a dike to assault the position. Armed with a rifle and several grenades, he and his comrade exposed themselves to intense fire from the bunkers as they charged the nearest one. Sp4c. Wright raced to the bunker, threw in a grenade, killing its occupant. The two soldiers then ran through a hail of fire to the second bunker. While his comrade covered him with his machinegun, Sp4c. Wright charged the bunker and succeeded in killing its occupant with a grenade. A third bunker contained an automatic rifleman who had pinned down much of the friendly platoon. While his comrade again covered him with machinegun fire, Sp4c. Wright charged in and killed the enemy rifleman with a grenade. The two soldiers worked their way through the remaining bunkers, knocking out four of them. Throughout their furious assault, Sp4c. Wright and his comrade had been almost continuously exposed to intense sniper fire from the tree line as the enemy desperately sought to stop their attack. Overcoming stubborn resistance from the bunker system, the men advanced into the tree line forcing the snipers to retreat, giving immediate chase, and driving the enemy away from the friendly unit so that it advanced across the open area without further casualty. When his ammunition was exhausted, Sp4c. Wright returned to his unit to assist in the evacuation of the wounded. This two man assault had driven an enemy platoon from a well prepared position, accounted for numerous enemy casualties, and averted further friendly casualties. Sp4c. Wright's extraordinary heroism, courage, and indomitable fighting spirit saved the lives of many of his comrades and inflicted serious damage on the enemy. His acts

were in keeping with the highest traditions of the military service and reflect great credit upon himself and the U.S. Army.

Note: The following is a newspaper account of the preceding battle for which both Sgt. Keller and Sp4c. Wright were awarded the Congressional Medal of Honor:

Fighting Rages in Delta

SAIGON, South Vietnam - Heavy fighting raged today between United States Ninth Infantry Division troops and a Viet Cong battalion in the Mekong Delta 39 miles southwest of Saigon.

A military spokesman said 181 Viet Cong of the 514th Battalion had been slain so far. A Viet Cong battalion consists of about 500 men. [The United States command said 15 Americans had been killed and 27 wounded in the engagement, The Associated Press reported.]

The spokesman said a battalion of the Third Brigade, Ninth Infantry Division, first made contact with the enemy in a marsh area near a branch of the Mekong River. He said contact continued throughout the evening "with increasing intensity."

After two and a half hours the fighting was described as heavy. American reinforcements arrived, and as night closed in, allied planes illuminated the scene while six Air Force tactical strike planes and artillery pounded the enemy.

†GRANDSTAFF, BRUCE ALAN

Rank and Organization: Platoon Sergeant, U.S. Army, Company B, 1st Battalion, 8th Infantry..

Born: June 2, 1934, Spokane, Washington

Entered Service At: Spokane, Washington

Place and Date: Pleiku Province, Republic of Vietnam, May 18, 1967

Citation: For conspicuous gallantry and intrepidity in action at the risk of his life above and beyond the call of duty. P/Sgt. Grandstaff distinguished himself while leading the Weapons Platoon, Company B, on a reconnaissance mission near the Cambodian border. His platoon was advancing through intermittent enemy contact when it was struck by heavy small arms and automatic weapons fire from three sides. As he established a defensive perimeter, P/Sgt. Grandstaff noted that several of his men had been struck down. He raced 30 meters through the intense fire to aid them but could only save one. Denied freedom to maneuver his unit by the intensity of the enemy onslaught, he adjusted artillery to within 45 meters of his position. When helicopter gunships arrived, he crawled outside the defensive position to mark the location with smoke grenades. Realizing his first marker was probably ineffective, he crawled to another location and threw his last smoke grenade but the smoke did not penetrate the jungle foliage. Seriously wounded in the leg during this effort he returned to his radio and, refusing medical aid, adjusted the artillery even closer as the enemy advanced on his position. Recognizing the need for additional firepower, he again braved the enemy fusillade, crawled to the edge of his position and fired several magazines of tracer ammunition through the jungle canopy. He succeeded in designating the location to the gunships but this action again drew the enemy fire and he was wounded in the other leg. Now enduring intense pain and bleeding profusely, he crawled to within 10 meters of an enemy machinegun which had caused many casualties among his men. He destroyed the position with hand grenades but received additional wounds. Rallying his remaining men to withstand the enemy assaults, he realized his position was being overrun and asked for artillery directly on his location. He fought until mortally wounded by an enemy rocket. Although every man in the platoon was a casualty, survivors attest to the indomitable spirit and exceptional courage of this outstanding combat leader who inspired his men to fight courageously against overwhelming odds and cost the enemy heavy casualties. P/Sgt. Grandstaff's selfless gallantry, above and beyond the call of duty, are in the highest traditions of the U.S. Army and reflect great credit upon himself and the Armed Forces of his country.

†WAYRYNEN, DALE EUGENE

Rank and Organization: Specialist Fourth Class, U.S. Army, Company B, 2d Battalion, 502d Infantry, 1st Brigade, 101st Airborne Division.

Born: January 18, 1947, Moose Lake, Minnesota

Entered Service At: Minneapolis, Minnesota

Place and Date: Quang Ngai, Province, Republic of Vietnam, May 18, 1967

Citation: For conspicuous gallantry and intrepidity in action at the risk of his life above and beyond the call of duty. Sp4c. Wayrynen distinguished himself with Company B, during combat operations near Duc Pho. His platoon was assisting in the night evacuation of the wounded from an earlier enemy contact when the leadman of the unit met face to face with a Viet Cong soldier. The American's shouted warning also alerted the enemy who immediately swept the area with automatic weapons fire from a strongly built bunker close to the trail and threw hand grenades from another nearby fortified position. Almost immediately, the leadman was wounded and knocked from his feet. Sp4c. Wayrynen, the second man in the formation, leaped beyond his fallen comrade to kill another enemy soldier who appeared on the trail, and he dragged his injured companion back to where the point squad had taken cover. Suddenly, a live enemy grenade landed in the center of the tightly grouped men. Sp4c. Wayrynen, quickly assessing the danger to the entire squad as well as to his platoon leader who was nearby, shouted a warning, pushed one soldier out of the way, and threw himself on the grenade at the moment it exploded. He was mortally wounded. His deep and abiding concern for his fellow soldiers was significantly reflected in his supreme and courageous act that preserved the lives of his comrades. Sp4c. Wayrynen's heroic actions are in keeping with the highest traditions of the service, and they reflect great credit upon himself and the U.S. Army.

†BELLRICHARD, LESLIE ALLEN

Rank and Organization: Private First Class, U.S. Army, Company C, 1st Battalion, 8th Infantry, 4th Infantry Division
Born: December 4, 1941, Janesville, Wisconsin
Entered Service At: Oakland, California
Place and Date: Kontum Province, Republic of Vietnam, May 20, 1967
Citation: For conspicuous gallantry and intrepidity in action at the risk of his life above and beyond the call of duty. Acting as a fire team leader with Company C, during combat operations Pfc. Bellrichard was with four fellow soldiers in a foxhole on their unit's perimeter when the position came under a massive enemy attack. Following a 30-minute mortar barrage, the enemy launched a strong ground assault. Pfc. Bellrichard rose in face of a group of charging enemy soldiers and threw hand grenades into their midst, eliminating several of the foe and forcing the remainder to withdraw. Failing in their initial attack, the enemy repeated the mortar and rocket bombardment of the friendly perimeter, then once again charged against the defenders in a concerted effort to overrun the position. Pfc. Bellrichard resumed throwing hand grenades at the on-rushing attackers. As he was about to hurl a grenade, a mortar round exploded just in front of his position, knocking him into the foxhole and causing him to lose his grip on the already armed grenade. Recovering instantly, Pfc. Bellrichard recognized the threat to the lives of his four comrades and threw himself upon the grenade, shielding his companions from the blast that followed. Although severely wounded, Pfc. Bellrichard struggled into an upright position in the foxhole and fired his rifle at the enemy until he succumbed to his wounds. His selfless heroism contributed greatly to the successful defense of the position, and he was directly responsible for saving the lives of several of his comrades. His acts are in keeping with the highest traditions of the military service and reflect great credit upon himself and the U.S. Army.

†**MOLNAR, FRANKIE ZOLY**
Rank and Organization: Staff Sergeant, U.S. Army, Company B,
1st Battalion, 8th Infantry, 4th Infantry Division.
Born: February 14, 1943, Logan, West Virginia
Entered Service At: Fresno, California
Place and Date: Kontum Province, Republic of Vietnam, May 20,
1967
Citation: For conspicuous gallantry and intrepidity in action at the
risk of his life above and beyond the call of duty. S/Sgt. Molnar distinguished himself while serving as a squad leader with Company B,
during combat operations. Shortly after the battalion's defensive perimeter was established, it was hit by intense mortar fire as the pre-
lude to a massive enemy night attack. S/Sgt. Molnar immediately
left his sheltered location to insure the readiness of his squad to meet
the attack. As he crawled through the position, he discovered a group
of enemy soldiers closing in on his squad area. His accurate rifle fire
killed five of the enemy and forced the remainder to flee. When the
mortar fire stopped, the enemy attacked in a human wave supported
by grenades, rockets, automatic weapons, and small-arms fire. After
assisting to repel the first enemy assault, S/Sgt. Molnar found that
his squad's ammunition and grenade supply was nearly expended.
Again leaving the relative safety of his position, he crawled through
intense enemy fire to secure additional ammunition and distribute it
to his squad. He rejoined his men to beat back the renewed enemy
onslaught, and he moved about his area providing medical aid and
assisting in the evacuation of the wounded With the help of several
men, he was preparing to move a severely wounded soldier when an
enemy hand grenade was thrown into the group. The first to see the
grenade, S/Sgt. Molnar threw himself on it and absorbed the deadly
blast to save his comrades. His demonstrated selflessness and inspirational leadership on the battlefield were a major factor in the successful defense of the American position and are in keeping with the
finest traditions of the U.S. Army. S/Sgt. Molnar's actions reflect
great credit upon himself, his unit, and the U.S. Army.

†**FLEEK, CHARLES CLINTON**
Rank and Organization: Sergeant, U.S. Army, Company C, 1st Battalion, 27th Infantry, 25th Infantry Division.
Born: August 28, 1947, Petersburg, Kentucky
Entered Service At: Cincinnati, Ohio
Place and Date: Binh Duong Province, Republic of Vietnam, May 27, 1967
Citation: For conspicuous gallantry and intrepidity in action at the risk of his life above and beyond the call of duty. Sgt. Fleek distinguished himself while serving as a squad leader in Company C, during an ambush operation. Sgt. Fleek's unit was deployed in ambush locations when a large enemy force approached the position. Suddenly, the leading enemy element, sensing the ambush, halted and started to withdraw. Reacting instantly, Sgt. Fleek opened fire and directed the effective fire of his men upon the numerically superior enemy force. During the fierce battle that followed, an enemy soldier threw a grenade into the squad position. Realizing that his men had not seen the grenade, Sgt. Fleek, although in a position to seek cover, shouted a warning to his comrades and threw himself onto the grenade, absorbing its blast. His gallant action undoubtedly saved the lives or prevented the injury of at least eight of his fellow soldiers. Sgt. Fleek's gallantry and willing self-sacrifice were in keeping with the highest traditions of the military service and reflect great credit on himself, his unit, and the U.S. Army.

†GRAHAM, JAMES A.

Rank and Organization: Captain, U.S. Marine Corps, Company F, 2d Battalion, 5th Marines, 1st Marine Division.

Born: August 24, 1940, Wilkinsburg, Allegheny County, Pennsylvania

Entered Service At: Prince Georges, Maryland

Place and Date: Republic of Vietnam, June 2, 1967

Citation: For conspicuous gallantry and intrepidity at the risk of his life above and beyond the call of duty. During Operation Union II, the 1st Battalion, 5th Marines, consisting of Companies A and D, with Capt. Graham's company attached launched an attack against an enemy occupied position with two companies assaulting and one in reserve. Company F, a leading company, was proceeding across a clear paddy area 1,000 meters wide, attacking toward the assigned objective, when it came under fire from mortars and small arms which immediately inflicted a large number of casualties. Hardest hit by the enemy fire was the 2d platoon of Company F, which was pinned down in the open paddy area by intense fire from two concealed machine-guns. Forming an assault unit from members of his small company headquarters, Capt. Graham boldly led a fierce assault through the second platoon's position, forcing he enemy to abandon the first machine-gun position, thereby relieving some of the pressure on his second platoon, and enabling evacuation of the wounded to a more secure area. Resolute to silence the second machine-gun, which continued its devastating fire, Capt. Graham's small force stood steadfast in its hard won enclave. Subsequently, during the afternoon's fierce fighting, he suffered two minor wounds while personally accounting for an estimated 15 enemy killed. With the enemy position remaining invincible upon each attempt to withdraw to friendly lines, and although knowing that he had no chance of survival, he chose to remain with one man who could not be moved due to the seriousness of his wounds. The last radio transmission from Capt. Graham reported that he was being assaulted by a force of 25 enemy soldiers; he died while protecting himself and the wounded man he chose not to abandon. Capt. Graham's actions throughout the day were a series of heroic achievements. His outstanding courage, superb leadership and indomitable fighting spirit undoubtedly saved the second platoon from annihilation and reflected great credit upon himself, the Marine Corps, and the U.S. Naval Service. He gallantly gave his life for his country.

McGONAGLE, WILLIAM L.

Rank and Organization: Captain (then Comdr.) U.S. Navy, U.S.S. *Liberty* (AGTR-5).
Born: November 19, 1925, Wichita, Kansas
Entered Service At: Thermal, California
Place and Date: International Waters, Eastern Mediterranean, June 8-9, 1967
Citation: For conspicuous gallantry and intrepidity at the risk of his life above and beyond the call of duty. Sailing in international waters, the *Liberty* was attacked without warning by jet fighter aircraft and motor torpedo boats which inflicted many casualties among the crew and caused extreme damage to the ship. Although severely wounded during the first air attack, Capt. McGonagle remained at his battle station on the badly damaged bridge and, with full knowledge of the seriousness of his wounds, subordinated his own welfare to the safety and survival of his command. Steadfastly refusing any treatment which would take him away from his post, he calmly continued to exercise firm command of his ship. Despite continuous exposure to fire, he maneuvered his ship, directed its defense, supervised the control of flooding and fire, and saw to the care of the casualties. Capt. McGonagle's extraordinary valor under these conditions inspired the surviving members of the *Liberty*'s crew, many of them seriously wounded, to heroic efforts to overcome the battle damage and keep the ship afloat. Subsequent to the attack, although in great pain and weak from the loss of blood, Captain McGonagle remained at his battle station and continued to command his ship for more than 17 hours. It was only after rendezvous with a U.S. destroyer that he relinquished personal control of the *Liberty* and permitted himself to be removed from the bridge. Even then, he refused much needed medical attention until convinced that the seriously wounded among his crew had been treated. Capt. McGonagle's superb professionalism, courageous fighting spirit, and valiant leadership saved his ship and many lives. His actions sustain and enhance the finest traditions of the U.S. Naval Service.

Note: Captain McGonagle was granted the Medal of Honor for actions which took place in international waters in the Eastern Mediterranean rather than in Vietnam.

†HARVEY, CARMEL BERNON, JR.

Rank and Organization: Specialist Fourth Class, U.S. Army, Company B, 1st Battalion, 5th Cavalry, 1st Cavalry Division (Airmobile).

Born: October 6, 1946, Montgomery, West Virginia

Entered Service At: Chicago, Illinois

Place and Date: Binh Dinh Province, Republic of Vietnam, June 21, 1967

Citation: For conspicuous gallantry and intrepidity in action at the risk of his life above and beyond the call of duty. Sp4c. Harvey distinguished himself as a fire team leader with Company B, during combat operations. Ordered to secure a downed helicopter, his platoon established a defensive perimeter around the aircraft, but shortly thereafter a large enemy force attacked the position from three sides. Sp4c. Harvey and two members of his squad were in a position directly in the path of the enemy onslaught, and their location received the brunt of the fire from an enemy machinegun. In short order, both of his companions were wounded, but Sp4c. Harvey covered this loss by increasing his deliberate rifle fire at the foe. The enemy machinegun seemed to concentrate on him and the bullets struck the ground all around his position. One round hit and armed a grenade attached to his belt. Quickly, he tried to remove the grenade but was unsuccessful. Realizing the danger to his comrades if he remained and despite the hail of enemy fire, he jumped to his feet, shouted a challenge at the enemy, and raced toward the deadly machinegun. He nearly reached the enemy position when the grenade on his belt exploded, mortally wounding Sp4c. Harvey, and stunning the enemy machinegun crew. His final act caused a pause in the enemy fire, and the wounded men were moved from the danger area. Sp4c. Harvey's dedication to duty, high sense of responsibility, and heroic actions inspired the others in his platoon to decisively beat back the enemy attack. His acts are in keeping with the highest traditions of the military service and reflect great credit upon himself and the U.S. Army.

†McWETHY, EDGAR LEE, JR.
Rank and Organization: Specialist Fifth Class, U.S. Army, Company B, 1st Battalion, 5th Cavalry, 1st Cavalry Division (Airmobile).
Born: November 22, 1944, Leadville, Colorado
Entered Service At: Denver, Colorado
Place and Date: Binh Dinh Province, Republic of Vietnam, June 21, 1967
Citation: For conspicuous gallantry and intrepidity in action at the risk of his life above and beyond the call of duty. Serving as a medical aidman with Company B, Sp5c, McWethy accompanied his platoon to the site of a downed helicopter. Shortly after the platoon established a defensive perimeter around the aircraft, a large enemy force attacked the position from three sides with a heavy volume of automatic weapons fire and grenades. The platoon leader and his radio operator were wounded almost immediately, and Sp5c. McWethy rushed across the fire-swept area to their assistance. Although he could not help the mortally wounded radio operator, Sp5c. McWethy's timely first aid enabled the platoon leader to retain command during this critical period. Hearing a call for aid, Sp5c. McWethy started across the open toward the injured men, but was wounded in the head and knocked to the ground. He regained his feet and continued on but was hit again, this time in the leg. Struggling onward despite his wounds, he gained the side of his comrades and treated their injuries. Observing another fallen rifleman lying in an exposed position raked by enemy fire, Sp5c. McWethy moved toward him without hesitation. Although the enemy fire wounded him a third time, Sp5c. McWethy reached his fallen companion. Though weakened and in extreme pain, Sp5c. McWethy gave the wounded man artificial respiration but suffered a fourth and fatal wound. Through his indomitable courage, complete disregard for his safety, and demonstrated concern for his fellow soldiers, Sp5c. McWethy inspired the members of his platoon and contributed in great measure to their successful defense of the position and the ultimate rout of the enemy force. Sp5c. McWethy's profound sense of duty, bravery, and his willingness to accept extraordinary risks in order to help the men of his unit are characteristic of the highest traditions of the military service and reflect great credit upon himself and the U.S. Army.

Note: The following is a, one paragraph, newspaper account of the preceding battle in which both Sp4c. Harvey and Sp5c. McWethy earned the Medal of Honor:

Fleeing Viet Cong Are Battered By U.S. Troops and Copters

SAIGON, South Vietnam - In Binh Dinh Province which adjoins Quangngai to the south, troops of the second brigade of the First Cavalry Division fought an all- day battle six miles southwest of Phumy. A military spokesman said that six United States Soldiers were killed and 22 wounded. Sixty enemy troops were killed.

†NEWLIN, MELVIN EARL

Rank and Organization: Private First Class, U.S. Marine Corps, 2d Battalion, 5th Marines, 1st Marine Division (Rein), FMF.
Born: September 27, 1948, Wellsville, Ohio
Entered Service At: Cleveland, Ohio
Place and Date: Quang Nam Province, Republic of Vietnam, July 4, 1967
Citation: For conspicuous gallantry and intrepidity at the risk of his life above and beyond the call of duty while serving as a machine gunner attached to the 1st Platoon, Company F, 2d Battalion, on July 3 and 4, 1967. Pfc. Newlin, with four other marines, was manning a key position on the perimeter of the Nong Son outpost when the enemy launched a savage and well coordinated mortar and infantry assault, seriously wounding him and killing his four comrades. Propping himself against his machinegun, he poured a deadly accurate stream of fire into the charging ranks of the Viet Cong. Though repeatedly hit by small-arms fire, he twice repelled enemy attempts to overrun his position. During the third attempt, a grenade explosion wounded him again and knocked him to the ground unconscious. The Viet Cong guerrillas, believing him dead, bypassed him and continued their assault on the main force. Meanwhile, Pfc. Newlin regained consciousness, crawled back to his weapon, and brought it to bear on the rear of the enemy causing havoc and confusion among them. Spotting the enemy attempting to bring a captured 106mm recoilless weapon to bear on other marine positions, he shifted his fire, inflicting heavy casualties on the enemy and preventing them from firing the captured weapon. He then shifted his fire back to the primary enemy force, causing the enemy to stop their assault on the marine bunkers and to once again attack his machinegun position. Valiantly fighting off two more enemy assaults, he firmly held his ground until mortally wounded. Pfc. Newlin had singlehandedly broken up and disorganized the entire enemy assault force, causing them to lose momentum and delaying them long enough for his fellow marines to organize a defense and beat off their secondary attack. His indomitable courage, fortitude, and unwavering devotion to duty in the face of almost certain death reflect great credit upon himself and the Marine Corps and upheld the highest traditions of the U.S. Naval Service.

†WHEAT, ROY M.

Rank and Organization: Lance Corporal, U.S. Marine Corps, Company K, 3d Battalion, 7th Marine, 1st Marine Division.
Born: July 24, 1947, Moselle, Mississippi
Entered Service At: Jackson, Mississippi
Place and Date: Republic of Vietnam, August 11, 1967
Citation: For conspicuous gallantry and intrepidity at the risk of his life above and beyond the call of duty. L/Cpl. Wheat and two other marines were assigned the mission of providing security for a Navy construction battalion crane and crew operating along Liberty Road in the vicinity of the Dien Ban District, Quang Nam Province. After the marines had set up security positions in a tree line adjacent to the work site, L/Cpl. Wheat reconnoitered the area to the rear of their location for the possible presence of guerrillas. He then returned to within 10 feet of the friendly position, and here unintentionally triggered a well concealed, bounding type, antipersonnel mine. Immediately, a hissing sound was heard which was identified by the three marines as that of a burning time fuse. Shouting a warning to his comrades, L/Cpl. Wheat in a valiant act of heroism hurled himself upon the mine, absorbing the tremendous impact of the explosion with his body. The inspirational personal heroism and extraordinary valor of his unselfish action saved his fellow marines from certain injury and possible death, reflected great credit upon himself, and upheld the highest traditions of the Marine Corps and the U.S. Naval Service. He gallantly gave his live for his country.

PLESS, STEPHEN W.
Rank and Organization: Major (then Capt.), U.S. Marine Corps, VMD-6, Mag-36, 1st Marine Aircraft Wing.
Born: September 6, 1939, Newman, Georgia
Entered Service At: Atlanta, Georgia
Place and Date: Near Quang Gnai, Republic of Vietnam, August 19, 1967
Citation: For conspicuous gallantry and intrepidity at the risk of his life above and beyond the call of duty while serving as a helicopter gunship pilot attached to Marine Observation Squadron 6 in action against enemy forces. During an escort mission Maj. Pless monitored an emergency call that four American soldiers stranded on a nearby beach were being overwhelmed by a large Viet Cong force. Maj. Pless flew to the scene and found 30 to 50 enemy soldiers in the open. Some of the enemy were bayonetting and beating the downed Americans. Maj. Pless displayed exceptional airmanship as he launched a devastating attack against the enemy force, killing or wounding many of the enemy and driving the remainder back into a tree line. His rocket and machinegun attacks were made at such low levels that the aircraft flew through debris created by explosions from its rockets. Seeing one of the wounded soldiers gesture for assistance, he maneuvered his helicopter into a position between the wounded men and the enemy, providing a shield which permitted his crew to retrieve the wounded. During the rescue the enemy directed intense fire at the helicopter and rushed the aircraft again and again, closing to within a few feet before being beaten back. When the wounded men were aboard, Maj. Pless maneuvered the helicopter out to sea. Before it became safely airborne, the overloaded aircraft settled four times into the water. Displaying superb airmanship, he finally got the helicopter aloft. Major Pless' extraordinary heroism coupled with his outstanding flying skill prevented the annihilation of the tiny force. His courageous actions reflect great credit upon himself and uphold the highest traditions of the Marine Corps and the U.S. Naval Service.

DAY, GEORGE E.
Rank and Organization: Colonel (then Major), U.S. Air Force, Forward Air Controller Pilot of an F-100 aircraft.
Born: February 24, 1925, Sioux City, Iowa
Entered Service At: Sioux City, Iowa
Place and Date: North Vietnam, August 26, 1967
Citation: On August 26, 1967, Col. Day was forced to eject from his aircraft over North Vietnam when it was hit by ground fire. His right arm was broken in three places, and his left knee was badly sprained. He was immediately captured by hostile forces and taken to a prison camp where he was interrogated and severely tortured. After causing the guards to relax their vigilance, Col. Day escaped into the jungle and began the trek toward South Vietnam. Despite injuries inflicted by fragments of a bomb or rocket, he continued southward surviving only on a few berries and uncooked frogs. He successfully evaded enemy patrols and reached the Ben Hai River, where he encountered U.S. artillery barrages. With the aid of a bamboo log float, Col. Day swam across the river and entered the demilitarized zone. Due to delirium, he lost his sense of direction and wandered aimlessly for several days. After several unsuccessful attempts to signal U.S. aircraft, he was ambushed and recaptured by the Viet Cong, sustaining gunshot wounds to his left hand and thigh. He was returned to prison from which he had escaped and later was moved to Hanoi after giving his captors false information to questions put before him. Physically, Col. Day was totally debilitated and unable to perform even the simplest task for himself. Despite his many injuries, he continued to offer maximum resistance. His personal bravery in the face of deadly enemy pressure was significant in saving the lives of fellow aviators who were still flying against the enemy. Col. Day's conspicuous gallantry and intrepidity at the risk of his life above and beyond the call of duty are in keeping with the highest traditions of the U.S. Air Force and reflect great credit upon himself and the U.S. Armed Forces.

†CAPODANNO, VINCENT R.

Rank and Organization: Lieutenant, U.S. Navy, Chaplain Corps, 3d Battalion, 5th Marines, 1st Marine Division (Rein), FMF.
Born: February 13, 1929, Staten Island, New York
Entered Service At: Staten Island, New York
Place and Date: Quang Tin Province, Republic of Vietnam, September 4, 1967
Citation: For conspicuous gallantry and intrepidity at the risk of his life above and beyond the call of duty as Chaplain of the 3d Battalion, in connection with operations against enemy forces. In response to reports that the 2d Platoon of M Company was in danger of being overrun by a massed enemy assaulting force, Lt. Capodanno left the relative safety of the company command post and ran through an open area raked with fire, directly to the beleaguered platoon. Disregarding the intense enemy small-arms, automatic-weapons, and mortar fire, he moved about the battlefield administering last rites to the dying and giving medical aid to the wounded. When an exploding mortar round inflicted painful multiple wounds to his arms and legs, and severed a portion of his right hand, he steadfastly refused all medical aid. Instead, he directed the corpsmen to help their wounded comrades and, with calm vigor, continued to move about the battlefield as he provided encouragement by voice and example to the valiant marines. Upon encountering a wounded corpsman in the direct line of fire of an enemy machine gunner positioned approximately 15 yards away, Lt. Capodanno rushed forward ina daring attempt to aid and assist the mortally wounded corpsman. At that instant, only inches from his goal, he was struck down by a burst of machinegun fire. By his heroic conduct on the battlefield, and his inspiring example, Lt. Capodanno upheld the finest traditions of the U.S. Naval Service. He gallantly gave his life in the cause of freedom.

†PETERS, LAWRENCE DAVID

Rank and Organization: Sergeant, U.S. Marine Corps, Company M, 3d Battalion, 5th Marines, 1st Marine Division.
Born: September 16, 1946, Johnson City, New York.
Entered Service At: Binghamton, New York
Place and Date: Quang Tin Province, Republic of Vietnam, September 4, 1967.
Citation: For conspicuous gallantry and intrepidity at the risk of his life above and beyond the call of duty while serving as squad leader with Company M. During Operation SWIFT, the marines of the 2d Platoon of Company M were struck by intense mortar, machinegun, and small-arms fire from an entrenched enemy force. As the company rallied its forces, Sgt. Peters maneuvered his squad in an assault on an enemy defended knoll. Disregarding his safety, as enemy rounds hit all around him, he stood in the open, pointing out enemy positions until he was painfully wounded in the leg. Disregarding his wound, he moved forward and continued to lead his men. As the enemy fire increased in accuracy and volume, his squad lost its momentum and was temporarily pinned down. Exposing himself to devastating enemy fire, he consolidated his position to render more effective fire. While directing the base of fire, he was wounded a second time in the face and neck from an exploding mortar round. As the enemy attempted to infiltrate the position of an adjacent platoon, Sgt. Peters stood erect, in the full view of the enemy, firing burst after burst forcing them to disclose their camouflaged positions. Sgt. Peters steadfastly continued to direct his squad in spite of two additional wounds, persisted in his efforts to encourage and supervise his men until he lost consciousness and succumbed. Inspired by his selfless actions, the squad regained fire superiority and once again carried the assault to the enemy. By his outstanding valor, indomitable fighting spirit and tenacious determination in the face of overwhelming odds, Sgt. Peters upheld the highest traditions of the Marine Corps and the U.S. Naval Service. He gallantly gave his life for his country.

Note: The following is a newspaper account of the preceding battle in which both Lt. Capodanno and Sgt. Peters earned the Medal of Honor:

Marines Lose 54 But Kill 143 Of Foe In 15-Hour Battle

DANANG, South Vietnam - Fifty four United States Marines were killed and 84 wounded in a 15-hour coastal battle in which they killed 143 North Vietnamese regulars and captured 25, a United States Military spokesman said here today.

The battle, fought through rice paddies, started yesterday morning and tapered off to sporadic contact early today, the spokesman said.

American artillery and machine-gun-firing Dakota aircraft pounded the North Vietnamese force, estimated at battalion strength. The North Vietnamese fought from heavily entrenched positions near Tamky, about 30 miles south of here in Quang Tin Province.

The spokesman said the battle, some 355 miles northeast of Saigon was part of a general intensification of the ground war following Sunday's Presidential and Senate elections in South Vietnam.

†**DAVIS, RODNEY MAXWELL**
Rank and Organization: Sergeant, U.S. Marine Corps, Company B, 1st Battalion, 5th Marines, 1st Marine Division.
Born: April 7, 1942, Macon, Georgia
Entered Service At: Macon, Georgia
Place and Date: Quang Nam Province, Republic of Vietnam, September 6, 1967
Citation: For conspicuous gallantry and intrepidity at the risk of his life above and beyond the call of duty while serving as the right guide of the 2d Platoon, Company B, in action against enemy forces. Elements of the 2d Platoon were pinned down by a numerically superior force of attacking North Vietnamese Army Regulars. Remnants of the platoon were located in a trench line where Sgt. Davis was directing the fire of his men in an attempt to repel the enemy attack. Disregarding the enemy hand grenades and high volume of small arms and mortar fire, Sgt. Davis moved from man to man shouting words of encouragement to each of them while firing and throwing grenades at the onrushing enemy. When an enemy grenade landed in the trench in the midst of his men. Sgt. Davis, realizing the gravity of the situation, and in a final valiant act of complete self-sacrifice, instantly threw himself upon the grenade, absorbing with his body the full and terrific force of the explosion. Through his extraordinary initiative and inspiring valor in the face of almost certain death, Sgt. Davis saved his comrades from injury and possible loss of life, enabled his platoon to hold its vital position, and upheld the highest traditions of the Marine Corps and the U.S. Naval Service. He gallantly gave his life for his country.

†BARKER, JEDH COLBY

Rank and Organization: Lance Corporal, U.S. Marine Corps, Company F, 2d Battalion, 4th Marines, 3d Marine Division (Rein), FMF.
Born: June 20, 1945, Franklin, New Hampshire
Entered Service At: Park Ridge, New Jersey
Place and Date: Near Con Thein, Republic of Vietnam, September 21, 1967
Citation: For conspicuous gallantry and intrepidity at the risk of his life above and beyond the call of duty while serving as a machine gunner with Company F. During a reconnaissance operation L/Cpl. Barker's squad was suddenly hit by enemy sniper fire. The squad immediately deployed to a combat formation and advanced to a strongly fortified enemy position, when it was again struck by small arms and automatic weapons fire, sustaining numerous casualties. Although wounded by the initial burst of fire, L/Cpl. Barker boldly remained in the open, delivering a devastating volume of accurate fire on the numerically superior force. The enemy was intent upon annihilating the small marine force and, realizing that L/Cpl. Barker was a threat to their position, directed the preponderance of their fire on his position. He was again wounded, this time in the right hand, which prevented him from operating his vitally needed machinegun. Suddenly and without warning, an enemy grenade landed in the midst of the few surviving marines. Unhesitatingly and with complete disregard for his personal safety, L/Cpl. Barker threw himself upon the deadly grenade, absorbing with his body the full and tremendous force of the explosion. In a final act of bravery, he crawled to the side of a wounded comrade and administered first aid before succumbing to his grievous wounds. His bold initiative, intrepid fighting spirit and unwavering devotion to duty in the face of almost certain death undoubtedly saved his comrades from further injury or possible death and reflected great credit upon himself, the Marine Corps, and the U.S. Naval Service. He gallantly gave his life for his country.

†PERKINS, WILLIAM THOMAS, JR.

Rank and Organization: Corporal, U.S. Marine Corps, Company C, 1st Battalion, 1st Marines, 1st Marine Division.
Born: August 10, 1947, Rochester, New York
Entered Service At: San Francisco, California
Place and Date: Quang Tri Province, Republic of Vietnam, October 12, 1967
Citation: For conspicuous gallantry and intrepidity at the risk of his life above and beyond the call of duty while serving as a combat photographer attached to Company C. During Operation MEDINA, a major reconnaissance in force southwest of Quang Tri, Company C made heavy combat contact with a numerically superior North Vietnamese Army force estimated at from two to three companies. The focal point of the intense fighting was a helicopter landing zone which was also serving as the Command Post of Company C. In the course of a strong hostile attack, an enemy grenade landed in the immediate area occupied by Cpl. Perkins and three other marines. Realizing the inherent danger, he shouted the warning, "Incoming Grenade" to his fellow marines, and in a valiant act of heroism, hurled himself upon the grenade absorbing the impact of the explosion with his body, thereby saving the lives of his comrades at the cost of his life. Through his exceptional courage and inspiring valor in the face of certain death, Cpl. Perkins reflected great credit upon himself and the Marine Corps and upheld the highest traditions of the U.S. Naval Service. He gallantly gave his life for his country.

†FOSTER, PAUL HELLSTROM

Rank and Organization: Sergeant, U.S. Marine Corps Reserve, 2d Battalion, 4th Marines, 3d Marine Division.

Born: April 17, 1939, San Mateo, California

Entered Service At: San Francisco, California

Place and Date: Near Con Thien, Republic of Vietnam, October 14, 1967

Citation: For conspicuous gallantry and intrepidity at the risk of his life above and beyond the call of duty while serving as an artillery liaison operations chief with the 2d Battalion. In the early morning hours the 2d Battalion was occupying a defensive position which protected a bridge on the road leading from con Thien to Cam Lo. Suddenly, the marines' position came under a heavy volume of mortar and artillery fire, followed by an aggressive enemy ground assault. In the ensuing engagement, the hostile force penetrated the perimeter and brought a heavy concentration of small arms, automatic weapons, and rocket fire to bear on the battalion command post. Although his position in the fire support coordination center was dangerously exposed to enemy fire and he was wounded when an enemy hand grenade exploded near his position, Sgt. Foster resolutely continued to direct accurate mortar and artillery fire on the advancing North Vietnamese troops. As the attack continued, a hand grenade landed in the midst of Sgt. Foster and his five companions. Realizing the danger, he shouted a warning, threw his armored vest over the grenade, and unhesitatingly placed his body over the armored vest. When the grenade exploded, Sgt. Foster absorbed the entire blast with his body and was mortally wounded. His heroic actions undoubtedly saved his comrades from further injury or possible death. Sgt. Foster's courage, extraordinary heroism, and unfaltering devotion to duty reflected great credit upon himself and the Marine Corps and upheld the highest traditions of the U.S. Naval Service. He gallantly gave his life for his country.

Note: The following is a newspaper account of the preceding battle in which Sgt. Foster earned the Medal of Honor:

BIG ENEMY FORCE ATTACKS MARINES NEAR BUFFER ZONE

At Lease 23 Americans Die South of Conthien
— 384 Artillery Rounds Pour In

SAIGON, South Vietnam, Saturday, Oct. 14 — Five hundred North Vietnamese troops attacked a United States Marine battalion near the demilitarized zone today under cover of the heaviest enemy shelling in nearly four weeks, military spokesmen reported.

At least 23 marines were reported killed and 36 wounded in the assault and the shelling.

The battalion was based south of Conthien, the Marine outpost that was held under siege by enemy artillery last month.

United States spokesmen reported that the ground fighting began before dawn, but broke off later in the morning. American planes and artillery struck back at the attackers, but there was no report on enemy casualties.

Foe Fires 384 Rounds

Enemy gunners struck the Marine outpost with 384 rounds of artillery in 24 hours, a Marine spokesman at Danang said. Damage reports were not available immediately.

After Sept. 25, when North Vietnamese gunners struck the Marine outpost at Conthien with 1,000 rounds of artillery fire, the month-long siege of the outpost began tapering to less than 100 rounds a day.

It was believed this morning that most of the marines' casualties had been suffered in the ground fighting. Unofficial reports said 20 of the 23 Marine dead and 21 of the 36 wounded were victims of the ground assault.

ANDERSON, WEBSTER

Rank and Organization: Sergeant First Class, U.S. Army, Battery A, 2d Battalion, 320th Artillery, 101st Airborne Division (Airmobile).
Born: July 15, 1933, Winnsboro, South Carolina
Entered Service At: Winnsboro, South Carolina
Place and Date: Tam Ky, Republic of Vietnam, October 15, 1967
Citation: Sfc. Anderson (then S/Sgt.), distinguished himself by conspicuous gallantry and intrepidity in action while serving as chief of section in Battery A, against a hostile force. During the early morning hours, Battery A's defensive position was attacked by a determined North Vietnamese Army infantry unit supported by heavy mortar, recoilless rifle, rocket propelled grenade and automatic weapon fire. The initial enemy onslaught breached the battery defensive perimeter. Sfc. Anderson, with complete disregard for his personal safety, mounted the exposed parapet of his howitzer position and became the mainstay of the defense of the battery position. Sfc. Anderson directed devastating direct howitzer fire on the assaulting enemy while providing rifle and grenade defensive fire against enemy soldiers attempting to overrun his gun section position. While protecting his crew and directing their fire against the enemy from his exposed position, two enemy grenades exploded at his feet knocking him down and severely wounding him in the legs. Despite the excruciating pain and though not able to stand, Sfc. Anderson valorously propped himself on the parapet and continued to direct howitzer fire upon the closing enemy and to encourage his men to fight on. Seeing an enemy grenade land within the gunpit near a wounded member of his guncrew, Sfc. Anderson heedless of his own safety, seized the grenade and attempted to throw it over the parapet to save his men. As the grenade was thrown from the position it exploded and Sfc. Anderson was again grievously wounded. Although only partially conscious and severely wounded. Sfc. Anderson refused medical evacuation and continued to encourage his men in the defense of the position. Sfc. Anderson by his inspirational leadership, professionalism, devotion to duty and complete disregard for his welfare was able to maintain the defense of his section position and to defeat a determined attack. Sfc. Anderson's gallantry and extraordinary heroism at the risk of his life above and beyond the call of duty are in the highest traditions of the military service and reflect great credit upon himself, his unit, and the U.S. Army.

†DURHAM, HAROLD BASCOM, JR.

Rank and Organization: Second Lieutenant, U.S. Army, Battery C, 6th Battalion, 15th Artillery, 1st Infantry Division.
Born: October 12, 1942, Rocky Mount, North Carolina
Entered Service At: Atlanta, Georgia
Place and Date: Republic of Vietnam, October 17, 1967
Citation: 2d Lt. Durham, Artillery, Distinguished himself by conspicuous gallantry and intrepidity at the cost of his life above and beyond the call of duty while assigned to Battery C. 2d Lt. Durham was serving as a forward observer with Company D, 2d Battalion, 28th Infantry during a battalion reconnaissance-in-force mission. At approximately 1015 hours contact was made with an enemy force concealed in well-camouflaged positions and fortified bunkers. 2d Lt. Durham immediately moved into an exposed position to adjust the supporting artillery fire onto the insurgents. During a brief lull in the battle he administered emergency first aid to the wounded in spite of heavy enemy sniper fire directed toward him. Moments later, as enemy units assaulted friendly positions, he learned that Company A, bearing the brunt of the attack, had lost its forward observer. While he was moving to replace the wounded observer, the enemy detonated a claymore mine, severely wounding him in the head and impairing his vision. In spite of the intense pain, he continued to direct the supporting artillery fire and to employ his individual weapon in support of the hard pressed infantrymen. As the enemy pressed their attack, 2d Lt. Durham called for supporting fire to be placed almost directly on his position. Twice the insurgents were driven back, leaving many dead and wounded behind. 2d Lt. Durham was then taken to a secondary defensive position. Even in his extremely weakened condition, he continued to call artillery fire onto the enemy. He refused to seek cover and instead positioned himself in a small clearing which offered a better vantage point from which to adjust the fire. Suddenly, he was severely wounded a second time by enemy machinegun fire. As he lay on the ground near death, he saw two Viet Cong approaching, shooting the defenseless wounded men. With his last effort, 2d Lt. Durham shouted a warning to a nearby soldier who immediately killed the insurgents. 2d Lt. Durham died moments later, still grasping the radio handset. 2d Lt. Durham's gallant actions in close combat with an enemy force are in keeping with the highest traditions of the military service and reflect great credit upon himself, his unit, and the U.S. Army.

†PITTS, RILEY L.

Rank and Organization: Captain, U.S. Army, Company C, 2d Battalion, 27th Infantry, 25th Infantry Division.
Born: October 15, 1937, Fallis, Oklahoma
Entered Service At: Wichita, Kansas
Place and Date: Ap Dong, Republic of Vietnam, October 31, 1967.
Citation: Distinguishing himself by exceptional heroism while serving as company commander during an airmobile assault. Immediately after his company landed in the area, several Viet Cong opened fire with automatic weapons. Despite the enemy fire, Capt. Pitts forcefully led an assault which overran the enemy positions. Shortly thereafter, Capt. Pitts was ordered to move his unit to the north to reinforce another company heavily engaged against a strong enemy force. As Capt. Pitts' company moved forward to engage the enemy, intense fire was received from three directions, including fire from four enemy bunkers, two of which were within 15 meters of Capt. Pitts' position. The severity of the incoming fire prevented Capt. Pitts from maneuvering his company. His rifle fire proving ineffective against the enemy due to the dense jungle foliage, he picked up an M-79 grenade launcher and began pinpointing the targets. Seizing a Chinese Communist grenade which had been taken from a captured Viet Cong's web gear, Capt. Pitts lobbed the grenade at a bunker to his front, but it hit the dense jungle foliage and rebounded. Without hesitation, Capt. Pitts threw himself on top of the grenade which, fortunately, failed to explode. Capt. Pitts then directed the repositioning of the company to permit friendly artillery to be fired. Upon completion of the artillery fire mission, Capt. Pitts again led his men toward the enemy positions, personally killing at least one more Viet Cong. The jungle growth still prevented effective fire to be placed on the enemy bunkers. Capt. Pitts, displaying complete disregard for his life and personal safety, quickly moved to a position which permitted him to place effective fire on the enemy. He maintained a continuous fire, pinpointing the enemy's fortified positions, while at the same time directing and urging his men forward, until he was mortally wounded. Capt. Pitts' conspicuous gallantry, extraordinary heroism, and intrepidity at the cost of his life, above and beyond the call of duty, are in the highest traditions of the U.S. Army and reflect great credit upon himself, his unit, and the Armed Services of his country.

†STRYKER, ROBERT F.

Rank and Organization: Specialist Fourth Class, U.S. Army, Company C, 1st Battalion, 26th Infantry, 1st Infantry Division.

Born: November 9, 1944, Auburn, New York

Entered Service At: Throop, New York

Place and Date: Near Loc Ninh, Republic of Vietnam, November 7, 1967.

Citation: For conspicuous gallantry and intrepidity at the risk of his life above and beyond the call of duty. Sp4c. Stryker, U.S. Army, distinguished himself while serving with Company C. Sp4c. Stryker was serving as a grenadier in a multi-company reconnaissance in force near Loc Ninh. As his unit moved through the dense underbrush, it was suddenly met with a hail of rocket, automatic weapons and small-arms fire from enemy forces concealed in fortified bunkers and in the surrounding trees. Reacting quickly, Sp4c. Stryker fired into the enemy positions with his grenade launcher. During the devastating exchange of fire, Sp4c. Stryker detected enemy elements attempting to encircle his company and isolate it from the main body of the friendly force. Undaunted by the enemy machinegun and small-arms fire, Sp4c. Stryker repeatedly fire grenades into the trees, killing enemy snipers and enabling his comrades to sever the attempted encirclement. As the battle continued, Sp4c. Stryker observed several wounded members of his squad in the killing zone of an enemy claymore mine. With complete disregard for his safety, he threw himself upon the mine as it was detonated. He was mortally wounded as his body absorbed the blast and shielded his comrades from the explosion. His unselfish actions were responsible for saving the lives of at least six of his fellow soldiers. Sp4c. Stryker's great personal bravery was in keeping with the highest traditions of the military service and reflect great credit upon himself, his unit, and the U.S. Army.

Note: The following is a newspaper account of the preceding battle in which Sp4c. Stryker earned the Medal of Honor:

NEW FIGHT FLARES IN LOC NINH REGION

Foe Apparently Ambushes U.S. Search Unit, Killing 18

SAIGON, South Vietnam, Nov. 7 — Two companies of the United States First Infantry Division, searching for remnants of the Vietcong regiments reported to have been eliminated in fighting last week near the Cambodian border, were apparently ambushed today.

Eighteen men were killed, including a battalion commander, and 20 were wounded during a one-hour clash, the division reported. The engagement took place about five miles northeast of Locninh, the rubber-plantation village that was the target of a Vietcong onslaught last week.

A division spokesman said that the command group was struck by a high-explosive rocket during the first moments of the attack. Snipers in trees accounted for many others of the killed and wounded.

The enemy unit, whose size was not estimated, was said to have lost 66 men killed and an undetermined number wounded. Contact was lost when the infantrymen pulled back to permit artillery, helicopter gunships and aircraft to blast the area.

†SIJAN, LANCE P.

Rank and Organization: Captain, U.S. Air Force, 4th Allied POW Wing, Pilot of an F-4C aircraft.
Born: April 13, 1942, Milwaukee, Wis.
Entered Service At: Milwaukee, Wis.
Place and Date: North Vietnam, November 9, 1967.
Citation: While on a flight over North Vietnam, Capt. Sijan ejected from his disabled aircraft and successfully evaded capture for more than six weeks. During this time, he was seriously injured and suffered from shock and extreme weight loss due to lack of food. After being captured by North Vietnamese soldiers, Capt. Sijan was taken to a holding point for subsequent transfer to a prisoner of war camp. In his emaciated and crippled condition, he overpowered one of his guards and crawled into the jungle, only to be recaptured after several hours. He was then transferred to another prison camp where he was kept in solitary confinement and interrogated at length. During interrogation, he was severely tortured; however, he did not divulge any information to his captors. Capt. Sijan lapsed into delirium and was placed in the care of another prisoner. During his intermittent periods of consciousness until his death, he never complained of his physical condition and, on several occasions, spoke of future escape attempts. Capt. Sijan's extraordinary heroism and intrepidity above and beyond the call of duty at the cost of his life are in keeping with the highest traditions of the U.S. Air Force and reflect great credit upon himself and the U.S. Armed Forces.

TAYLOR, JAMES ALLEN

Rank and Organization: Captain (then 1st Lt.), U.S. Army, Troop B, 1st Cavalry, Americal Division.
Born: December 31, 1937, Arcata, California.
Entered Service At: San Francisco, California
Place and Date: West of Que Son, Republic of Vietnam, November 9, 1967.
Citation: Capt. Taylor, Armor, was serving as executive officer of Troop B, 1st Squadron. His troop was engaged in an attack on a fortified position west of Que Son when it came under intense enemy recoilless rifle, mortar, and automatic weapons fire from an enemy strong point located immediately to its front. One armored cavalry assault vehicle was hit immediately by recoilless rifle fire and all five crew members were wounded. Aware that the stricken vehicle was in grave danger of exploding, Capt. Taylor rushed forward and personally extracted the wounded to safety despite the hail of enemy fire and exploding ammunition. Within minutes a second armored cavalry assault vehicle was hit by multiple recoilless rifle rounds. Despite the continuing intense enemy fire, Capt. Taylor moved forward on foot to rescue the wounded men from the burning vehicle and personally removed all the crewmen to the safety of a nearby dike. Moments later the vehicle exploded. As he was returning to his vehicle, a bursting mortar round painfully wounded Capt. Taylor, Yet he valiantly returned to his vehicle to relocate the medical evacuation landing zone to an area closer to the front lines. As he was moving his vehicle, it came under machinegun fire from an enemy position not 50 yards away. Capt. Taylor engaged the position with his machinegun, killing the three man crew. Upon arrival at the new evacuation site, still another vehicle was struck. Once again Capt. Taylor rushed forward and pulled the wounded from the vehicle, loaded them aboard his vehicle, and returned them safely to the evacuation site. His actions of unsurpassed valor were a source of inspiration to his entire troop, contributed significantly to the success of the overall assault on the enemy position, and were directly responsible for saving the lives of a number of his fellow soldiers. His actions were in keeping with the highest traditions of the military profession and reflect great upon himself, his unit, and the U.S. Army.

YOUNG, GERALD O.

Rank and Organization: Captain, U.S. Air Force, 37th ARS Da Nang AFB.

Born: May 9, 1930, Chicago, Ill.

Entered Service At: Colorado Springs, Colorado

Place and Date: Khesanh, Republic of Vietnam, November 9, 1967.

Citation: For conspicuous gallantry and intrepidity at the risk of his life above and beyond the call of duty. Capt. Young distinguished himself while serving as a helicopter rescue crew commander. Capt. Young was flying escort for another helicopter attempting the night rescue of an Army ground reconnaissance team in imminent danger of death or capture. Previous attempts had resulted in the loss of two helicopters to hostile ground fire. The endangered team was positioned on the side of a steep slope which required unusual airmanship on the part of Capt. Young to effect pickup. Heavy automatic weapons fire from surrounding enemy severely damaged one rescue helicopter, but was able to extract three of the team. The commander of this aircraft recommended to Capt. Young that further rescue attempts be abandoned because it was not possible to suppress the concentrated fire from enemy automatic weapons. With full knowledge of the danger involved, and the fact that supporting helicopter gunships were low on fuel and ordinance, Capt. Young hovered under intense fire until the remaining survivors were aboard. As he maneuvered the aircraft for takeoff, the enemy appeared at point-blank range and raked the aircraft with automatic weapons fire. The aircraft crashed, inverted, and burst into flames. Capt. Young escaped through a window of the burning aircraft. Disregarding serious burns, Capt. Young aided one of the wounded men and attempted to lead the hostile forces away from his position. Later, despite intense pain from his burns, he declined to accept rescue because he had observed hostile forces setting up automatic weapons positions to entrap any rescue aircraft. For more than 17 hours he evaded the enemy until rescue aircraft could be brought into the area. Through his extraordinary heroism, aggressiveness, and concern for his fellow man, Capt. Young reflected the highest credit upon himself, the U.S. Air Force, and the Armed Forces of his country.

†BARNES, JOHN ANDREW III

Rank and Organization: Private First Class, U.S. Army, Company C, 1st Battalion, 503d Infantry, 173d Airborne Brigade.
Born: April 16, 1945, Boston, Mass.
Entered Service At: Boston, Mass.
Place and Date: Dak To, Republic of Vietnam, November 12, 1967.
Citation: For conspicuous gallantry and intrepidity in action at the risk of his life above and beyond the call of duty. Pfc. Barnes distinguished himself by exceptional heroism while engaged in combat against hostile forces. Pfc. Barnes was serving as a grenadier when his unit was attacked by a North Vietnamese force, estimated to be a battalion. Upon seeing the crew of a machinegun team killed, Pfc. Barnes, without hesitation, dashed through the bullet swept area, manned the machinegun, and killed nine enemy soldiers as they assaulted his position. While pausing just long enough to retrieve more ammunition, Pfc. Barnes observed an enemy grenade thrown in the midst of some severely wounded personnel close to his position. Realizing that the grenade could further injure or kill the majority of the wounded personnel, he sacrificed his life by throwing himself directly onto the hand grenade as it exploded. Through his indomitable courage, complete disregard for his own safety, and profound concern for his fellow soldiers, he averted a probable loss of life and injury to the wounded members of his unit. Pfc. Barnes' extraordinary heroism, and intrepidity at the cost of his life, above and beyond the call of duty, are in the highest traditions of the military service and reflect great credit upon himself, his unit, and the U.S. Army.

Note: The following is a newspaper account of the preceding battle in which Pfc. Barnes earned the Medal of Honor:

VIETNAM FIGHTING GROWS IN HIGHLANDS WITH 2 NEW BATTLES

SAIGON, South Vietnam, Nov. 11 — Fighting in the central highlands exploded with new fury today as American paratroopers of the 173d Airborne Brigade and foot soldiers of the United States

Fourth Infantry Division fought two battles near the Cambodian border southwest of Dakto.

The paratroopers, with two companies totaling about 300 men, lost more than half their number in killed and wounded in fighting that broke out at 8:30 A.M. and ended at 4:30 P.M.

A spokesman for the United States command said 20 soldiers of the airborne unit had been killed and 132 wounded. He said the North Vietnamese lost 103 killed.

The other action, involving three companies of Fourth Division troops, or about 450 men, broke out at 2 this afternoon and ended at nightfall. The spokesman described the action as a "very hot contact."

The spokesman said preliminary reports indicated that six Americans had been killed and 30 wounded in this action. Enemy casualties were not known.

The spokesman said casualty totals since fighting first began in the area Nov. 3, stood at 527 North Vietnamese killed, 76 Americans killed and 368 United States soldiers wounded. About half of the wounded did not require hospital treatment and were returned to duty.

The paratroopers found the enemy today while patrolling 12 miles southwest of Dakto. The North Vietnamese were dug in atop high land three or four miles from the Cambodian border. The fighting raged as the Americans assaulted the enemy positions.

The paratroopers overran the enemy positions at 3:30 P.M., the spokesman said. A half hour later, the North Vietnamese withdrew.

The second action broke out when troops of both sides "bumped into each other" the spokesman said, in an area five miles southwest of Dakto.

B-52's saturated an area near Dakto with high explosives, supporting air strikes and armed helicopters, which were back on the job after stormy weather yesterday.

Intelligence estimates place enemy strength in the Dakto area at about two regiments of perhaps 5,000 men.

Two North Vietnamese divisions, the First and the Sixth, of perhaps 20,000 men, were known to be in Cambodia along the border in the Dakto region. The North Vietnamese objective is believed to be to down large numbers of Americans and to score heavy casualties on them.

This outbreak of fighting is the first sizable contact since last July, when North Vietnamese units attacked several United States Special Forces camps. South Vietnamese battalions fought North Vietnamese regulars there in late July and early August.

DAVIS, SAMMY L.

Rank and Organization: Sergeant, U.S. Army, Battery C, 2d Battalion, 4th Artillery, 9th Infantry Division.
Born: November 1, 1946, Dayton, Ohio
Entered Service At: Indianapolis, Indiana
Place and Date: West of Cai Lay, Republic of Vietnam, November 18, 1967.
Citation: For conspicuous gallantry and intrepidity in action at the risk of his life above and beyond the call of duty. Sgt. Davis (then Pfc.) distinguished himself during the early morning hours while serving as a cannoneer with Battery C, at a remote fire support base. At approximately 0200 hours, the fire support base came under heavy enemy mortar attack. Simultaneously, an estimated reinforced Viet Cong battalion launched a fierce ground assault upon the fire support base. The attacking enemy drove to within 25 meters of the friendly positions. Only a river separated the Viet Cong from the fire support base. Detecting a nearby enemy position, Sgt. Davis seized a machinegun and provided covering fire for his gun crew, as they attempted to bring direct artillery fire on the enemy. Despite his efforts, an enemy recoilless rifle round scored a direct hit upon the artillery piece. The resultant blast hurled the gun crew from their weapon and blew Sgt. Davis into a foxhole. He struggled to his feet and returned to the howitzer, which was burning furiously. Ignoring repeated warnings to seek cover, Sgt. Davis rammed a shell into the gun. Disregarding a withering hail of enemy fire directed against his position, he aimed and fired the howitzer which rolled backward, knocking Sgt. Davis to the ground. Undaunted, he returned to the weapon to fire again when an enemy mortar round exploded within 20 meters of his position, injuring him painfully. Nevertheless, Sgt. Davis loaded the artillery piece, aimed and fired. Again he was knocked down by the recoil. In complete disregard for his safety, Sgt. Davis loaded and fired three more shells into the enemy. Disregarding his extensive injuries and his inability to swim, Sgt. Davis picked up an air mattress and struck out across the deep river to rescue three wounded comrades on the far side. Upon reaching the three wounded men, he stood upright and fired into the dense vegetation to prevent the Viet Cong from advancing. While the most seriously wounded soldier was helped across the river, Sgt. Davis protected the two remaining casualties until he could pull them across the river

to the fire support base. Though suffering from painful wounds, he refused medical attention, joining another howitzer crew which fired at the large Viet Cong force until it broke contact and fled. Sgt. Davis' extraordinary heroism, at the risk of his life, are in keeping with the highest traditions of the military service and reflect great credit upon himself and the U.S. Army.

†WATTERS, CHARLES JOSEPH

Rank and Organization: Chaplain (Maj.), U.S. Army, Company A, 173d Support Battalion, 173d Airborne Brigade.
Born: January 17, 1927, Jersey City, New Jersey
Entered Service At: Ford Dix, New Jersey
Place and Date: Near Dak To Province, Republic of Vietnam, November 19, 1967
Citation: For conspicuous gallantry and intrepidity in action at the risk of his life above and beyond the call of duty. Chaplain Watters distinguished himself during an assault in the vicinity of Dak To. Chaplain Watters was moving with one of the companies when it engaged a heavily armed enemy battalion. As the battle raged and the casualties mounted, Chaplain Watters, with complete disregard for his safety, rushed forward to the line of contact. Unarmed and completely exposed, he moved among, as well as in front of the advancing troops, giving aid to the wounded, assisting in their evacuation, giving words of encouragement, and administering the last rites to the dying. When a wounded paratrooper was standing in shock in front of the assaulting forces, Chaplain Watters ran forward, picked the man up on his shoulders and carried him to safety. As the troopers battled to the first enemy entrenchment, Chaplain Watters ran through the intense enemy fire to the front of the entrenchment to aid a fallen comrade. A short time later, the paratroopers pulled back in preparation for a second assault. Chaplain Watters exposed himself to both friendly and enemy fire between the two forces in order to recover two wounded soldiers. Later, when the battalion was forced to pull back into a perimeter, Champlain Watters noticed that several wounded soldiers were lying outside the newly formed perimeter. Without hesitation and ignoring attempts to restrain him, Chaplain Watters left the perimeter three times in the face of small arms, automatic weapons, and mortar fire to carry and to assist the injured troopers to safety. Satisfied that all of the wounded were inside the perimeter, he began aiding the medics – applying field bandages to open wounds, obtaining and serving food and water, giving spiritual and mental strength and comfort. During his ministering he moved out to the perimeter from position to position redistributing food and water, and tending to the needs of his men. Chaplain Watters was giving aid to the wounded when he himself was mortally wounded. Chaplain Watters' unyielding perseverance and selfless devotion to his comrades was in keeping with the highest traditions of the U.S. Army.

†LOZADA, CARLOS JAMES

Rank and Organization: Private First Class, U.S. Army, Company A, 2d Battalion, 503d Infantry, 173d Airborne Brigade.
Born: September 6, 1946, Caguas, Puerto Rico.
Entered Service At: New York, New York
Place and Date: Dak To, Republic of Vietnam, November 20, 1967.
Citation: For conspicuous gallantry and intrepidity in action at the risk of his life above and beyond the call of duty. Pfc. Lozada, U.S. Army, distinguished himself in the battle of Dak To. While serving as a machine gunner with 1st Platoon, Company A, Pfc. Lozada was part of a four man early warning outpost, located 35 meters from his company's lines. At 1400 hours a North Vietnamese company rapidly approached the outpost along a well defined trail. Pfc. Lozada alerted his comrades and commenced firing at the enemy who were within 10 meters of the outpost. His heavy and accurate machinegun fire killed at least 20 North Vietnamese soldiers and completely disrupted their initial attack. Pfc. Lozada remained in an exposed position and continued to pour deadly fire upon the enemy despite the urgent pleas of his comrades to withdraw. The enemy continued their assault, attempting to envelop the outpost. At the same time enemy forces launched a heavy attack on the forward west flank of Company A with the intent to cut them off from their battalion. Company A was given the order to withdraw. Pfc. Lozada apparently realized that if he abandoned his position there would be nothing to hold back the surging North Vietnamese soldiers and the entire company withdrawal would be jeopardized. He called for his comrades to move back and that he would stay and provide cover for them. He made this decision realizing that the enemy was converging on three sides of his position and only meters away, and a delay in withdrawal meant almost certain death. Pfc. Lozada continued to deliver a heavy, accurate volume of suppressive fire against the enemy until he was mortally wounded and had to be carried during the withdrawal. His heroic deed served as an example and an inspiration to his comrades throughout the ensuing 4-day battle. Pfc. Lozada's actions are in the highest traditions of the U.S. Army and reflect great credit upon himself, his unit, and the Armed Forces of his country.

Note: The following is a newspaper account of the preceding battle in which both Chaplain Watters and Pfc. Lozada earned the Medal of Honor:

40 Americans Die In Highland Fight
Paratroops Battle Foe Near Dak To Base

SAIGON, South Vietnam, Mon. Nov. 20 - Forty American paratroopers were killed yesterday during heavy fighting near Dak To in the Central Highlands, a United States spokesman said today.

Fighting flared up in the early afternoon between troops of the 173d Airborne Brigade and North Vietnamese regulars entrenched in the hills around the mountain outpost.

After a minor skirmish between a company of paratroopers and about 15 to 20 North Vietnamese in prepared positions a second company of Americans clashed with a force of unknown size about half a mile away.

[The United States command spokesman said seven North Vietnamese were killed in one of the actions and gave no account of enemy dead in the other, The Associated Press reported.]

The North Vietnamese used small arms and high powered automatic rifles and backed their attack with mortars.

Third Company Joins Battle

A third United States company joined the battle and engaged a North Vietnamese force about 240 yards away. The North Vietnamese broke off contact soon after dusk.

The casualties raised total United States deaths since fighting began in the area to 197 killed and 750 wounded.

LITEKY, ANGELO J.
Rank and Organization: Chaplain (Captain), U.S. Army, Headquarters and Headquarters Company, 199th Infantry Brigade.
Born: February 14, 1931, Washington, D.C.
Entered Service At: Fort Hamilton, New York
Place and Date: Near Phuoc-Lac, Bien Hoa Province, Republic of Vietnam, December 6, 1967.
Citation: Chaplain Liteky distinguished himself while serving with Company A, 4th battalion, 12th Infantry, 199th Light Infantry Brigade. He was participating in a search and destroy operation when Company A came under intense fire from a battalion size enemy force. Momentarily stunned from the immediate encounter that ensued, the men hugged the ground for cover. Observing two wounded men, Chaplain Liteky moved to within 15 meters of an enemy machinegun position to reach them, placing himself between the enemy and the wounded men. When there was a brief respite in the fighting, he managed to drag them to the relative safety of the landing zone. Inspired by his courageous actions, the company rallied and began placing heavy volume of fire upon the enemy's positions. In a magnificent display of courage and leadership, Chaplain Liteky began moving upright through the enemy fire, administering last rites to the dying and evacuating the wounded. Noticing another trapped and seriously wounded man, Chaplain Liteky crawled to his aid. Realizing that the wounded man was to heavy to carry, he rolled on his back, placed the man on his chest and through sheer determination and fortitude crawled back to the landing zone using his elbows and heels to push himself along. Pausing for breath momentarily, he returned to the action and came upon a man entangled in the dense, thorny underbrush. Once more intense enemy fire was directed at him, but Chaplain Liteky stood his ground and calmly broke the vines and carried the man to the landing zone for evacuation. On several occasions when the landing zone was under small-arms and rocket fire, Chaplain Liteky stood up in the face of hostile fire and personally directed the medivac helicopters into and out of the area. With the wounded safely evacuated, Chaplain Liteky returned to the perimeter, constantly encouraging and inspiring the men. Upon the unit's relief on the morning of 7 December 1967, it was discovered that despite painful wounds in the neck and foot, Chaplain Liteky had

personally carried over 20 men to the landing zone for evacuation during the savage fighting. Through his indomitable inspiration and heroic actions, Chaplain Liteky saved the lives of a number of his comrades and enabled the company to repulse the enemy. Chaplain Liteky's actions reflect great credit upon himself and were in keeping with the highest traditions of the U.S. Army.

LYNCH, ALLEN JAMES

Rank and Organization: Sergeant, U.S. Army, Company D, 1st Battalion, 12th Cavalry, 1st Cavalry Division (Airmobile).
Born: October 28, 1945, Chicago, Ill.
Entered Service At: Chicago, Ill.
Place and Date: Near My An (2), Binh Dinh Province, Republic of Vietnam, December 15, 1967.
Citation: For conspicuous gallantry and intrepidity in action at the risk of his life above and beyond the call of duty. Sgt. Lynch (then Sp4c.) distinguished himself while serving as a radio telephone operator with Company D. While serving in the forward element of an operation near the village of My An, his unit became heavily engaged with a numerically superior enemy force. Quickly and accurately assessing the situation, Sgt. Lynch provided his commander with information which subsequently proved essential to the unit's successful actions. Observing three wounded comrades lying exposed to enemy fire, Sgt. Lynch dashed across 50 meters of open ground through a withering hail of enemy fire to administer aid. Reconnoitering a nearby trench for a covered position to protect the wounded from the intense hostile fire, he killed two enemy soldiers at point-blank range. With the trench cleared, he unhesitatingly returned to the fire-swept area three times to carry the wounded men to safety. When his company was forced to withdraw by the superior firepower of the enemy, Sgt. Lynch remained to aid his comrades at the risk of his life rather than abandon them. Alone, he defended his isolated position for two hours against the advancing enemy. Using only his rifle and a grenade, he stopped them just short of his trench, killing five. Again, disregarding his safety in the face of the withering hostile fire, he crossed 70 meters of exposed terrain five times to carry his wounded comrades to a more secure area. Once he assured their comfort and safety, Sgt. Lynch located the counterattacking friendly company to assist in directing the attack and evacuating the three casualties. His gallantry at the risk of his life is in the highest traditions of the military service. Sgt. Lynch has reflected great credit upon himself, the 12th Cavalry, and the U.S. Army.

†SMEDLEY, LARRY E.

Rank and Organization: Corporal, U.S. Marine Corps, Company D, 1st Battalion, 7th Marines, 1st Marine Division.
Born: March 4, 1949, Front Royal, Virginia
Entered Service At: Orlando, Florida
Place and Date: Quang Nam Province, Republic of Vietnam, December 21, 1967.
Citation: For conspicuous gallantry and intrepidity at the risk of his life above and beyond the call of duty while serving as a squad leader with Company D, in connection with operations against the enemy. On the evenings of 20-21 December 1967, Cpl. Smedley led his six-man squad to an ambush site at the mouth of Happy Valley, near Phouc Ninh (2) in Quang Nam Province. Later that night an estimated 100 Viet Cong and North Vietnamese Army regulars, carrying 122mm rocket launchers and mortars, were observed moving toward Hill 41. Realizing that this was a significant enemy move to launch an attack on the vital Danang complex, Cpl. Smedley immediately took sound and courageous action to stop the enemy threat. After he radioed for a reaction force, he skillfully maneuvered his men to a more advantageous position and led an attack on the numerically superior enemy force. A heavy volume of fire from an enemy machinegun positioned on the left flank of the squad inflicted several casualties on Cpl. Smedley's unit. Simultaneously, an enemy grenade exploded nearby, wounding him in the right foot and knocking him to the ground. Cpl. Smedley disregarded this serious injury, valiantly struggled to his feet and shouted words of encouragement to his men. He fearlessly led a charge against the enemy machinegun emplacement, firing his rifle and throwing grenades, until he was again struck by the enemy fire and knocked to the ground. Gravely wounded and weak from loss of blood, he rose and commenced a one-man assault against the enemy position. Although his aggressive and single handed attack resulted in the destruction of the machinegun, he was struck in the chest by enemy fire and fell mortally wounded. Cpl. Smedley's inspiring and courageous actions, bold initiative, and selfless devotion to duty in the face of certain death were in keeping with the highest traditions of the Marine Corps and the U.S. Naval Service. He gallantly gave his life for his country.

CHAPTER 5
1968

(† - Indicates Posthumous Award)

Note: The following newspaper article concerning Vietnam appeared on the front page of *The New York Times* on Jan. 1, 1968:

U.S. Said To Press Sharply
For Good Vietnam Reports

SAIGON, South Vietnam, Dec. 31 - American officials at almost all levels, both in Saigon and in the provinces, say they are under steadily increasing pressure from Washington to produce convincing evidence of progress, especially by the South Vietnamese, in the next few months.

The pressure began to increase about three months ago, the officials report, and became more intense in December. They expect no lessening, and probably a further increase, as the American elections approach.

"I was in a briefing the other day," a middle-level civilian said, "and the briefing us came out and said it: "An election year is about to begin. And the people we work for are in the business of re-electing President Johnson in November."

Washington's latest campaign for "results" appears to differ from some in the past in that it is directed more toward South Vietnamese, military and civilian, than Americans.

A well-informed Saigon source said that recent cable-grams from the State Department and the Pentagon had been full of such instructions as these:

Get the South Vietnamese Army moving. Not only the regulars but the militia and the national guardsmen. And get the idea across to the American public that they are fighting well.

Do something-anything-about Government corruption.

Get President Nguyen Van Thieu to demonstrate his commitment to the war as well as his determination to demand sacrifices from the public.

"What it all adds up to" an officer in the American Embassy said "is a simple, straight-forward message: Washington is telling us that the American people will no longer tolerate the Vietnamese caring less about winning than we do.

Reflecting the same view, a senior American provincial representative in the Mekong Delta said recently: "They're telling us to find some way to get the Vietnamese moving-that we aren't going to have forever to get it on the road."

A junior official tells of receiving several cablegrams with the specific instruction that "this can't wait until after Tet." The Government traditionally all but closes down during the weeks immediately preceding the lunar new year, which is called Tet in Vietnam. The 1968 Tet is at the end of January.

To illustrate what he calls the "Washington squeeze play," another official said he recently received a private cablegram whose sole message was that another cablegram, marked "top secret," was on its way and that he should be sure to read it quickly.

Whether the pressure will result in action by the Vietnamese is, of course, highly problematical. Already, the efforts by Ambassador Ellsworth Bunker to push President Thieu into action on several fronts have produced anti-American speeches in the Legislature and diatribes in the newspapers.

BRADY, PATRICK HENRY

Rank and Organization: Major, U.S. Army, Medical Service Corps, 54th Medical Detachment, 67th Medical Group, 44th Medical Brigade.

Born: October 1, 1936, Philip, South Dakota

Entered Service At: Seattle, Washington

Place and Date: Near Chu Lai, Republic of Vietnam, January 6, 1968

Citation: For conspicuous gallantry and intrepidity in action at the risk of his life above and beyond the call of duty, Maj. Brady distinguished himself while serving in the Republic of Vietnam commanding a UH-1H ambulance helicopter, volunteered to rescue wounded men from a site in enemy held territory which was reported to be heavily defended and to be blanketed by fog. To reach the site he descended through heavy fog and smoke and hovered slowly along a valley trail, turning his ship sideward to blow away the fog with the backwash from his rotor blades. Despite the unchallenged, close-range enemy fire, he found the dangerously small site, where he successfully landed and evacuated two badly wounded South Vietnamese soldiers. He was then called to another area completely covered by dense fog where American casualties lay only 50 meters from the enemy. Two aircraft had previously been shot down and others had made unsuccessful attempts to reach this site earlier in the day. With unmatched skill and extraordinary courage, Maj. Brady made four flights to this embattled landing zone and successfully rescued all the wounded. On his third mission of the day Maj. Brady once again landed at a site surrounded by the enemy. The friendly ground force, pinned down by enemy fire, had been unable to reach and secure the landing zone. Although his aircraft had been badly damaged and his controls partially shot away during his initial entry into this area, he returned minutes later and rescued the remaining injured. Shortly thereafter, obtaining a replacement aircraft, Maj. Brady was requested to land in an enemy mine-field where a platoon of American soldiers was trapped. A mine detonated near his helicopter, wounding two crew members and damaging his ship. In spite of this, he managed to fly six severely injured patients to medical aid. Throughout that day Maj. Brady utilized three helicopters to evacuate a total of 51 seriously wounded men, many of whom would have perished without prompt medical treatment. Maj. Brady's bravery was in the highest traditions of the military service and reflects great credit upon himself and the U.S. Army.

Note: Maj. Brady never refused to go into any area to evacuate a wounded soldier. In his two tours of duty he picked up over 5000 wounded soldiers.

†WICKAM, JERRY WAYNE

Rank and Organization: Corporal, U.S. Army, Troop F, 2d Squadron, 11th Armored Cavalry Regiment.
Born: January 19, 1942, Rockford, Illinois
Entered Service At: Chicago, Illinois
Place and Date: Near Loc Ninh, Republic of Vietnam, January 6, 1968
Citation: For conspicuous gallantry and intrepidity in action at the risk of his life above and beyond the call of duty. Cpl. Wickam, distinguished himself while serving with Troop F. Troop F was conducting a reconnaissance in force mission southwest of Loc Ninh when the lead element of the friendly force was subjected to a heavy barrage of rocket, automatic weapons, and small-arms fire from a well concealed enemy bunker complex. Disregarding the intense fire, Cpl. Wickam leaped from his armored vehicle and assaulted one of the enemy bunkers and threw a grenade into it, killing two enemy soldiers. He moved into the bunker, and with the aid of another soldier, began to remove the body of one Viet Cong when he detected the sound of an enemy grenade being charged. Cpl. Wickam warned his comrade and physically pushed him away from the grenade thus protecting him from the force of the blast. When a second Viet Cong bunker was discovered, he ran through a hail of enemy fire to deliver deadly fire into the bunker, killing one enemy soldier. He also captured one Viet Cong who later provided valuable information on enemy activity in the Loc Ninh area. After the patrol withdrew and an airstrike was conducted, Cpl. Wickam led his men back to evaluate the success of the strike. They were immediately attacked again by enemy fire. Without hesitation, he charged the bunker from which the fire was being directed, enabling the remainder of his men to seek cover. He threw a grenade inside of the enemy's position killing two Viet Cong and destroying the bunker. Moments later he was mortally wounded by enemy fire. Cpl. Wickam's extraordinary heroism at the cost of his life were in keeping with the highest traditions of the military service and reflect great credit upon himself and the U.S. Army.

WETZEL, GARY GEORGE

Rank and Organization: Specialist Fourth Class (then Pfc.), U.S. Army, 173d Assault Helicopter Company.
Born: September 29, 1947, South Milwaukee, Wisconsin
Entered Service At: Milwaukee, Wisconsin
Place and Date: Near Ap Dong An, Republic of Vietnam, January 8, 1968
Citation: Sp4c. Wetzel, 173d Assault Helicopter Company, distinguished himself by conspicuous gallantry and intrepidity at the risk of his life, above and beyond the call of duty. Sp4c. Wetzel was serving as door gunner aboard a helicopter which was part of an insertion force trapped in a landing zone by intense and deadly hostile fire. Sp4c. Wetzel was going to the aid of his aircraft commander when he was blown into a rice paddy and critically wounded by two enemy rockets that exploded just inches from his location. Although bleeding profusely due to the loss of his left arm and severe wounds in his right arm, chest, and left leg, Sp4c. Wetzel staggered back to his original position in his gun-well and took the enemy forces under fire. His machinegun was the only weapon placing effective fire on the enemy at that time. Through a resolve that overcame the shock and intolerable pain of his injuries, Sp4c. Wetzel remained at his position until he had eliminated the automatic weapons emplacement that had been inflicting heavy casualties on the American troops and preventing them from moving against this strong enemy force. Refusing to attend his own extensive wounds, he attempted to return to the aid of his aircraft commander but passed out from loss of blood. Regaining consciousness, he persisted in his efforts to drag himself to the aid of his fellow crewman. After an agonizing effort, he came to the side of the crew chief who was attempting to drag the wounded aircraft commander to the safety of a nearby dike. Unswerving in his devotion to his fellow man, Sp4c. Wetzel assisted his crew chief even though he lost consciousness once again during this action. Sp4c. Wetzel displayed extraordinary heroism in his efforts to aid his fellow crewmen. His gallant actions were in keeping with the highest traditions of the U.S. Army and reflect great credit upon himself and the Armed Forces of his country.

SASSER, CLARENCE EUGENE

Rank and Organization: Specialist Fifth Class (then Pfc.), U.S. Army, Headquarters Company, 3d Battalion, 60th Infantry, 9th Infantry Division.

Born: September 12, 1947, Chenango, Texas

Entered Service At: Houston, Texas

Place and Date: Ding Tuong Province, Republic of Vietnam, January 10, 1968

Citation: For conspicuous gallantry and intrepidity in action at the risk of his life above and beyond the call of duty. Sp5c. Sasser distinguished himself while assigned to Headquarters and Headquarters Company, 3d Battalion. He was serving as a medical aidman with Company A, 3d Battalion, on a reconnaissance in force operation. His company was making an air assault when suddenly it was taken under heavy small arms, recoilless rifle, machinegun and rocket fire from well fortified enemy positions on three sides of the landing zone. During the first few minutes, over 30 casualties were sustained. Without hesitation, Sp5c. Sasser ran across an open rice paddy through a hail of fire to assist the wounded. After helping one man to safety, he was painfully wounded in the left shoulder by fragments of an exploding rocket. Refusing medical attention, he ran through a barrage of rocket and automatic weapons fire to aid casualties of the initial attack and, after giving them urgently needed treatment, continued to search for other wounded. Despite two additional wounds immobilizing his legs, he dragged himself through the mud toward another soldier 100 meters away. Although in agonizing pain and faint from loss of blood, Sp5c. Sasser reached the man, treated him, and proceeded on to encourage another group of soldiers to crawl 200 meters to relative safety. There he attended their wounds for five hours until they were evacuated. Sp5c. Sasser's extraordinary heroism is in keeping with the highest traditions of the military service and reflects great credit upon himself, his unit, and the U.S. Army.

†PORT, WILLIAM D.

Rank and Organization: Sergeant (then Pfc.), U.S. Army, Company C, 5th Battalion, 7th Cavalry, 1st Air Cavalry Division.

Born: October 13, 1941, Petersburg, Pa.

Entered Service At: Harrisburg, Pa.

Place and Date: Que Son Valley, Heip Duc Province, Republic of Vietnam, January 12, 1968.

Citation: For conspicuous gallantry and intrepidity at the risk of his life above and beyond the call of duty. Sgt. Port distinguished himself while serving as a rifleman with Company C, which was conducting combat operations against an enemy force in the Que Son Valley. As Sgt. Port's platoon was moving to cut off a reported movement of enemy soldiers, the platoon came under heavy fire from an entrenched enemy force. The platoon was forced to withdraw due to the intensity and ferocity of the fire. Although wounded in the hand as the withdrawal began, Sgt. Port, with complete disregard for his safety, ran through the heavy fire to assist a wounded comrade back to the safety of the platoon perimeter. As the enemy forces assaulted in the perimeter, Sgt. Port and three comrades were in position behind an embankment when an enemy grenade landed in their midst. Sgt. Port, realizing the danger to his fellow soldiers, shouted the warning "grenade," and unhesitatingly hurled himself towards the grenade to shield his comrades from the explosion. Through his exemplary courage and devotion he saved the lives of his fellow soldiers and gave the members of his platoon the inspiration they needed to hold their position. Sgt. Port's selfless concern for his comrades, at the risk of his life above and beyond the call of duty are in keeping with the highest tradition of the military service and reflect great credit upon himself, his unit, and the U.S. Army.

JOHNSON, DWIGHT H.

Rank and Organization: Specialist Fifth Class, U.S. Army, Company B, 1st Battalion, 69th Armor, 4th Infantry Division.
Born: May 7, 1947, Detroit, Michigan
Entered Service At: Detroit, Michigan
Place and Date: Near Dak To, Kontum Province, Republic of Vietnam, January 15, 1968.
Citation: For conspicuous gallantry and intrepidity at the risk of his life above and beyond the call of duty. Sp5c. Johnson, a tank driver with Company B, was a member of a reaction force moving to aid other elements of his platoon, which was in heavy contact with a battalion size North Vietnamese force. Sp5c. Johnson's tank, upon reaching the point of contact, threw a track and became immobilized. Realizing that he could do no more as a driver, he climbed out of the vehicle, armed only with a .45 caliber pistol. Despite intense hostile fire, Sp5c. Johnson killed several enemy soldiers before he had expended his ammunition. Returning to his tank through a heavy volume of antitank rocket, small-arms and automatic weapons fire, he obtained a sub-machinegun with which to continue his fight against the advancing enemy. Armed with this weapon, Sp5c. Johnson again braved deadly enemy fire to return to the center of the ambush site where he courageously eliminated more of the determined foe. Engaged in extremely close combat when the last of his ammunition was expended, he killed an enemy soldier with the stock end of his sub-machinegun. Now weaponless, Sp5c. Johnson ignored the enemy fire around him, climbed into his platoon sergeant's tank, extricated a wounded crew member and carried him to an armored personnel carrier. He then returned to the same tank and assisted in firing the main gun until it jammed. In a magnificent display of courage, Sp5c. Johnson exited the tank and armed only with a .45 caliber pistol, engaged several North Vietnamese troops in close proximity to the vehicle. Fighting his way through devastating fire and remounting his own immobilized tank, he remained fully exposed to the enemy as he bravely and skillfully engaged them with the tank's externally-mounted .50 caliber machinegun; where he remained until the situation was brought under control. Sp5c. Johnson's profound concern for his fellow soldiers, at the risk of his life above and beyond the call of duty are in keeping with the highest traditions of the military service and reflect great credit upon himself and the U.S. Army.

Note: The following is a newspaper account of the preceding battle in which Sp5c. Johnson received the Medal of Honor:

U.S. Units Escape Traps In Vietnam
37 of Foe Killed Attacking
Convoys in the Highlands
– 23 Americans Injured

SAIGON, South Vietnam, Tue., Jan. 16 - Enemy forces ambushed two American convoys in the Central Highlands yesterday, but U.S. tanks, armed helicopters and infantrymen killed 37 of the attackers and captured four.

Twenty-three American soldiers were wounded and damage to the convoy was described as light.

The first convoy, of the Fourth Infantry Division, was taking supplies from Kontum up Route 14 to units in the Dak To area. The second convoy was a 40-truck column traveling between Ankhe and Pleiku.

In the first attack 24 North Vietnamese soldiers were killed, while 13 American soldiers were wounded.

An American spokesman said that when enemy troops hiding in the steep mountains alongside the road fired on the lead armored vehicles, two tanks from the 69th Armored Battalion, which happened to be nearby, moved in and pumped cannon fire at the attackers.

Two helicopter gunships quickly flew in to strike the North Vietnamese with rockets and machine-gun fire. Then about 100 men of the 4th Division were rushed up the road, the spokesman said.

In the second ambush, three mines buried in the road were set off to halt the convoy. Then the enemy troops fired machine-guns and rifles.

The spokesman said that the fight raged for an hour and a half until Fourth Division reinforcements arrived.

Thirteen enemy soldiers were killed and four captured, the spokesman said, and 10 Americans were wounded.

Last Saturday, an American convoy was ambushed just south of the demilitarized zone. Nineteen U.S. soldiers were killed in that action, and the bodies of 10 enemy soldiers were found.

†YNTEMA, GORDON DOUGLAS
Rank and Organization: Sergeant, U.S. Army, Company D, 5th Special Forces Group (Airborne).
Born: June 26, 1945, Bethesda, Md.
Entered Service At: Detroit, Michigan
Place and Date: Near Thong Binh, Republic of Vietnam, January 16 to 18, 1968.
Citation: For conspicuous gallantry and intrepidity in action at the risk of his life above and beyond the call of duty. Sgt. Yntema, U.S, Army, distinguished himself while assigned to Detachment A-431, Company D. As part of a larger force of civilian irregulars from Camp Cai Cai, he accompanied two platoons to a blocking position east of the village of Thong Binh, where they became heavily engaged in a small-arms fire fight with the Viet Cong. Assuming control of the force when the Vietnamese commander was seriously wounded, he advanced his troops to within 50 meters of the enemy bunkers. After a fierce 30 minute fire fight, the enemy forced Sgt. Yntema to withdraw his men to a trench in order to afford them protection and still perform their assigned blocking mission. Under cover of machinegun fire, approximately one company of Viet Cong maneuvered into a position which pinned down the friendly platoons from three sides. A dwindling ammunition supply, coupled with a Viet Cong mortar barrage which inflicted heavy losses on the exposed friendly troops, caused many of the irregulars to withdraw. Seriously wounded and ordered to withdraw himself, Sgt. Yntema refused to leave his fallen comrades. Under withering small-arms and machinegun fire, he carried the wounded Vietnamese commander and a mortally wounded American Special Forces adviser to a small gully 50 meters away in order to shield them from the enemy fire. Sgt. Yntema then continued to repulse the attacking Viet Cong attempting to overrun his position until, out of ammunition and surrounded, he was offered the opportunity to surrender. Refusing, Sgt. Yntema stood his ground, using his rifle as a club to fight the approximately 15 Viet Cong attempting his capture. His resistance was so fierce that the Viet Cong were forced to shoot in order to overcome him. Sgt. Yntema's personal bravery in the face of insurmountable odds and supreme self-sacrifice were in keeping with the highest traditions of the military service and reflect the utmost credit upon himself, the 1st Special Forces, and the U.S. Army.

FERGUSON, FREDERICK EDGAR

Rank and Organization: Chief Warrant Officer, U.S. Army, Company C, 227th Aviation Battalion, 1st Cavalry Division (Airmobile).
Born: August 18, 1939, Pilot Point, Texas
Entered Service At: Phoenix, Arizona
Place and Date: Hue, Republic of Vietnam, January 31, 1968
Citation: For conspicuous gallantry and intrepidity in action at the risk of his life above and beyond the call of duty. CWO Ferguson, U.S. Army, distinguished himself while serving with Company C. CWO Ferguson, commander of a resupply helicopter monitoring an emergency call from wounded passengers and crewmen of a downed helicopter under heavy attack within the enemy controlled city of Hue, unhesitatingly volunteered to attempt evacuation. Despite warnings from all aircraft to stay clear of the area due to heavy antiaircraft fire, CWO Ferguson began a low-level flight at maximum airspeed along the Perfume River toward the tiny, isolated South Vietnamese Army compound in which the crash survivors had taken refuge. Coolly and skillfully maintaining his course in the face of intense, short range fire from enemy occupied buildings and boats, he displayed superior flying skill and tenacity of purpose by landing his aircraft in an extremely confined area in a blinding dust cloud under heavy mortar and small-arms fire. Although the helicopter was severely damaged by mortar fragments during the loading of the wounded, CWO Ferguson disregarded the damage and, taking off through the continuing hail of mortar fire, he flew his crippled aircraft on the return route through the rain of fire that he had experienced earlier and safely returned his wounded passengers to friendly control. CWO Ferguson's extraordinary determination saved the lives of five of his comrades. His actions are in the highest traditions of the military service and reflect great credit on himself and the U.S. Army.

†DIX, DREW DENNIS

Rank and Organization: Staff Sergeant, U.S. Army, U.S. Senior Advisor Group, IV Corps, Military Assistance Command.
Born: December 14, 1944, West Point, New York
Entered Service At: Denver, Colorado
Place and Date: Chau Doc Province, Republic of Vietnam, January 31, and February 1, 1968
Citation: For conspicuous gallantry and intrepidity in action at the risk of his life above and beyond the call of duty. S/Sgt. Dix distinguished himself by exceptional heroism while serving as a unit adviser. Two heavily armed Viet Cong battalions attacked the Province capital city of Chau Phu resulting in the complete breakdown and fragmentation of the defenses of the city. S/Sgt. Dix, with a patrol of Vietnamese soldiers, was recalled to assist in the defense of Chau Phu. Learning that a nurse was trapped in a house near the center of the city, S/Sgt. Dix organized a relief force, successfully rescued the nurse, and returned her to the safety of the Tactical Operations Center. Being informed of other trapped civilians within the city, S/Sgt. Dix voluntarily led another force to rescue eight civilian employees located in a building which was under heavy mortar and small-arms fire. S/Sgt. Dix then returned to the center of the city. Upon approaching a building, he was subjected to intense automatic rifle and machine-gun fire from an unknown number of Viet Cong. He personally assaulted the building, killing six Viet Cong, and rescuing two Filipinos. The following day S/Sgt. Dix, still on his own volition, assembled a 20-man force and though under intense enemy fire cleared the Viet Cong out of the hotel, theater, and other adjacent buildings within the city. During this portion of the attack, Army Republic of Vietnam soldiers inspired by the heroism and success of S/Sgt. Dix, rallied and commenced firing upon the Viet Cong. S/Sgt. Dix captured 20 prisoners, including a high ranking Viet Cong official. He then attacked enemy troops who had entered the residence of the Deputy Province Chief and was successful in rescuing the official's wife and children. S/Sgt. Dix's personal heroic actions resulted in 14 confirmed Viet Cong killed in action and possibly 25 more, the capture of 20 prisoners, 15 weapons, and the rescue of the 14 United States and free world civilians. The heroism of S/Sgt. Dix was in the highest tradition and reflects great credit upon the U.S. Army.

†MAXAM, LARRY LEONARD

Rank and Organization: Corporal, U.S. Marine Corps, Company D, 1st Battalion, 4th Marines, 3d Marine Division (Rein), FMF.
Born: January 9, 1948, Glendale, California
Entered Service At: Los Angeles, California
Place and Date: Cam Lo District, Quang Tri Province, Republic of Vietnam, February 2, 1968
Citation: For conspicuous gallantry and intrepidity at the risk of his life above and beyond the call of duty while serving as a fire team leader with Company D. The Cam Lo District Headquarters came under extremely heavy rocket, artillery, mortar, and recoilless rifle fire from a numerically superior enemy force, destroying a portion of the defensive perimeter. Cpl. Maxam, observing the enemy massing for an assault into the compound across the remaining defensive wire, instructed his assistant fire team leader to take charge of the fire team, and unhesitatingly proceeded to the weakened section of the perimeter. Completely exposed to the concentrated enemy fire, he sustained multiple fragmentation wounds from exploding grenades as he ran to an abandoned machine-gun position. Reaching the emplacement, he grasped the machine-gun and commenced to deliver effective fire on the advancing enemy. As the enemy directed maximum firepower against the determined marine, Cpl. Maxam's position received a direct hit from a rocket propelled grenade, knocking him backwards and inflicting severe fragmentation wounds to his face and right eye. Although momentarily stunned and in intense pain, Cpl. Maxam courageously resumed his firing position and subsequently was struck again by small-arms fire. With resolute determination, he gallantly continued to deliver intense machine-gun fire, causing the enemy to retreat through the defensive wire to positions of cover. In a desperate attempt to silence his weapon, the North Vietnamese threw hand-grenades and directed recoilless rifle fire against him inflicting two additional wounds. Too weak to reload his machine-gun, Cpl. Maxam fell to a prone position and valiantly continued to deliver effective fire with his rifle. After 1-1/2 hours, during which he was hit repeatedly by fragments from exploding grenades and concentrated small-arms fire, he succumbed to his wounds, having successfully defended nearly half of the perimeter singlehandedly. Cpl. Maxam's aggressive fighting spirit, inspiring valor and selfless devotion to duty reflected great credit upon himself and the Marine Corps and upheld the highest traditions of the U.S. Naval Service. He gallantly gave his life for his country.

†GONZALEZ, ALFREDO

Rank and Organization: Sergeant, U.S. Marine Corps, Company A, 1st Battalion, 1st Marines, 1st Marine Division (Rein), FMF.
Born: May 23, 1946, Edinburg, Texas
Entered Service At: San Antonio, Texas
Place and Date: Near Thua Thien, Republic of Vietnam, February 4, 1968
Citation: For conspicuous gallantry and intrepidity at the risk of his life above and beyond the call of duty while serving as platoon commander, 3d Platoon, Company A. On January 31, 1968, during the initial phase of Operation Hue City, Sgt. Gonzalez' unit was formed as a reaction force and deployed to Hue to relieve the pressure on the beleaguered city. While moving by truck convoy along Route No. 1, near the village of Lang Van Lrong, the marines received a heavy volume of enemy fire. Sgt. Gonzalez aggressively maneuvered the marines in his platoon, and directed their fire until the area was cleared of snipers. Immediately after crossing a river south of Hue, the column was again hit by intense enemy fire. One of the marines on top of a tank was wounded and fell to the ground in an exposed position. With complete disregard for his safety, Sgt. Gonzalez ran through the fire-swept area to the assistance of his injured comrade. He lifted him up and though receiving fragmentation wounds during the rescue, he carried the wounded marine to a covered position for treatment. Due to the increased volume and accuracy of enemy fire from a fortified machine-gun bunker on the side of the road, the company was temporarily halted. Realizing the gravity of the situation, Sgt. Gonzalez exposed himself to the enemy fire and moved his platoon along the east side of a bordering rice paddy to a dike directly across from the bunker. Though fully aware of the danger involved, he moved to the fire-swept road and destroyed the hostile position with hand-grenades. Although seriously wounded again on February 3, he steadfastly refused medical treatment and continued to supervise his men and lead the attack. On February 4, the enemy had again pinned the company down, inflicting heavy casualties with automatic weapons and rocket fire. Sgt. Gonzalez, utilizing a number of light antitank assault weapons, fearlessly moved from position to position firing numerous rounds at the heavily fortified enemy emplacements. He successfully knocked out a rocket position and suppressed much of the enemy fire before falling mortally wounded. The heroism, cour-

age, and dynamic leadership displayed by Sgt. Gonzalez reflected great credit upon himself and the Marine Corps, and were in keeping with the highest traditions of the U.S. Naval Service. He gallantly gave his life for his country.

Note: The following are two newspaper accounts of the preceding battle in which Sgt. Gonzales earned the Medal of Honor:

ENEMY MAINTAINS TIGHT GRIP ON HUE

U.S. Marines Hold Two Square Blocks of City

HUE, South Vietnam, Feb. 2 - Enemy battalions weathered repeated attacks by Marine tanks and South Vietnamese aircraft today to maintain a tight grip on the ancient city of Hue.

At nightfall, the Marines held only two square blocks of the smoking city. Seven South Vietnamese Army battalions struggled unsuccessfully to push North Vietnamese and Viet Cong troops from the Citadel-a 19th century fortress built to shield the nation's historic imperial palace.

The strength of the enemy resistance caught the South Vietnamese by surprise. As late as yesterday, Vietnamese commanders in the area were saying that the enemy troops in Hue were week and ill supplied and would fall with the first major allied push.

But today the assessment has changed. "Enemy forces in the ancient Citadel are believed to number five battalions," the regional Vietnamese command said in a late communique that gave the Hue battle more attention than any other engagement under way in the country.

The battle is significant for both the allies and the enemy because of the city's unique position in the spiritual, cultural and educational life of the country. It is the center of strength for the anti-Government sect of Buddhism.

Recognizing the psychological importance of the enemy's gains in Hue, marines and South Vietnamese alike make it clear, in background statements to newsmen, that they will step up their efforts to secure the city.

3rd Day Of Fighting

But troops in Hue said the going would be tough. "I was in Conthien last fall and that was rough, but this is even rougher," said a marine, one of 700 sent here since Wednesday afternoon to reinforce an embattled compound of 200 American military advisers. Meanwhile, as the fighting continued for the third day, the city was in chaos.

The chief of Thuathien Province, of which Hue is the capitol, was wounded and is receiving medical treatment at an undisclosed place. His house is in ruins.

The province headquarters is in the hands of soldiers, who are using it as a sniper post, and the flag of the National Liberation Front, the Viet Cong's political organization, flutters from the imperial palace.

The streets of this normally bustling city are deserted except for the fighting forces and the wreckage. Parents hold their children tightly by the hand, and move sideways with their backs pressed against the buildings. When they reach an open space-an intersection or a gap between a house-they run quickly and flatten themselves against the first wall they reach.

Scores of them have reached Hue University and the American advisory compound next to it in search of food and shelter. American advisers are trying to assist them from offices that only four days were abuzz with the bookkeeping chores of the Government's pacification program. The pacification project is a shambles.

"Until the enemy moved into the city we were doing great-making real progress," said Lt. Col. Howard L. Moon, the senior American adviser to the province chief. "Now we'll have to start all over again."

While Col. Moon talked, smoke was billowing from buildings along the city's riverfront and rockets from South Vietnamese installations streaked across the river toward the citadel.

Fred Blackwell, a bespectacled Army specialist from Los Angeles, waited until the roar of a tank-mounted cannon had subsided and then spoke above the clatter of a machine gun.

"I'll tell you the truth" he said. "I was never so happy to see a marine in my life."

A few steps away an Army Captain, Herbert Wilfring of the Bronx, repeated the view. "The greatest news we had was that the Marines were coming with four tanks," he said. "It made you feel somebody was thinking about you."

Until a special unit of 500 marines broke through 48 hours ago, the 200 United States advisers, most of them with the Army, and more than 50 American civilians were cut off from the rest of Hue for 12 hours. Enemy forces battered them with rocket and mortar fire.

The marines fought their way from Phubai airfield through more than six miles of Viet Cong controlled roads to reach the embattled advisers. Then they fought house to house over a half mile of city streets. Another company of marines joined them yesterday by helicopter – the only means of supply and reinforcement now available.

In breaking through to Hue, the marines suffered 10 dead and 20 to 30 wounded. They reported that they had killed 50 Viet Cong and wounded many others.

The South Vietnamese Army estimated that they had killed 200 enemy soldiers and described its own losses as light.

The two allied forces are working separately rather then as a coordinated unit.

"Hue is South Vietnam's leading cultural, educational and religious center," said one high Marine officer. "We want the South Vietnamese themselves to liberate it – not the Americans."

But another Marine officer said the American command was reluctant to send marines into the area because of the city's many historic buildings.

"If buildings have to be destroyed to get the enemy out of here, we want the South Vietnamese to be the ones to do it – not us," he said.

With the enemy in strong positions, the marines and the South Vietnamese face the prospect of lengthy house-to-house fighting. In several parts of Hue, the lines between the allies and the enemy is a narrow one-a situation that could make all of the fighting bitter. The situation was dramatized yesterday when a lean Marine sergeant stood by a brick column near an intersection, waving his arms like a traffic officer and ordering his men to move behind a low concrete wall.

"Friendlies on the left," he told each passing marine. "Enemies on the right."

U.S. MARINES SEIZE A 3D BLOCK OF HUE

Reinforcements Enter City -32 American Civilians Are Listed as Missing

HUE, South Vietnam, Feb. 3 - United States Marines were in firm control of three square blocks of Hue today, compared with two blocks yesterday. They steadily increased the length of their probes in search of the enemy.

Marine units were also searching for 32 American civilians listed as unaccounted for by American military advisers.

Col. S. S. Hughes, commander of the First Regiment of the First Marine Division, said tonight that more than 300 bodies of North Vietnamese and Vietcong had been counted in the last four days by his force and by the 200 American military advisers in the section of the city south of the Namngum (Perfume) River.

Hundreds of other enemy deaths were reported by South Vietnamese troops who are fighting on the river's north bank.

"We expect even heavier contact with the enemy as the battle wears on," said Colonel Hughes. He added that he thought the South Vietnamese estimate of five enemy battalions in the city was reasonable.

Marine casualties are mounting also. More than 20 men were evacuated by helicopter today. Others were awaiting evacuation when night fell.

But military commanders here believe that the cost of wresting Hue from enemy control may be worth it because the ancient city is both an Athens and a Mecca to Vietnamese. Meanwhile American forces are moving steadily into the city. Elements of the First Armored Cavalry were massing tonight on the northwest fringe of the city and elements of the 101st Airborne Division have also been airlifted into the vicinity of Hue.

A Marine company blasted its way into the city today from the Phubai Airfield, seven miles away, raising the total number of marines to 1,000.

Minutes later marine tanks were rumbling out to engage enemy forces that had fired on a convoy.

"That convoy smashed out a whole mess of the goods," said a Marine private as he shoved 106-mm projectiles into the breach of a recoilless rifle. "We'll get them with these."

Often the battle scenes were bizarre.

A half-filled cup of lemonade rested at the elbow of P.F.C. Tony Davis of Greenwood, Miss., as he blasted away at the Vietcong front's flag flying over the imperial palace. He fired from the roof of the four-story building housing the American military compound.

On the third floor, two Army advisers listened to a portable radio while they crouched near a window with their rifles.

"Hot damn," one of them yelled. "The announcer just said they are going to rebroadcast the Senior Bowl game."

Tanks continued tonight to fire at houses known to conceal the enemy. Marines and military advisers alternated sleeping on the floor.

Lieut. Col. Howard L. Moon, the senior American adviser to the province chief of Hue, identified the 32 missing Americans as 20 employees of the United States aid agency, six teachers and six employees of the World Relief Organization.

But hope for their safety was raised last night when Donald Bradley, a 44-year-old water works superintendent from Greenfield, Calif., clambered into the compound under a hail of machine-gun bullets fired by South Vietnamese who mistook him for a guerilla.

Mr. Bradley had hidden in an attic above his apartment a block from the compound for 65 hours before escaping through a gaping hole torn in the roof by an artillery shell.

He said that one night as many as 200 North Vietnamese and Vietcong soldiers were within 25 feet of the house.

"I watched one of them fire a mortar all night," he said.

With that comment Mr. Bradley sat down on a corner of the porch of the compound, sipped a cup of cold coffee and reflected for a minute.

"God, was I lucky," he said finally. "Everyone has had their chance to get me, but none did. I must be bulletproof."

†ASHLEY, EUGENE, JR.

Rank and Organization: Sergeant First Class, U.S. Army, Company C, 5th Special Forces Group (Airborne), 1st Special Forces.
Born: October 1, 1931, Wilmington, North Carolina
Entered Service At: New York, New York
Place and Date: Near Lang Vei, Republic of Vietnam, February 6, and 7, 1968
Citation: Sfc. Ashley, distinguished himself by conspicuous gallantry and intrepidity while serving with Detachment A-101, Company C. Sfc. Ashley was the senior special forces Advisor of a hastily organized assault force whose mission was to rescue entrapped U.S. Special forces advisors at Camp Lang Vei. During the initial attack on the special forces camp by North Vietnamese army forces, Sfc. Ashley supported the camp with high explosive and illumination mortar rounds. When communications were lost with the main camp, he assumed the additional responsibility of directing air strikes and artillery support. Sfc. Ashley organized and equipped a small assault force composed of local friendly personnel. During the ensuing battle, Sfc. Ashley led a total of five vigorous assaults against the enemy, continuously exposing himself to a voluminous hail of enemy grenades, machine-gun and automatic weapons fire. Throughout these assaults, he was plagued by numerous boobytrapped satchel charges in all bunkers on his avenue of approach. During his fifth and final assault, he adjusted air strikes nearly on top of his assault element, forcing the enemy to withdraw and resulting in friendly control of the summit of the hill. While exposing himself to intense enemy fire, he was seriously wounded by machine-gun fire but continued his mission without regard for his personal safety. After the fifth assault he lost consciousness and was carried from the summit by his comrades only to suffer a fatal wound when an enemy artillery round landed in the area. Sfc. Ashley displayed extraordinary heroism in risking his life in an attempt to save the lives of his entrapped comrades and commanding officer. His total disregard for his personal safety while exposed to enemy observation and automatic weapons fire was an inspiration to all men committed to the assault. The resolute valor with which he led five gallant charges placed critical diversionary pressure on the attacking enemy and his valiant efforts carved a channel in the overpowering enemy forces and weapons

positions through which the survivors of Camp Lang Vei eventually escaped to freedom. Sfc. Ashley's bravery at the cost of his life was in the highest traditions of the military service, and reflects great credit upon himself, his unit, and the U.S. Army.

KINSMAN, THOMAS JAMES

Rank and Organization: Specialist Fourth Class, U.S. Army, Company B, 3d Battalion, 60th Infantry, 9th Infantry Division.
Born: March 4, 1945, Renton, Washington
Entered Service At: Seattle, Washington
Place and Date: Near Vinh Long, Republic of Vietnam, February 6, 1968
Citation: For conspicuous gallantry and intrepidity in action at the risk of his life above and beyond the call of duty Sp4c Kinsman (then Pfc.) distinguished himself in action in the afternoon while serving as a rifleman with Company B, on a reconnaissance-in-force mission. As his company was proceeding up a narrow canal in armored troops carriers, it came under sudden and intense rocket, automatic weapons and small-arms fire from a well entrenched Viet Cong force. The company immediately beached and began assaulting the enemy bunker complex. Hampered by exceedingly dense undergrowth which limited visibility to 10 meters, a group of eight men became cut off from the main body of the company. As they were moving through heavy enemy fire to effect a line-up, an enemy soldier in a concealed position hurled a grenade into their midst. Sp4c. Kinsman immediately alerted his comrades of the danger, then unhesitatingly threw himself on the grenade and blocked the explosion with his body. As a result of his courageous action, he received severe head and chest wounds. Through his indomitable courage, complete disregard for his personal safety and profound concern for his fellow soldiers, Sp4c. Kinsman averted loss of life and injury to the other seven men of his element. Sp4c. Kinsman's extraordinary heroism at the risk of his life, above and beyond the call of duty, are in keeping with the highest traditions of the military service and reflect great credit upon himself, his unit, and the U.S. Army.

†GRAVES, TERRENCE COLLINSON

Rank and Organization: Second Lieutenant, U.S. Marine Corps, 3d Force Reconnaissance Company, 3d Reconnaissance Battalion, 3d Marine Division (Rein), FMF
Born: July 6, 1945, Corpus Christi, Texas
Entered Service At: New York, New York
Place and Date: Quang Tri Province, Republic of Vietnam, February 16, 1968
Citation: For conspicuous gallantry and intrepidity at the risk of his life above and beyond the call of duty as a platoon commander with the 3d Force Reconnaissance Company. While on a long-range reconnaissance mission, 2d Lt. Graves' eight-man patrol observed seven enemy soldiers approaching their position. Reacting instantly, he deployed his men and directed their fire on the approaching enemy. After the fire had ceased, he and two patrol members commenced a search of the area, and suddenly came under a heavy volume of hostile small arms and automatic weapons fire from a numerically superior enemy force. When one of his men was hit by the enemy fire, 2d Lt. Graves moved through the fire-swept area to his radio and, while directing suppressive fire from his men, requested air support and adjusted a heavy volume of artillery and helicopter gunship fire upon the enemy. After attending the wounded, 2d Lt. Graves, accompanied by another marine, moved from his relatively safe position to confirm the results of the earlier engagement. Observing that several of the enemy were still alive, he launched a determined assault, eliminating the remaining enemy troops. he then began moving the patrol to a landing zone for extraction, when the unit again came under intense fire which wounded two more marines and 2d Lt. Graves. Refusing medical attention, he once more adjusted air strikes and artillery fire upon the enemy while directing the fire of his men. He led his men to a new landing site into which he skillfully guided the incoming aircraft and boarded his men while remaining exposed to the hostile fire. Realizing that one of the wounded had not embarked, he directed the aircraft to depart and, along with another marine, moved to the side of the casualty. Confronted with a shortage of ammunition, 2d Lt. Graves utilized supporting arms and directed fire until a second helicopter arrived. At this point, the volume of enemy fire intensified, hitting the helicopter and causing it to crash shortly after liftoff. All aboard were killed. 2d Lt. Graves' outstanding cour-

age, superb leadership and indomitable fighting spirit throughout the day were in keeping with the highest traditions of the Marine Corps and the U.S. Naval Service. He gallantly gave his life for his country.

ZABITOSKY, FRED WILLIAM

Rank and Organization: Sergeant First Class (then S/Sgt.), U.S. Army, 5th Special Forces Group (Airborne).

Born: October 27, 1942, Trenton, New Jersey

Entered Service At: Trenton, New Jersey

Place and Date: Republic of Vietnam, February 19, 1968

Citation: For conspicuous gallantry and intrepidity in action at the risk of his life above and beyond the call of duty. Sfc. Zabitosky, U.S. Army, distinguished himself while serving as an assistant team leader of a nine-man Special Forces long-range reconnaissance patrol. Sfc. Zabitosky's patrol was operating deep within enemy controlled territory when they were attacked by a numerically superior North Vietnamese Army unit. Sfc. Zabitosky rallied his team members, deployed them into defensive positions, and, exposing himself to concentrated enemy automatic weapons fire, directed their return fire. Realizing the gravity of the situation, Sfc. Zabitosky ordered his patrol to move to a landing zone for helicopter extraction while he covered their withdrawal with rifle fire and grenades. Rejoining the patrol under increasing enemy pressure, he positioned each man in a tight perimeter defense and continually moved from man to man, encouraging them and controlling their defensive fire. Mainly due to his example, the outnumbered patrol maintained its precarious position until the arrival of tactical air support and a helicopter extraction team. As the rescue helicopters arrived, the determined North Vietnamese pressed their attack. Sfc. Zabitosky repeatedly exposed himself to their fire to adjust suppressive helicopter gunship fire around the land zone. After boarding one of the rescue helicopters, he positioned himself in the door delivering fire on the enemy as the ship took off. The helicopter was engulfed in a hail of bullets and Sfc. Zabitosky was thrown from the craft as it spun out of control and crashed. Recovering consciousness, he ignored his extremely painful injuries and moved to the flaming wreckage. Heedless of the danger of exploding ordnance and fuel, he pulled the severely wounded pilot from the searing blaze and made repeated attempts to rescue his patrol members but was driven back by the intense heat. Despite his serious burns and crushed ribs, he carried and dragged the unconscious pilot through a curtain of enemy fire to within 10 feet of a hovering rescue helicopter before collapsing. Sfc. Zabitosky's extraordinary heroism and devotion to duty were in keeping with the highest traditions of the military service and reflect great credit upon himself, his unit, and the U.S. Army.

HOOPER, JOE R.

Rank and Organization: Staff Sergeant, U.S. Army, Company D, 2d Battalion (Airborne), 501st Infantry, 101st Airborne Division.
Born: August 8, 1938, Piedmont, South Carolina
Entered Service At: Los Angeles, California
Place and Date: Near Hue, Republic of Vietnam, February 21, 1968
Citation: For conspicuous gallantry and intrepidity in action at the risk of his life above and beyond the call of duty. Staff Sergeant (then Sgt.) Hooper, U.S. Army, distinguished himself while serving as squad leader with Company D. Company D was assaulting a heavily defended enemy position along a river bank when it encountered a withering hail of fire from rockets, machine-guns and automatic weapons. S/Sgt. Hooper rallied several men and stormed across the river, overrunning several bunkers on the opposite shore. Thus inspired, the rest of the company moved to the attack. With utter disregard for his own safety, he moved out under the intense fire again and pulled back the wounded, moving them to safety. During this act S/Sgt. Hooper was seriously wounded, but he refused medical aid and returned to his men. With the relentless enemy fire disrupting the attack, he singlehandedly stormed three enemy bunkers, destroying them with hand-grenade and rifle fire, and shot two enemy soldiers who had attacked and wounded the Chaplain. Leading his men forward in a sweep of the area, S/Sgt. Hooper destroyed three buildings housing enemy riflemen. At this point he was attacked by a North Vietnamese officer whom he fatally wounded with his bayonet. Finding his men under heavy fire from a house to the front, he proceeded alone to the building, killing its occupants with rifle fire and grenades. By now his initial body wound had been compounded by grenade fragments, yet despite the multiple wounds and loss of blood, he continued to lead his men against the intense enemy fire. As his squad reached the final line of enemy resistance, it received devastating fire from four bunkers in line on its left flank. S/Sgt. Hooper gathered several hand-grenades and raced down a small trench which ran the length of the bunker line, tossing grenades into each bunker as he passed by, killing all but two of the occupants. With these positions destroyed, he concentrated on the last bunkers facing his men, destroying the first with an incendiary grenade and neutralizing two more by rifle fire. he then raced across an open field, still under enemy fire, to rescue a wounded man who was trapped in a trench. Upon reaching the man, he was faced by an armed enemy soldier

whom he killed with a pistol. Moving his comrade to safety and re-turning to his men, he neutralized the final pocket of enemy resistance by fatally wounding three North Vietnamese officers with rifle fire. S/Sgt. Hooper then established a final line and reorganized his men, not accepting treatment until this was accomplished and not consenting to evacuation until the following morning. His supreme valor, inspiring leadership and heroic self-sacrifice were directly responsible for the company's success and provided a lasting example in personal courage for every man on the field. S/Sgt. Hooper's actions were in keeping with the highest traditions of the military service and reflect great credit upon himself and the U.S. Army.

†SIMS, CLIFFORD CHESTER

Rank and Organization: Staff Sergeant, U.S. Army, Company D, 2d Battalion (Airborne) 501st Infantry, 101st Airborne Division.
Born: June 18, 1942, Port St. Joe, Florida
Entered Service At: Jacksonville, Florida
Place and Date: Near Hue, Republic of Vietnam, February 21, 1968
Citation: For conspicuous gallantry and intrepidity in action at the risk of his life above and beyond the call of duty. S/Sgt. Sims distinguished himself while serving as a squad leader with Company D. Company D was assaulting a heavily fortified enemy position concealed within a dense wooded area when it encountered strong enemy defensive fire. Once within the woodline, S/Sgt. Sims led his squad in a furious attack again an enemy force which had pinned down the 1st Platoon and threatened to overrun it. His skillful leadership provided the platoon with freedom of movement and enabled it to regain the initiative. S/Sgt. Sims was then ordered to move his squad to a position where he could provide covering fire for the company command group and to link up with the 3d Platoon, which was under heavy enemy pressure. After moving no more than 30 meters S/Sgt. Sims noticed that a brick structure in which ammunition was stocked was on fire. Realizing the danger, S/Sgt. Sims took immediate action to move his squad from this position. Though in the process of leaving the area two member of his squad were injured by the subsequent explosion of the ammunition, S/Sgt. Sims' prompt actions undoubtedly prevented more serious casualties from occurring. While continuing through the dense woods amidst heavy enemy fire, S/Sgt. Sims and his squad were approaching a bunker when they heard the unmistakable noise of a concealed boobytrap being triggered immediately to their front. S/Sgt. Sims warned his comrades of the danger and unhesitatingly hurled himself upon the device as it exploded, taking the full impact of the blast. In so protecting his fellow soldiers, he willingly sacrificed his life. S/Sgt. Sims' extraordinary heroism at the cost of his life is in keeping with the highest traditions of the military service and reflects great credit upon himself and the U.S. Army.

†CUTINHA, NICHOLAS J.

Rank and Organization: Specialist Fourth Class, U.S. Army, Company C, 4th Battalion, 9th Infantry Regiment, 25th Infantry Division.

Born: January 13, 1945, Fernandina Beach, Florida

Entered Service At: Coral Gables, Florida

Place and Date: Near Gia Dinh, Republic of Vietnam, March 2, 1968

Citation: For conspicuous gallantry and intrepidity in action at the risk of his life above and beyond the call of duty. While serving as a machine gunner with Company C, Sp4c. Cutinha accompanied his unit on a combat mission near Gia Dinh. Suddenly his company came under small arms, automatic weapons, mortar and rocket propelled grenade fire, from a battalion size enemy unit. During the initial hostile attack, communication with the battalion was lost and the company commander and numerous members of the company became casualties. When Sp4c. Cutinha observed that his company was pinned down and disorganized, he moved to the front with complete disregard for his safety, firing his machine-gun at the charging enemy. As he moved forward he drew fire on his own position and was seriously wounded in the leg. As the hostile fire intensified and half of the company was killed or wounded, Sp4c. Cutinha assumed command of all the survivors in his area and initiated a withdrawal while providing covering fire for the evacuation of the wounded. He killed several enemy soldiers but sustained another leg wound when his machine-gun was destroyed by incoming rounds. Undaunted, he crawled through a hail of enemy fire to an operable machine-gun in order to continue the defense of his injured comrades who were being administered medical treatment. Sp4c. Cutinha maintained this position, refused assistance, and provided defensive fire for his comrades until he fell mortally wounded. He was solely responsible for killing 15 enemy soldiers while saving the lives of at least nine members of his own unit. Sp4c. Cutinha's gallantry and extraordinary heroism were in keeping with the highest traditions of the military service and reflect great credit upon himself, his unit, and the U.S. Army.

†JOHNSON, RALPH H.

Rank and Organization: Private First Class, U.S. Marine Corps, Company A, 1st Reconnaissance Battalion, 1st Marine Division (Rein), FMF.
Born: January 11, 1949, Charleston, South Carolina
Entered Service At: Oakland, California
Place and Date: Near the Quan Duc Valley, Republic of Vietnam, March 5, 1968.
Citation: For conspicuous gallantry and intrepidity at the risk of his life above and beyond the call of duty while serving as a reconnaissance scout with Company A, in action against the North Vietnamese Army and Viet Cong forces. In the early morning hours during Operation ROCK, Pfc. Johnson was a member of a 15-man reconnaissance patrol manning an observation post on Hill 146 overlooking the Quan Duc Valley deep in enemy controlled territory. They were attacked by a platoon-size hostile force employing automatic weapons, satchel charges and handgrenades. Suddenly, a handgrenade landed in the three-man fighting hole occupied by Pfc. Johnson and two fellow marines. Realizing the inherent danger to his two comrades, he shouted a warning and unhesitatingly hurled himself upon the explosive device. When the grenade exploded, Pfc. Johnson absorbed the tremendous impact of the blast and was killed instantly. His prompt and heroic act saved the life of one marine at the cost of his life and undoubtedly prevented the enemy from penetrating his sector of the patrol's perimeter. Pfc. Johnson's courage, inspiring valor and selfless devotion to duty were in keeping with the highest traditions of the Marine Corps and the U.S. Naval Service. He gallantly gave his life for his country.

JACOBS, JACK H.

Rank and Organization: Captain, U.S. Army, U.S. Army Element, U.S. Military Assistance Command, Republic of Vietnam.
Born: August 2, 1945, Brooklyn, New York
Entered Service At: Trenton, New Jersey
Place and Date: Kien Phong Province, Republic of Vietnam, March 9, 1968
Citation: For conspicuous gallantry and intrepidity in action at the risk of his life above and beyond the call of duty. Capt. Jacobs (then 1st Lt.), Infantry, distinguished himself while serving as assistant battalion advisor, 2d Battalion, 16th Infantry, 9th Infantry Division, Army of the Republic of Vietnam. The 2d Battalion was advancing to contact when it came under intense heavy machine-gun and mortar fire from a Viet Cong battalion positioned in well fortified bunkers. As the 2d Battalion deployed into attack formation its advance was halted by devastating fire. Capt. Jacobs, with the command element of the lead company, called for and directed air strikes on the enemy positions to facilitate a renewed attack. Due to the intensity of the enemy fire and heavy casualties to the command group, including the company commander, the attack stopped and the friendly troops became disorganized. Although wounded by mortar fragments, Capt. Jacobs assumed command of the allied company, ordered a withdrawal from the exposed position and established a defensive perimeter. Despite profuse bleeding from head wounds which impaired his vision, Capt. Jacobs, with complete disregard for his safety, returned under intense fire to evacuate a seriously wounded advisor to the safety of a wooded area where he administered lifesaving first aid. He then returned through heavy automatic weapons fire to evacuate the wounded company commander. Capt. Jacobs made repeated trips across the fire-swept open rice paddies evacuating wounded and their weapons. On three separate occasions, Capt. Jacobs contacted and drove off Viet Cong squads who were searching for allied wounded and weapons, singlehandedly killing three and wounding several others. His gallant actions and extraordinary heroism saved the lives of one U.S. Advisor and 13 allied soldiers. Through his effort the allied company was restored to an effective fighting unit and prevented defeat of the friendly forces by a strong and determined enemy. Capt. Jacobs, by his gallantry and bravery in action in the highest traditions of the military service, has reflected great credit upon himself, his unit, and the U.S. Army.

BUCHA, PAUL WILLIAM

Rank and Organization: Captain, U.S. Army, Company D, 3d Battalion. 187th Infantry, 3d Brigade, 101st Airborne Division.
Born: August 1, 1943, Washington, D.C.
Entered Service At: U.S. Military Academy, West Point, New York
Place and Date: Near Phuoc Vinh, Binh Duon province, Republic of Vietnam, March 16-19, 1968
Citation: For conspicuous gallantry and intrepidity in action at the risk of his life above and beyond the call of duty. Capt. Bucha distinguished himself while serving as commanding officer, Company D, on a reconnaissance-in-force mission against enemy forces near Phuoc Vinh. The company was inserted by helicopter into the suspected enemy stronghold to locate and destroy the enemy. During this period Capt. Bucha aggressively and courageously led his men in the destruction of enemy fortifications and base areas and eliminated scattered resistance impeding the advance of the company. On March 18, while advancing to contact, the lead elements of the company became engaged by the heavy automatic weapon, heavy machine-gun, rocket propelled grenade, claymore mine and small-arms fire of an estimated battalion-size force. Capt. Bucha, with complete disregard for his safety, moved to the threatened area to direct the defense and ordered reinforcements to the aid of the lead element. Seeing that his men were pinned down by heavy machine-gun fire from a concealed bunker located some 40 meters to the front of the positions, Capt. Bucha crawled through the hail of fire to singlehandedly destroy the bunker with grenades. During this heroic action Capt. Bucha received a painful shrapnel wound. Returning to the perimeter, he observed that his unit could not hold its positions and repel the human wave assaults launched by the determined enemy. Capt. Bucha ordered the withdrawal of the unit elements and covered the withdrawal to positions of a company perimeter from which he could direct fire upon the charging enemy. When one friendly element retrieving casualties was ambushed and cut off from the perimeter, Capt. Bucha ordered them to feign death and he directed artillery fire around them. During the night Capt. Bucha moved throughout the position, distributing ammunition, providing encouragement and insuring the integrity of the defense. He directed artillery, helicopter gunship and Air Force gunship fire on the enemy strong points and attacking forces, marking the positions with smoke-grenades. Using

flashlights in complete view of enemy snipers, he directed the medical evacuation of three air-ambulance loads of seriously wounded personnel and helicopter supply of his company. At daybreak Capt. Bucha led a rescue party to recover the dead and wounded members of the ambushed element. During the period of intensive combat, Capt. Bucha, by his extraordinary heroism, inspirational example, outstanding leadership and professional competence, led his company in the decimation of a superior enemy force which left 156 dead on the battlefield. His bravery and gallantry at the risk of his life are in the highest traditions of the military service, Capt. Bucha has reflected great credit on himself, his unit, and the U.S. Army.

Note: Capt. Bucha's company started the battle with just 89 men and they held out all night against an enemy force estimated to be between 1000 and 1500 men. The men of Company D certainly performed heroically.

†DEVORE, EDWARD A., JR.

Rank and Organization: Specialist Fourth Class, U.S. Army, Company B, 4th Battalion, 39th Infantry, 9th Infantry Division.
Born: June 15, 1947, Torrance, California
Entered Service At: Harbor City, California
Place and Date: Near Saigon, Republic of Vietnam, March 17, 1968
Citation: For conspicuous gallantry and intrepidity in action at the risk of his life above and beyond the call of duty. Sp4c. DeVore, distinguished himself by exceptionally valorous actions on the afternoon of March 17, 1968, while serving as a machine gunner with Company B, on a reconnaissance-in-force mission approximately five kilometers south of Saigon. Sp4c. DeVore's platoon, the company's lead element, abruptly came under intense fire from automatic weapons, claymore mines, rockets and grenades from well-concealed bunkers in a nipa palm swamp. One man was killed and three wounded about 20 meters from the bunker complex. Sp4c. DeVore raced through a hail of fire to provide a base of fire with his machine-gun, enabling the point element to move the wounded back to friendly lines. After supporting artillery, gunships and airstrikes had been employed on the enemy positions, a squad was sent forward to retrieve their fallen comrades. Intense enemy frontal and enfilading automatic weapons fire pinned down this element in the kill zone. With complete disregard for his personal safety, Sp4c. DeVore assaulted the enemy positions. Hit in the shoulder and knocked down about 35 meters short of his objectives, Sp4c. DeVore, ignoring his pain and the warnings of his fellow soldiers, jumped to his feet and continued his assault under intense hostile fire. Although mortally wounded during this advance, he continued to place highly accurate suppressive fire upon the entrenched insurgents. By drawing the enemy fire upon himself, Sp4c. DeVore enabled the trapped squad to rejoin the platoon in safety. Sp4c. DeVore's extraordinary heroism and devotion to duty in close combat were in keeping with the highest traditions of the military service and reflect great credit upon himself, the 39th Infantry and the U.S. Army.

Note: The following is a newspaper account of the preceding battle in which Sp4c. Devore earned the Medal of Honor:

ALLIED UNITS OPEN THE BIGGEST DRIVE OF THE VIETNAM WAR

50,000 Men Seek To Capture or Destroy Enemy Forces Believed Near Saigon

SAIGON, South Vietnam, March 16 - The allied forces announced yesterday that they had begun the largest offensive operation of the war in an effort to capture or destroy the 8,000 to 10,000 enemy troops believed to be near Saigon.

More than 50 battalions of United States and South Vietnamese soldiers-plus air, artillery and national police support units-have been committed to the maneuver, which will extend from Saigon to the Cambodian border.

It adds up to a force of about 50,000 men, one high American military official said.

Command Was Eager

There has been an eagerness within the military command "to respond to the enemy's Tet offensive with a major offensive of our own," the officer continued, "and this is a major one."

The operation began Monday, but military authorities prevented any public discussion of it until yesterday by invoking their ground rules on news coverage, which can be used to revoke accreditation of any correspondent who writes about secret operations.

Units in the operation report that they have killed 296 of the enemy and captured many weapons and large supplies of ammunition. Eleven United States servicemen have been killed and 115 wounded, a military spokesman reported. South Vietnamese losses were described as light.

Cavalrymen Draw Fire

The major battle, so far, came late yesterday when enemy soldiers fired on a company of armored cavalrymen about 15 miles northwest of Saigon. Artillery, armed helicopters and Air Force fighter-bombers supported the Americans.

Army spokesmen said 81 of the enemy had been killed. Twenty-one of the American troops were listed as wounded.

Assigned to the operation from the American military structure are units of the First, Ninth and 25th Infantry Divisions and helicopter and artillery support teams. The South Vietnamese Government has sent in units of the Fifth and 25th Infantry Divisions, an airborne task force, a Marine task force and elements of the Fifth Ranger Group and the national police forces.

Some of the units began offensive actions immediately after the enemy launched the Lunar New Year offensive. Others have joined them during the last three weeks.

"But this week we put still more units on the offensive near Saigon and joined them into a single, highly coordinated operation," the high military official said.

"The purpose of this is to catch the enemy," he added, "and barring this, to drive him as far away from Saigon as possible."

Parts of 2 Divisions

The objects of the search are elements of two enemy divisions - containing both Vietcong and North Vietnamese troops - that soon after the Lunar New Year offensive began maneuvering in a belt three to eight miles from Saigon.

While the danger of any second wave attack on Saigon appears to have faded, a military spokesman said, the high command wants to take no chances.

As the operation was explained, the allied units will try to trap the enemy with a series of pincer-like movements in Binhduong, Longan, Haunghia, Giadinh Provinces and part of Bienhoa Province.

The action has been named Operation Quyet Thang. The Vietnamese term means "straight arrow."

The only operation ever to have approached it in size, military spokesmen said, was Operation Junction City, which was made up of 31 United States and 3 South Vietnamese battalions. That mission was carried out about a year ago along the Cambodian border.

SPRAYBERRY, JAMES M.
Rank and Organization: Captain (then 1st lt.), U.S. Army, Company D, 5th Battalion, 7th Cavalry, 1st Cavalry Division (Airmobile).
Born: April 24, 1947, LaGrange, Georgia
Entered Service At: Montgomery, Alabama
Place and Date: Republic of Vietnam, April 25, 1968
Citation: For conspicuous gallantry and intrepidity in action at the risk of his life above and beyond the call of duty. Capt. Sprayberry, Armor, U.S. Army, distinguished himself by exceptional bravery while serving as executive officer of Company D. His company commander and a great number of the men were wounded and separated from the main body of the company. A daylight attempt to rescue them was driven back by the well entrenched enemy's heavy fire. Capt. Sprayberry then organized and led a volunteer night patrol to eliminate the intervening enemy bunkers and to relieve the surrounded element. The patrol soon began receiving enemy machine-gun fire. Capt. Sprayberry quickly moved the men to protective cover and without regard for his own safety, crawled within close range of the bunker from which the fire was coming. he silenced the machine-gun with a hand grenade. Identifying several one man enemy positions nearby, Capt. Sprayberry immediately attacked them with the rest of his grenades. He crawled back for more grenades and when two grenades were thrown at his men from a position to the front, Capt. Sprayberry, without hesitation, again exposed himself and charged the enemy-held bunker killing its occupants with a grenade. Placing two men to cover his advance, he crawled forward and neutralized three more bunkers with grenades. Immediately thereafter, Capt. Sprayberry was surprised by an enemy soldier who charged from a concealed position. He killed the soldier with his pistol and with continuing disregard for the danger neutralized another enemy emplacement. Capt. Sprayberry then established radio contact with the isolated men, directing them toward his position. When the two elements made contact he organized his men into litter parties to evacuate the wounded. As the evacuation was nearing completion, he observed an enemy machine-gun position which he silenced with a grenade. Capt. Sprayberry returned to the rescue party, established security, and moved to friendly lines with the wounded. This rescue operation, which lasted approximately 7-1/2 hours, saved the lives

of many of his fellow soldiers. Capt. Sprayberry personally killed 12 enemy soldiers, eliminated two machine-guns, and destroyed numerous enemy bunkers. Capt. Sprayberry's indomitable spirit and gallant action at great personal risk to his life are in keeping with the highest traditions of the military service and reflect great credit upon himself, his unit, and the U.S. Army.

†LEE, MILTON A.

Rank and Organization: Private First Class, U.S. Army, Company B, 2d Battalion, 502d Infantry, 1st Brigade, 101st Airborne Division (Airmobile)
Born: February 28, 1949, Shreveport, Louisiana
Entered Service At: San Antonio, Texas
Place and Date: Near Phu Bai, Thua Thien Province, Republic of Vietnam, April 26, 1968
Citation: For conspicuous gallantry and intrepidity in action at the risk of his life above and beyond the call of duty. Pfc. Lee distinguished himself near the city of Phu Bai in the Province of Thua Thien. Pfc. Lee was serving as the radio telephone operator with the 3d Platoon, Company B. As lead element for the company, the 3d Platoon received intense surprise hostile fire from a force of North Vietnamese Army regulars in well concealed bunkers. With 50 percent casualties, the platoon maneuvered to a position of cover to treat their wounded and reorganize, while Pfc. Lee moved through the heavy enemy fire giving lifesaving first aid to his wounded comrades. During the subsequent assault on the enemy defensive positions, Pfc. Lee continuously kept close radio contact with the company commander, relaying precise and understandable orders to his platoon leader. While advancing with the front rank toward the objective, Pfc. Lee observed four North Vietnamese soldiers with automatic weapons and a rocket launcher lying in wait for the lead element of the platoon. As the element moved forward, unaware of the concealed danger, Pfc. Lee immediately and with utter disregard for his own personal safety, passed his radio to another soldier and charged through the murderous fire. Without hesitation he continued his assault, overrunning the enemy position, killing all occupants and capturing four automatic weapons and a rocket launcher. Pfc. Lee continued his one-man assault on the second position through a heavy barrage of enemy automatic weapons fire. Grievously wounded, he continued to press the attack, crawling forward into a firing position and delivering accurate covering fire to enable his platoon to maneuver and destroy the position. Not until the position was overrun did Pfc. Lee falter in his steady volume of fire and succumb to his wounds. Pfc. Lee's heroic actions saved the lives of the lead element and were instrumental in the destruction of the key position of the enemy de-

fense. Pfc. Lee's gallantry at the risk of life above and beyond the call of duty are in keeping with the highest traditions of the military service and reflect great credit on himself, the 502d Infantry, and the U.S. Army.

VARGAS, M. SANDO, JR.

Rank and Organization: Major (then Capt.), U.S. Marine Corps, Company G, 2d Battalion, 4th Marines, 9th Marine Amphibious Brigade.
Born: July 29, 1940, Winslow, Arizona
Entered Service At: Winslow, Arizona
Place and Date: Dai Do, Republic of Vietnam, April 30, to May 3, 1968
Citation: For conspicuous gallantry and intrepidity at the risk of his life above and beyond the call of duty while serving as commanding officer, Company G, in action against enemy forces from April 30, to May 2, 1968. On May 1, 1968, though suffering from wounds he had incurred while relocating his unit under heavy enemy fire the preceding day, Maj. Vargas combined Company G with two other companies and led his men in an attack on the fortified village of Dai Co. Exercising expert leadership, he maneuvered his marines across 700 meters of open rice paddy while under intense enemy mortar, rocket and artillery fire and obtained a foothold in two hedgerows on the enemy perimeter, only to have elements of his company become pinned down by the intense enemy fire. Leading his reserve platoon to the aid of his beleaguered men, Maj. Vargas inspired his men to renew their relentless advance, while destroying a number of enemy bunkers. Again wounded by grenade fragments, he refused aid as he moved about the hazardous area reorganizing his unit into a strong defense perimeter at the edge of the village. Shortly after the objective was secured the enemy commenced a series of counterattacks and probes which lasted throughout the night but were unsuccessful as the gallant defenders of Company G stood firm in their hard-won enclave. Reinforced the following morning, the marines launched a renewed assault through Dai Do on the village of Dinh To, to which the enemy retaliated with a massive counterattack resulting in hand-to-hand combat. Maj. Vargas remained in the open, encouraging and rendering assistance to his marines when he was hit for the third time in the three day battle. Observing his battalion commander sustain a serious wound, he disregarded his excruciating pain, crossed the fire-swept area and carried his commander to a covered position, then resumed supervising and encouraging his men while simultaneously assisting in organizing the battalion's perimeter defense. His gallant actions uphold the highest traditions of the Marine Corps and the U.S. Naval Service.

Note; The following is a newspaper account of the preceding battle in which Maj. Vargas and Capt. Livingston were awarded the Medal of Honor:

Village Dies in a Battle

DAI DO, South Vietnam, May 3 - It was not much of a village, even when the buildings were standing. Now there is nothing but rubble and the smell of death and destruction.

In the last three days, Dai Do has received more attention than ever before in its history. It has changed hands three times. American marines now occupy the southern half of the village and enemy troops are in the northern part, hanging on despite a fiery canopy of napalm and 500-pound bombs.

At the start of the week there were only civilians here, cultivating their rice and sweet potatoes. On Monday the enemy swept in after brushing aside the lightly armed militia.

By Tuesday the civilians had melted into the surrounding countryside.

From their base at Dongha, only two miles away, the marines came down the Cua Viet, an estuary, late Tuesday and established a beachhead on the northern bank.

Attack Drives Out Enemy

The Americans, in battalion strength, attacked Dai Do on Wednesday, temporarily driving out the North Vietnamese and Viet Cong. A first counterattack was repulsed by the marines. A second counterattack in the afternoon pushed the marines back to the southern half of the village.

This afternoon the exhausted marines were reinforced while jet fighter-bombers screamed out of the blue sky to drop napalm and high explosive bombs on the enemy positions, only 500 yards from the American perimeter.

In the rice fields around the Marine position and especially to their rear, where the Americans advanced through rifle and machine-gun fire, lie the bodies of enemy soldiers.

It was through these same rice fields that the marines carried out a steady stream of their own dead and wounded. An armored personnel carrier, hit by mortar fire and burned out, lies on a slight rise above the river.

In three days of fighting, the marines estimate that they have killed more than 100 of the enemy. And this is only part of the battle raging in the Dongha area near Rt.1. Elements of the South Vietnamese and the United States Army are reported to have killed more than 300 in other actions.

Today, Maj. Charles W. Knapp of Oceanside, California, who took command of the battalion on Wednesday when the commanding officer, a Lieutenant Colonel, was wounded by fragments of a rocket grenade, said he thought he was facing a regiment of North Vietnamese.

"They may have pulled out by now," he said. His face was haggard from three days of battle.

"We'll let artillery and air strikes soften him up for a while," he said.

A Marine Lance Corporal, his fatigues covered with red dust, said the colonel had been hit Wednesday while standing with his radio operator and the battalion sergeant-major.

"The Colonel, as we were treating him, kept saying "I can't find the sergeant-major, I think he's got himself lost."

"We didn't have the heart to tell him that the sergeant-major was dead," the corporal said.

BENAVIDEZ, ROY P.

Rank and Organization: Master Sergeant, Detachment B-56, 5th Special Forces Group, Republic of Vietnam.
Born: August 5, 1935, DeWitt County, Cuero, Texas
Entered Service At: Houston, Texas
Place and Date: West of Loc Ninh, May 2, 1968
Citation: Master Sergeant (then Staff Sergeant) Roy P. Benavidez, United States Army, who distinguished himself by a series of daring and extremely valorous actions on May 2, 1968, while assigned to Detachment B-56, 5th Special Forces Group (Airborne), 1st Special Forces, Republic of Vietnam. On the morning of May 2, 1968, a 12-man Special Forces Reconnaissance Team was inserted by helicopters in a dense jungle area west of Loc Ninh, Vietnam to gather intelligence information about confirmed large-scale enemy activity. This area was controlled and routinely patrolled by the North Vietnamese Army. After a short period of time on the ground, the team met heavy enemy resistance, and requested emergency extraction. Three helicopters attempted extraction, but were unable to land due to intense enemy small arms and anti-aircraft fire. Sergeant Benavidez was at the Forward Operating Base in Loc Ninh monitoring the operation by radio when these helicopters returned to off-load wounded crewmembers and to assess aircraft damage. Sergeant Benavidez voluntarily boarded a returning aircraft to assist in another extraction attempt. Realizing that all the team members were either dead or wounded and unable to move to the pickup zone, he directed the aircraft to a nearby clearing where he jumped from the hovering helicopter, and ran approximately 75 meters under withering small arms fire to the crippled team. Prior to reaching the team's position he was wounded in his right leg, face, and head. Despite these painful injuries, he took charge, repositioning the team members and directing their fire to facilitate the landing of an extraction aircraft, and the loading of wounded and dead team members. He then threw smoke canisters to direct the aircraft to the team's position. Despite his severe wounds and under intense enemy fire, he carried and dragged half of the wounded team members to the awaiting aircraft. He then provided protective fire by running alongside the aircraft as it moved to pick up the remaining team members. As the enemy's fire intensified, he hurried to recover the body and classified documents on the

dead team leader. When he reached the leader's body, Sergeant Benavidez was severely wounded by small arms fire in the abdomen and grenade fragments in his back. At nearly the same moment, the aircraft pilot was mortally wounded, and his helicopter crashed. Although in extremely critical condition due to his multiple wounds. Sergeant Benavidez secured the classified documents and made his way back to the wreckage, where he aided the wounded out of the overturned aircraft, and gathered the stunned survivors into a defensive perimeter. Under increasing enemy automatic weapons and grenade fire, he moved around the perimeter distributing water and ammunition to his weary men, reinstilling in them a will to live and fight. Facing a buildup of enemy opposition with a beleaguered team, Sergeant Benavidez mustered his strength, began calling in tactical air strikes and directed the fire from supporting gunships to suppress the enemy's fire and so permit another extraction attempt. He was wounded again in his thigh by small arms fire while administering first aid to a wounded team member just before another extraction helicopter was able to land. His indomitable spirit kept him going as he began to ferry his comrades to the craft. On his second trip with the wounded, he was clubbed from additional wounds to his head and arms before killing his adversary. He then continued under devastating fire to carry the wounded to the helicopter. Upon reaching the aircraft, he spotted and killed two enemy soldiers who were rushing the craft from an angle that prevented the aircraft door gunner from firing upon them. With little strength remaining, he made one last trip to the perimeter to ensure that all classified material had been collected or destroyed, and to bring in the remaining wounded. Only then, in extremely serious condition from numerous wounds and loss of blood, did he allow himself to be pulled into the extraction aircraft. Sergeant Benavidez' gallant choice to join voluntarily his comrades who were in critical straits, to expose himself constantly to withering enemy fire, and his refusal to be stopped despite numerous severe wounds, saved the lives of at least eight men. His fearless personal leadership, tenacious devotion to duty, and extremely valorous actions in the face of overwhelming odds were in keeping with the highest traditions of the military service, and reflect the utmost credit on him and the United States Army. (This award supersedes the Distinguished Service Cross awarded to Master Sergeant Roy P. Benavidez for extraordinary heroism on May 2, 1968, as announced in United States Army, Vietnam, General Orders 3752, 1968.)

101st Airborne Division near Dak To, 1966. (U.S. Army)

Marines during Operation "Prairie" near the DMZ, 1966. (U.S. Marine Corps)

Troops of the 101st Airborne Division near Kontum, 1966. (U.S. Army)

Soldiers of the 1st Infantry Division in Tay Ninh Province, 1966. (U.S. Army)

Soldiers of the 1st Cavalry Division in Operation "Byrd", 1966. (U.S. Army)

Soldiers of the 101st Airborne Division on Hill 882 near Dak To, 1967. (U.S. Army)

Marines landing near LZ Catapult. (U.S. Marine Corps)

Navy river patrol boat in the Mekong Delta. (U.S. Navy)

Soldiers of the 101st Airborne Division near Phuoc Vinh, 1968. The soldier on the radio is Capt. Paul Bucha, a Medal of Honor recipient. (U.S. Army)

Troops of the 9th Infantry Division near the "Y" Bridge, 1968. (U.S. Army)

Navy Seal team on the Ca Mau Peninsula, 1968. (U.S. Navy)

Marines attending services near Da Nang, 1968. (U.S. Marine Corps)

Marines on Mutter's Ridge near the DMZ, 1968. (U.S. Marine Corps)

A monitor boat – called a "Zippo" – in the Mekong Delta, 1968. (U.S. Navy)

Navy Seal team in the Mekong Delta, 1968. (U.S. Navy)

Soldiers of the 9th Infantry Division in the Mekong Delta, 1968. (U.S. Army)

Marines of the 1st Division in Hue City, February, 1968. (Courtesy of John Ligato)

Marines of the 1st Division in Hue City, February, 1968. (Courtesy of John Ligato)

Marines of the 1st Division in Hue City, February, 1968. (Courtesy of John Ligato)

Marines of the 1st Division in Hue City, February, 1968. (Courtesy of John Ligato)

Three F-100 Super Sabres during Operation "Rolling Thunder." (U.S. Air Force)

**An A-4 Skyhawk taking off from the U.S.S. Coral Sea during Operation "Rolling Thunder."
(U.S. Navy)**

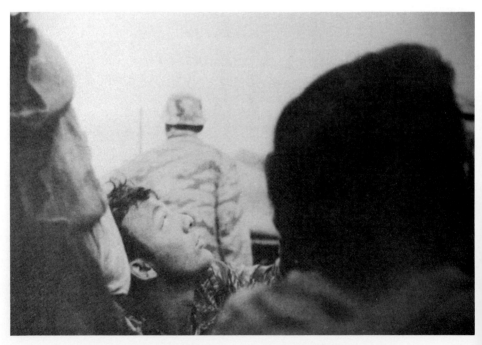

Soldiers of the Special Forces camp at Ben Het, 1969. (U.S. Army)

Soldiers of the Americal Division in the Hiep Duc Valley northwest of Chu Lai, 1969. (U.S. Army)

Soldiers of the 9th Infantry Division near Dong Tam, 1969. (U.S. Army)

Never have so few been so Fool (Foul?) to so many

Marines of the 1st Btn., 26th Marines during Operation "Daring Rebel", 1969. (U.S. Marine Corps)

Marine tanks on Barrier Island, southeast of Da Nang, 1969. (U.S. Marine Corps)

Helicopters with troops of the 25th Infantry Division near Tay Ninh, 1970. (U.S. Army)

3rd Battalion, 21st Infantry at Da Nang, 1972. (Courtesy of Gary Senger)

Navy Seal in the Mekong Delta, 1970. (U.S. Navy)

LIVINGSTON, JAMES E.

Rank and Organization: Captain, U.S. Marine Corps, Company E, 2d Battalion, 4th Marines, 9th Marine Amphibious Brigade.
Born: January 12, 1940, Towns, Telfair County, Georgia
Entered Service At: McRae, Georgia
Place and Date: Dai Do, Republic of Vietnam, May 2, 1968
Citation: For conspicuous gallantry and intrepidity at the risk of his life above and beyond the call of duty while serving as Commanding Officer, Company E, in action against enemy forces. Company E launched a determined assault on the heavily fortified village of Dai Do, which had been seized by the enemy on the preceding evening isolating a marine company from the remainder of the battalion. Skillfully employing screening agents, Capt. Livingston maneuvered his men to assault positions across 500 meters of dangerous open rice paddy while under intense enemy fire. Ignoring hostile rounds impacting near him, he fearlessly led his men in a savage assault against enemy emplacements within the village. While adjusting supporting arms fire, Capt. Livingston moved to the points of heaviest resistance, shouting words of encouragement to his marines, directing their fire, and spurring the dwindling momentum of the attack on repeated occasions. Although twice painfully wounded by grenade fragments, he refused medical treatment and courageously led his men in the destruction of over 100 mutually supporting bunkers, driving the remaining enemy from their positions, and relieving the pressure on the stranded marine company. As the two companies consolidated positions and evacuated casualties, a third company passed through the friendly lines launching an assault on the adjacent village of Dinh To, only to be halted by a furious counterattack of an enemy battalion. Swiftly assessing the situation and disregarding the heavy volume of enemy fire, Capt. Livingston boldly maneuvered the remaining effective men of his company forward, joined forces with the heavily engaged marines, and halted the enemy's counterattack. Wounded a third time and unable to walk, he steadfastly remained in the dangerously exposed area, deploying his men to more tenable positions and supervising the evacuation of casualties. Only when assured of the safety of his men did he allow himself to be evacuated. Capt. Livingston's gallant actions uphold the highest traditions of the Marine Corps and the U.S. Naval Service.

†FOURNET, DOUGLAS B.

Rank and Organization: First Lieutenant, U.S. Army, Company B, 1st Battalion, 7th Cavalry, 1st Cavalry Division (Airmobile).
Born: May 7, 1943, Lake Charles, Louisiana
Entered Service At: New Orleans, Louisiana
Place and Date: A Shau Valley, Republic of Vietnam, May 4, 1968
Citation: For conspicuous gallantry and intrepidity in action at the risk of his life above and beyond the call of duty. 1st Lt. Fournet, Infantry, distinguished himself in action while serving as rifle platoon leader of the 2d Platoon, Company B. While advancing uphill against fortified enemy positions in the A Shau Valley, the platoon encountered intense sniper fire, making movement very difficult. The right flank man suddenly discovered an enemy claymore mine covering the route of advance and shouted a warning to his comrades. Realizing that the enemy would also be alerted, 1st Lt. Fournet ordered his men to take cover and ran uphill toward the mine, drawing a sheath knife as he approached it. With complete disregard for his safety and realizing the imminent danger to members of his command, he used his body as a shield in front of the mine as he attempted to slash the control wires leading from the enemy positions to the mine. As he reached for the wire the mine was detonated, killing him instantly. Five men nearest the mine were slightly wounded, but 1st Lt. Fournet's heroic and unselfish act spared his men of serious injury or death. His gallantry and willing self-sacrifice are in keeping with the highest traditions of the military service and reflect great credit upon himself, his unit, and the U.S. Army.

Note: The following is a newspaper account of the preceding battle in which 1st Lt. Fournet was awarded the Medal of Honor:

Ashau Valley Drive Ends

SAIGON, South Vietnam, May 17 - Operation Delaware, the offensive aimed at clearing North Vietnamese troops from the Ashau Valley, has been concluded, the military command said today.

In making the announcement the spokesman declined for security reasons to say whether United States and South Vietnamese troops had left the valley or were remaining in an effort to block enemy supply routes.

The operation began on April 18 and involved units of the First Cavalry Division (Airmobile) and the 101st Airborne Division, as well as a regiment of South Vietnamese paratroopers.

American and South Vietnamese casualties for the month-long offensive were put at 139 dead and 662 wounded. The North Vietnamese were said to have lost 726 men.

Heavy fighting was reported during the first few days of Operation Delaware, but only light to moderate action has been disclosed since then. One high-ranking American officer said a few weeks ago that the fighting had "not been what we expected."

The allies, however, did capture or destroy an enormous amount of enemy equipment and supplies, including heavy weapons, ammunition, trucks, bulldozers, explosives, rice and other foodstuffs.

PATTERSON, ROBERT MARTIN

Rank and Organization: Sergeant, U.S. Army, Troop B, 2d Squadron, 17th Cavalry.
Born: April 16, 1948, Durham, North Carolina
Entered Service At: Raleigh, North Carolina
Place and Date: Near LaChu, Republic of Vietnam, May 6, 1968
Citation: For conspicuous gallantry and intrepidity in action at the risk of his life above and beyond the call of duty. Sgt. Patterson (then Sp4c.) distinguished himself while serving as a fire team leader of the 3d Platoon, Troop B, during an assault against a North Vietnamese Army battalion which was entrenched in a heavily fortified position. When the leading squad of the 3d Platoon was pinned down by heavy interlocking automatic weapon and rocket propelled grenade fire from two enemy bunkers, Sgt. Patterson and the two other members of his assault team moved forward under a hail of enemy fire to destroy the bunkers with grenade and machine-gun fire. Observing that his comrades were being fired on from a third enemy bunker covered by enemy gunners in one-man spider holes. Sgt. Patterson, with complete disregard for his safety and ignoring the warning of his comrades that he was moving into a bunker complex, assaulted and destroyed the position. Although exposed to intensive small arm and grenade fire from the bunkers and their mutually supporting emplacements, Sgt. Patterson continued his assault upon the bunkers which were impeding the advance of his unit. Sgt. Patterson singlehandedly destroyed by rifle and grenade fire five enemy bunkers, killed eight enemy soldiers and captured seven weapons. His dauntless courage and heroism inspired his platoon to resume the attack and to penetrate the enemy defensive position. Sgt. Patterson's action at the risk of his life has reflected great credit upon himself, his unit, and the U.S. Army.

JACKSON, JOE M.

Rank and Organization: Lieutenant Colonel, U.S. Air Force, 311th Air Commando Squadron, Da Nang, Republic of Vietnam.
Born: March 14, 1923, Newman, Georgia
Entered Service At: Newman, Georgia
Place and Date: Kham Duc, Republic of Vietnam, May 12, 1968.
Citation: For conspicuous gallantry and intrepidity in action at the risk of his lie above and beyond the call of duty. Lt. Col. Jackson distinguished himself as a pilot of a C-123 aircraft. Lt. Col. Jackson volunteered to attempt the rescue of a three-man USAF Combat Control Team from the special forces camp at Kham Duc. Hostile forces had overrun the forward outpost and established gun positions on the airstrip. They were raking the camp with small-arms, mortars, light and heavy automatic weapons, and recoilless rifle fire. The camp was engulfed in flames and ammunition dumps were continuously exploding and littering the runway with debris. In addition, eight aircraft had been destroyed by the intense enemy fire and one aircraft remained on the runway reducing its usable length to only 2,200 feet. To further complicate the landing, the weather was deteriorating rapidly, thereby permitting only one airstrike prior to his landing. Although fully aware of the extreme danger and likely failure of such an attempt, Lt. Col. Jackson elected to land his aircraft and attempt the rescue. Displaying superb airmanship and extraordinary heroism, he landed his aircraft near the point where the combat control team was reported to be hiding. While on the ground, his aircraft was the target of intense hostile fire. A rocket landed in front of the nose of the aircraft but failed to explode. Once the combat control team was aboard, Lt. Col. Jackson succeeded in getting airborne despite the hostile fire directed across the runway in front of his aircraft. Lt. Col. Jackson's profound concern for his fellow man, at the risk of his life above and beyond the call of duty are in keeping with the highest traditions of the U.S. Air Force and reflect great credit upon himself and the Armed Forces of his country.

†OLSON, KENNETH L.

Rank and Organization: Specialist Fourth Class, U.S. Army, Company A, 5th Battalion, 12th Infantry, 199th Infantry Brigade (Separate) (Light).
Born: May 26, 1945, Willmar, Minn.
Entered Service At: Minneapolis, Minn.
Place and Date: Republic of Vietnam, May 13, 1968.
Citation: For conspicuous gallantry and intrepidity in action at the risk of his life above and beyond the call of duty. Sp4c. Olson distinguished himself at the cost of his life while serving as a team leader with Company A. Sp4c. Olson was participating in a mission to reinforce a reconnaissance platoon which was heavily engaged with a well-entrenched Viet Cong force. When his platoon moved into the area of contact and had overrun the first line of enemy bunkers, Sp4c. Olson and a fellow soldier moved forward of the platoon to investigate another suspected line of bunkers. As the two men advanced they were pinned down by intense automatic weapons fire from an enemy position 10 meters to their front. With complete disregard for his safety, Sp4c. Olson exposed himself and hurled a hand grenade into the Viet Cong position. Failing to silence the hostile fire, he again exposed himself to the intense fire in preparation to assault the enemy position. As he prepared to hurl the grenade, he was wounded, causing him to drop the activated device within his own position. Realizing that it would explode immediately, Sp4c. Olson threw himself upon the grenade and pulled it in to his body to take the full force of the explosion. By this unselfish action Sp4c. Olson sacrificed his own life to save the lives of his fellow comrades-in-arms. His extraordinary heroism inspired his fellow soldiers to renew their efforts and totally defeat the enemy force. Sp4c. Olson's profound courage and intrepidity were in keeping with the highest traditions of the military service and reflect great credit upon himself, his unit. and the U.S. Army.

McCLEERY, FINNIS D.

Rank and Organization: Platoon Sergeant, U.S. Army, Company A, 1st Battalion, 6th U.S. Infantry.

Born: December 25, 1927, Stephenville, Texas

Entered Service At: San Angelo, Texas

Place and Date: Quang Tin Province, Republic of Vietnam, May 14, 1968

Citation: For conspicuous gallantry and intrepidity in action at the risk of his life above and beyond the call of duty. P/Sgt. McCleery, U.S. Army, distinguished himself while serving as platoon leader of the 1st Platoon of Company A. A combined force was assigned the mission of assaulting a reinforced company of North Vietnamese Army regulars, well entrenched on Hill 352, 17 miles west of Tam Ky. As P/Sgt. McCleery led his men up the hill and across an open area to close with the enemy, his platoon and other friendly elements were pinned down by tremendously heavy fire coming from the fortified enemy positions. Realizing the severe damage that the enemy could inflict on the combined force in the event that their attack was completely halted, P/Sgt. McCleery rose from his sheltered position and began a one-man assault on the bunker complex. With extraordinary courage, he moved across 60 meters of open ground as bullets struck all around him and rockets and grenades literally exploded at his feet. As he came within 30 meters of the key enemy bunker, P/Sgt. McCleery began firing furiously from the hip and throwing hand grenades. At this point in his assault, he was painfully wounded by shrapnel, but, with complete disregard for his wound, he continued his advance on the key bunker and killed all of its occupants. Having successfully and singlehandedly breached the enemy perimeter, he climbed to the top of the bunker he had just captured and, in full view of the enemy, shouted encouragement to his men to follow his assault. As the friendly forces moved forward, P/Sgt. McCleery began a lateral assault on the enemy bunker line. He continued to expose himself to the intense enemy fire as he moved from bunker to bunker, destroying each in turn. He was wounded a second time by shrapnel as he destroyed and routed the enemy from the hill. P/Sgt. McCleery is personally credited with eliminating several key enemy positions and inspiring the assault that resulted in gaining control of Hill 352. His extraordinary heroism at the risk of his life, above and beyond the call of duty, was in keeping with the highest standards of the military service, and reflects great credit on him, the American Division, and the U.S. Army.

†FOUS, JAMES W.
Rank and Organization: Private First Class, U.S. Army, Company E, 4th Battalion, 47th Infantry, 9th Infantry Division.
Born: October 14, 1946, Omaha, Nebraska
Entered Service At: Omaha, Nebraska
Place and Date: Kien Hoa Province, Republic of Vietnam, May 14, 1968
Citation: For conspicuous gallantry and intrepidity in action at the risk of his life above and beyond the call of duty. Pfc. Fous distinguished himself at the risk of his life while serving as a rifleman with Company E. Pfc. Fous was participating in a reconnaissance-in-force mission when his unit formed its perimeter defense for the night. Pfc. Fous, together with three other American soldiers, occupied a position in a thickly vegetated area facing a woodline. Pfc. Fous detected three Viet Cong maneuvering toward his position and, after alerting the other men, directed accurate fire upon the enemy soldiers, silencing two of them. The third Viet Cong soldier managed to escape in the thick vegetation after throwing a hand grenade into Pfc. Fous' position. Without hesitation, Pfc. Fous shouted a warning to his comrades and leaped upon the lethal explosive, absorbing the blase with his body to save the lives of the three men in the area at the sacrifice of his life. Pfc. Fous' extraordinary heroism at the cost of his life were in keeping with the highest traditions of the military service and reflect great credit upon himself, his unit, and the U.S. Army.

Note: The following article appeared in *The New York Times* **on May 14, 1968:**

4 Men Awarded Medals Of Honor
President Honors Soldier, Sailor, Marine and Airman
—Voices Hope for Peace

WASHINGTON, May 14 - President Johnson voiced hope today that the negotiations in Paris between the United States and the North Vietnamese would "silence the guns in a free Vietnam."

He spoke at a rare ceremony at the pentagon—the first in which the century-old Medal of Honor was given at one time to four men, one from each of the military services.

"The world prays that the way to peace will be found at that distant table – the peace with honor for which these men, and their comrades, have fought so long and so nobly," the President said.

Mr. Johnson conferred the nation's highest military award for bravery in combat on a soldier, sailor, marine and Air Force officer.

He then dedicated the pentagon's new "Hall of Heros," where the medals and names of the 3,210 winners, including those honored today, are displayed. In the huge gray building's leafy central court, while a mockingbird sang in a tree, the President spoke of another gathering far away.

"As we meet here, other men-in Paris-are beginning the very hard negotiations that we hope will one day silence the guns in a free Vietnam," he said. "Diplomacy's painful work now is to forge, from the fires of hostility, the way in which men can live without conflict and in mutual accord.

The President then hung the medal, suspended from a pale blue moire ribbon, on these four men in turn:

Army Specialist 5 Charles C. Hagemeister, 21 years old, of Lincoln, Neb.

Marine Sgt. Richard A. Pittman, 22, of Stockton, Calif., who finally got into the service after fighting a draft board rating of 4-F for poor eyesight.

Navy Boatswain's Mate James E. Williams, 37, of Darlington S.C., with 20 years of service.

Air Force Capt. Gerald O. Young, 37, of Anacortes, Wash., who first served as an enlisted man in the Navy after World War II.

Including those decorated today, 37 men have now won the Medal of Honor in the Vietnam War.

Larger groups of men have previously received the medal simultaneously but never has such a group represented all the services.

BALLARD, DONALD E.

Rank and Organization: Hospital Corpsman Second Class, U.S. Navy, Company M, 3d Battalion, 4th Marines, 3d Marine Division.
Born: December 5, 1945, Kansas City, Mo.
Entered Service At: Kansas City, Mo.
Place and Date: Quang Tri Province, Republic of Vietnam, May 16, 1968.
Citation: For conspicuous gallantry and intrepidity at the risk of his life above and beyond the call of duty while serving as a HC2c. with Company M, in connection with operations against enemy aggressor forces. During the afternoon hours, Company M was moving to join the remainder of the 3d Battalion in Quang Tri Province. After treating and evacuating two heat casualties, HC2c. Ballard was returning to his platoon from the evacuation landing zone when the company was ambushed by a North Vietnamese Army unit employing automatic weapons and mortars, and sustained numerous casualties. Observing a wounded marine, HC2c. Ballard unhesitatingly moved across the fire-swept terrain to the injured man and swiftly rendered medical assistance to his comrade. HC2c. Ballard then directed four marines to carry the casualty to a position of relative safety. As the four men prepared to move the wounded marine, an enemy soldier suddenly left his concealed position and, after hurling a hand grenade which landed near the casualty, commenced firing upon the small group of men. Instantly shouting a warning to the marines, HC2c. Ballard fearlessly threw himself upon the lethal explosive device to protect his comrades from the deadly blast. When the grenade failed to detonate, he calmly arose from his dangerous position and resolutely continued his determined efforts in treating other marine casualties. HC2c. Ballard's heroic actions and selfless concern for the welfare of his companions served to inspire all who observed him and prevented possible injury or death to his fellow marines. His courage, daring initiative, and unwavering devotion to duty in the face of extreme personal danger, sustain and enhance the finest traditions of the U.S. Naval Service.

†ROARK, ANUND C.

Rank and Organization: Sergeant, U.S. Army, Company C, 1st Battalion, 12th Infantry, 4th Infantry Division.
Born: February 17, 1948, Vallejo, California
Entered Service At: Los Angeles, California
Place and Date: Kontum Province, Republic of Vietnam, May 16, 1968
Citation: For conspicuous gallantry and intrepidity in action at the risk of his life above and beyond the call of duty. Sgt. Roark distinguished himself by extraordinary gallantry while serving with Company C. Sgt. Roark was the point squad leader of a small force which had the mission of rescuing 11 men in a hilltop observation post under heavy attack by a company-size force, approximately 1,000 meters from the battalion perimeter. As lead elements of the relief force reached the besieged observation post, intense automatic weapons fire from enemy occupied bunkers halted their movement. Without hesitation, Sgt. Roark maneuvered his squad, repeatedly exposing himself to withering enemy fire to hurl grenades and direct the fire of his squad to gain fire superiority and cover the withdrawal of the outpost and evacuation of its casualties. Frustrated in their effort to overrun the position, the enemy swept the hilltop with small arms and volleys of grenades. Seeing a grenade land in the midst of his men. Sgt. Roark, with complete disregard for his safety, hurled himself upon the grenade, absorbing its blast with his body. Sgt. Roark's magnificent leadership and dauntless courage saved the lives of many of his comrades and were the inspiration for the successful relief of the outpost. His actions which culminated in the supreme sacrifice of his life were in keeping with the highest traditions of the military service, and reflect great credit on himself and the U.S. Army.

Note: The following is a newspaper account of the preceding battle in which Sgt. Roark was awarded the Medal of Honor:

Base Near Kontum Attacked

SAIGON, May 16 (AP) - North Vietnamese troops advanced in darkness about 20 miles west of the city of Kontum today and opened fire with mortars, rocket-propelled grenades, flame throwers and small-arms on a patrol base and an outpost of the United States Fourth Infantry Division.

The defenders retaliated with mortars and artillery, and Air Force planes armed with rapid firing guns sprayed thousands of rounds into the enemy positions under the light of flares.

As Dawn broke, the North Vietnamese pulled back, but an hour later they renewed the mortar attack. Sporadic shelling continued during the day.

Initial reports said that four United States soldiers had been killed and 22 wounded. Enemy casualties could not be determined.

†**BURKE, ROBERT C.**
Rank and Organization: Private First Class, U.S. Marine Corps, Company I, 3d Battalion 27th Marines, 1st Marine Division (Rein), FMF.
Born: November 7, 1949, Monticello, Illinois
Entered Service At: Chicago, Illinois
Place and Date: Southern Quang Nam Province, Republic of Vietnam, May 17, 1968
Citation: For conspicuous gallantry and intrepidity at the risk of his life above and beyond the call of duty for service as a machine gunner with Company I. While on Operation ALLEN BROOK, Company I was approaching a dry river bed with a heavily wooded treeline that borders the hamlet of Le Nam (1), when they suddenly came under intense mortar, rocket propelled grenades, automatic weapons and small-arms fire from a large, well concealed enemy force which halted the company's advance and wounded several marines. Realizing that key points of resistance had to be eliminated to allow the units to advance and casualties to be evacuated, Pfc. Burke, without hesitation, seized his machinegun and launched a series of one-man assaults against the fortified emplacements. As he aggressively maneuvered to the edge of the steep river bank, he delivered accurate suppressive fire upon several enemy bunkers, which enabled his comrades to advance and move the wounded marines to positions of relative safety. As he continued his combative actions, he located an opposing automatic weapons emplacement and poured intense fire into the position, killing three North Vietnamese soldiers as they attempted to flee. Pfc. Burke then fearlessly moved from one position to another, quelling the hostile fire until his weapon malfunctioned. Obtaining a casualty's rifle and hand grenades, he advanced further into the midst of the enemy fire in an assault against another pocket of resistance, killing two more of the enemy. Observing that a fellow marine had cleared his malfunctioning machinegun he grasped his weapon and moved into a dangerously exposed area and saturated the hostile treeline until he fell mortally wounded. Pfc. Burke's gallant actions upheld the highest traditions of the Marine Corps and the U.S. Naval Service. He gallantly gave his life for his country.

†GUENETTE, PETER M.

Rank and Organization: Specialist Fourth Class, U.S. Army, Company D, 2d Battalion (Airborne), 506th Infantry, 101st Airborne Division (Airmobile).
Born: January 4, 1948, Troy, New York
Entered Service At: Albany, New York
Place and Date: Quan Tan Uyen Province, Republic of Vietnam, May 18, 1968
Citation: For conspicuous gallantry and intrepidity in action at the risk of his life above and beyond the call of duty. Sp4c. Guenette distinguished himself while serving as a machine gunner with Company D, during combat operations. While Sp4c. Guenette's platoon was sweeping a suspected enemy base camp, it came under light harassing fire from a well equipped and firmly entrenched squad of North Vietnamese Army regulars which was serving as a delaying force at the entrance to their base camp. As the platoon moved within 10 meters of the fortified positions, the enemy fire became intense. Sp4c. Guenette and his assistant gunner immediately began to provide a base of suppressive fire, ceasing momentarily to allow the assistant gunner time to throw a grenade into a bunker. Seconds later, an enemy grenade was thrown to Sp4c. Guenette's right flank. Realizing that the grenade would kill or wound at least four men and destroy the machinegun, he shouted a warning and smothered the grenade with his body, absorbing its blast. Through his actions, he prevented loss of life or injury to at least three men and enabled his comrades to maintain their fire superiority. By his gallantry at the cost of his life in keeping with the highest traditions of the military service, Sp4c. Guenette has reflected great credit on himself, his unit, and the U.S. Army.

†McDONALD, PHILL G.

Rank and Organization: Private First Class, U.S. Army, Company A, 1st Battalion, 14th Infantry, 4th Infantry Division.
Born: September 13, 1941, Avondale, West Virginia
Entered Service At: Beckley, West Virginia
Place and Date: Near Kontum City, Republic of Vietnam, June 7, 1968
Citation: For conspicuous gallantry and intrepidity in action at the risk of his life above and beyond the call of duty. Pfc. McDonald distinguished himself while serving as a team leader with the 1st Platoon of Company A. While on a combat mission his platoon came under heavy barrage of automatic weapons fire from a well concealed company-size enemy force. Volunteering to escort two wounded comrades to an evacuation point, Pfc. McDonald crawled through intense fire to destroy with a grenade an enemy automatic weapon threatening the safety of the evacuation. Returning to his platoon, he again volunteered to provide covering fire for the maneuver of the platoon from its exposed position. Realizing the threat he posed, enemy gunners concentrated their fire on Pfc. McDonald's position, seriously wounding him. Despite his painful wounds, Pfc. McDonald recovered the weapon of a wounded machine gunner to provide accurate covering fire for the gunner's evacuation. When other soldiers were pinned down by a heavy volume of fire from a hostile machinegun to his front, Pfc. McDonald crawled toward the enemy position to destroy it with grenades. He was mortally wounded in this intrepid action. Pfc. McDonald's gallantry at the risk of his life which resulted in the saving of the lives of his comrades, is in keeping with the highest traditions of the military service and reflects great credit upon himself, his unit, and the U.S. Army.

†KEDENBURG, JOHN J.

Rank and Organization: Specialist Fifth Class, U.S. Army, 5th Special Forces Group (Airborne), 1st Special Forces.
Born: July 31, 1946, Brooklyn, New York
Entered Service At: Brooklyn, New York
Place and Date: Republic of Vietnam, June 13, 1968
Citation: For conspicuous gallantry and intrepidity in action at the risk of his life above and beyond the call of duty. Sp5c. Kedenburg, U.S. Army, Command and Control Detachment North, Forward Operating Base 2, 5th Special Forces Group (Airborne), distinguished himself while serving as advisor to a long-range reconnaissance team of South Vietnamese irregular troops. The team's mission was to conduct counter-guerrilla operations deep within enemy-held territory. Prior to reaching the day's objective, the team was attacked and encircled by a battalion-size North Vietnamese Army force. Sp5c. Kedenburg assumed immediate command of the team which succeeded, after a fierce fight, in breaking out of the encirclement. As the team moved through thick jungle to a position from which it could be extracted by helicopter, Sp5c. Kedenburg conducted a gallant rear guard fight against the pursuing enemy and called for tactical air support and rescue helicopters. His withering fire against the enemy permitted the team to reach a preselected landing zone with the loss of only one man, who was unaccounted for. Once in the landing zone, Sp5c. Kedenburg deployed the team into a perimeter defense against the numerically superior enemy force. When tactical air support arrived, he skillfully directed air strikes against the enemy, suppressing their fire so that helicopters could hover over the area and drop slings to be used in the extraction of the team. After half of the team was extracted by helicopter, Sp5c. Kedenburg and the remaining three members of the team harnessed themselves to the sling on a second hovering helicopter. Just as the helicopter was to lift them out of the area, the South Vietnamese team member who had been unaccounted for after the initial encounter with the enemy appeared in the landing zone. Sp5c. Kedenburg unhesitatingly gave up his place in the sling to the man and directed the helicopter pilot to leave the area. He then continued to engage the enemy who were swarming into the landing zone, killing six enemy soldiers before he was overpowered. Sp5c. Kedenburg's inspiring leadership, consum-

mate courage and willing self-sacrifice permitted his small team to inflict heavy casualties on the enemy and escape almost certain annihilation. His actions reflect great credit upon himself and the U.S. Army.

LASSEN, CLYDE EVERETT

Rank and Organization: Lieutenant, U.S. Navy, Helicopter Support Squadron 7, Detachment 104, embarked in U.S.S. *Preble* (DLG-15).
Born: March 14, 1942, Fort Myers, Florida
Entered Service At: Jacksonville, Florida
Place and Date: Republic of Vietnam, June 19, 1968
Citation: For conspicuous gallantry and intrepidity at the risk of his life above and beyond the call of duty as pilot and aircraft commander of a search and rescue helicopter, attached to Helicopter Support Squadron 7, during operations against enemy forces in North Vietnam. Launched shortly after midnight to attempt the rescue of two downed aviators, Lt. (then Lt. [jg.]) Lassen skillfully piloted his aircraft over unknown and hostile terrain to a steep, tree-covered hill on which the survivors had been located. Although enemy fire was being directed at he helicopter, he initially landed in a clear area near the base of the hill, but, due to the dense undergrowth, the survivors could not reach the helicopter. With the aid of flare illumination, Lt. Lassen successfully accomplished a hover between two trees at the survivors' position. Illumination was abruptly lost as the last of the flares were expended, and the helicopter collided with a tree, commencing a sharp descent. Expertly righting his aircraft and maneuvering clear, Lt. Lassen remained in the area, determined to make another rescue attempt, and encouraged the downed aviators while awaiting resumption of flare illumination. After another unsuccessful, illuminated rescue attempt, and with his fuel dangerously low and his aircraft significantly damaged, he launched again and commenced another approach in the face of the continuing enemy opposition. When flare illumination was again lost, Lt. Lassen, fully aware of the dangers in clearly revealing his position to the enemy, turned on his landing lights and completed the landing. On this attempt, the survivors were able to make their way to the helicopter. Enroute to the coast he encountered and successfully evaded additional hostile antiaircraft fire and, with fuel for only five minutes of flight remaining, landed safely aboard U.S.S. *Jouett* (DLG-19).

†SANTIAGO-COLON, HECTOR

Rank and Organization: Specialist Fourth Class, U.S. Army, Company B, 5th Battalion, 7th Cavalry, 1st Cavalry Division (Airmobile).
Born: December 20, 1942, Salinas, Puerto Rico
Entered Service At: New York, New York
Place and Date: Quang Tri Province, Republic of Vietnam, June 28, 1968
Citation: For conspicuous gallantry and intrepidity in action at the risk of his life above and beyond the call of duty. Sp4c. Santiago-Colon distinguished himself at the cost of his life while serving as a gunner in the mortar platoon of Company B. While serving as a perimeter sentry, Sp4c. Santiago-Colon heard distinct movement in the heavily wooded area to his front and flanks. Immediately he alerted his fellow sentries in the area to move to their foxholes and remain alert for any enemy probing forces. From the wooded area around his position heavy enemy automatic weapons and small-arms fire suddenly broke out, but extreme darkness rendered difficult the precise location and identification of the hostile force. Only the muzzle flashes from enemy weapons indicated their position. Sp4c. Santiago-Colon and the other members of his position immediately began to repel the attackers, utilizing hand grenades, antipersonnel mines and small-arms fire. Due to the heavy volume of enemy fire and exploding grenades around them, a North Vietnamese soldier was able to crawl, undetected, to their position. Suddenly, the enemy soldier lobbed a hand grenade into Sp4c. Santiago-Colon's foxhole. Realizing that there was not time to throw the grenade out of his position, Sp4c. Santiago-Colon retrieved the grenade, tucked it into his stomach and, turning away from his comrades. absorbed the full impact of the blast. His heroic self-sacrifice saved the lives of those who occupied the foxhole with him, and provided them with the inspiration to continue fighting until they has forced the enemy to retreat from the perimeter. By his gallantry at the cost of his life and in the highest traditions of the military service, Sp4c. Santiago-Colon has reflected great credit upon himself, his unit, and the U.S. Army.

Note: The following is a newspaper account of the preceding battle in which Sp4c. Santiago-Colon was awarded the Medal of Honor:

300 Enemy Soldiers Are Killed In Heavy Fighting Near DMZ

SAIGON, South Vietnam, Sat. June 29 - Heavy fighting in the jungles just south of the demilitarized zone has taken the lives of 300 enemy soldiers in the last few days, according to the allied command.

The renewed fighting began three days ago when units of the South Vietnamese First Regiment engaged a force of North Vietnamese regulars five miles east of Quang Tri.

The South Vietnamese said 148 enemy soldiers had been killed and 10 captured during the fight. The South Vietnamese also reported finding a number of weapons and three radios of Chinese Communist manufacture.

In another battle in the same area, units of the United States First Cavalry Division (Airmobile) fought an enemy force of about 200 men, 11 miles east of the large Marine base at Dongha.

152 Bodies Counted

The clash began early Thursday morning and ended at nightfall. A sweep of the battlefield yesterday showed the enemy had lost 152 men to the cavalrymen, who were supported by artillery, naval gunfire and tactical air strikes. United States losses were three killed and 36 wounded.

HERDA, FRANK A.

Rank and Organization: Specialist Fourth Class, U.S. Army, Company A, 1st Battalion (Airborne), 506th Infantry, 101st Airborne Division (Airmobile).
Born: September 13, 1947, Cleveland, Ohio
Entered Service At: Cleveland, Ohio
Place and Date: Near Dak To, Quang Trang Province, Republic of Vietnam, June 29, 1968
Citation: For conspicuous gallantry and intrepidity in action at the risk of his life above and beyond the call of duty. Sp4c. Herda (then Pfc.) distinguished himself while serving as a grenadier with Company A. Company A was part of a battalion-size night defensive perimeter when a large enemy force initiated an attack on the friendly units. While other enemy elements provided diversionary fire and indirect weapons fire to the west, a sapper force of approximately 30 men armed with hand grenades and small charges attacked Company A;s perimeter from the east. As the sappers were making a last, violent assault, five of them charged the position defended by Sp4c. Herda and two comrades, one of whom was wounded and lay helpless in the bottom of the foxhole. Sp4c. Herda fired at the aggressors until they were within 10 feet of his position and one of their grenades landed in the foxhole. He fired one last round from his grenade launcher, hitting one of the enemy soldiers in the head, and then, with no concern for his safety, Sp4c. Herda immediately covered the blase of the grenade with his body. The explosion wounded him grievously, but his selfless action prevented his two comrades from being seriously injured or killed and enabled the remaining defender to kill the other sappers. By his gallantry at the risk of his life in the highest traditions of the military service, Sp4c. Herda has reflected great credit on himself, his unit, and the U.S. Army.

†CARON, WAYNE MAURICE

Rank and Organization: Hospital Corpsman Third Class, U.S. Navy, Headquarters and Service Company, 3d Battalion, 7th Marines, 1st Marine Division (Rein), FMF.

Born: November 2, 1946, Middleboro, Mass.

Entered Service At: Boston, Mass.

Place and Date: Quang Nam Province, Republic of Vietnam, July 28, 1968.

Citation: For conspicuous gallantry and intrepidity at the risk of his life above and beyond the call of duty while serving as platoon corpsman with Company K, during combat operations against enemy forces. While on a sweep through an open rice field HC3c. Caron's unit started receiving enemy small-arms fire. Upon seeing two marine casualties fall, he immediately ran forward to render first aid, but found that they were dead. At this time, the platoon was taken under intense small-arms and automatic weapons fire, sustaining additional casualties. As he moved to the aid of his wounded comrades, HC3c. Caron was hit in the arm by enemy fire. Although knocked to the ground, he regained his feet and continued toward the injured marines. He rendered medical assistance to the first marine he reached, who was grievously wounded, and undoubtedly was instrumental in saving the man's life. HC3c. Caron then ran toward the second marine, but was again hit by enemy fire, this time in the leg. Nonetheless, he crawled the remaining distance and provided medical aid to this severely wounded man. HC3c. Caron started to make his way to yet another injured comrade, when he was again struck by enemy small-arms fire. Courageously and with unbelievable determination, HC3c. Caron continued his attempt to reach the third marine until he was killed by an enemy rocket round. His inspiring valor, steadfast determination and selfless dedication in the face of extreme danger, sustain and enhance the finest traditions of the U.S. Naval Service.

†**WORLEY, KENNETH L.**

Rank and Organization: Lance Corporal, U.S. Marine Corps, 3d Battalion, 7th Marines, 1st Marine Division (Rein), FMF.

Born: April 27, 1948, Farmington, New Mexico.

Entered Service At: Fresno, California

Place and Date: Bo Ban, Quang Nam Province, Republic of Vietnam, August 12, 1968.

Citation: For conspicuous gallantry and intrepidity at the risk of his life above and beyond the call of duty while serving as a machine gunner with Company L, 3d battalion, in action against enemy forces. After establishing a night ambush position in a house in the Bo Ban Hamlet of Quang Nam Province, security was set up and the remainder of the patrol members retired until their respective watch. During the early morning hours the marines were abruptly awakened by the platoon leader's warning that "grenades" had landed in the house. Fully realizing the inevitable result of his actions, L/Cpl. Worley, in a valiant act of heroism, instantly threw himself upon the grenade nearest him and his comrades, absorbing with his body, the full and tremendous force of the explosion. Through his extraordinary initiative and inspiring valor in the face of almost certain death, he saved his comrades from serious injury and possible loss of life although five of his fellow marines incurred minor wounds as the other grenades exploded. L/Cpl. Worley's gallant actions upheld the highest traditions of the Marine Corps and the U.S. Naval Service. He gallantly gave his life for his country.

LAMBERS, PAUL RONALD
Rank and Organization: Staff Sergeant, U.S. Army, Company A, 2d Battalion, 27th Infantry, 25th Infantry Division.
Born: June 25, 1942, Holland, Michigan.
Entered Service At: Holland, Michigan
Place and Date: Tay Ninh Province, Republic of Vietnam, August 20, 1968.
Citation: For conspicuous gallantry and intrepidity in action at the risk of his life above and beyond the call of duty. S/Sgt. (then Sgt.) Lambers distinguished himself in action while serving with the 3d Platoon, Company A. The unit had established a night defensive position astride a suspected enemy infiltration route, when it was attacked by an estimated Viet Cong battalion. During the initial enemy onslaught, the platoon leader fell seriously wounded and S/Sgt. Lambers assumed command of the platoon. Disregarding the intense enemy fire, S/Sgt. Lambers left his covered position, secured the platoon radio and moved to the command post to direct the defense. When his radio became inoperative due to enemy action, S/Sgt. Lambers crossed the fire-swept position to secure the 90mm recoilless rife crew's radio in order to re-establish communications. Upon discovering that the 90mm recoilless rifle was not functioning, S/Sgt. Lambers assisted in the repair of the weapon and directed canister fire at point blank range against the attacking enemy who had breached the defensive wire of the position. When the weapon was knocked out by enemy fire, he singlehandedly repulsed a penetration of the position by detonating claymore mines and throwing grenades into the midst of the attackers, killing four more of the Viet Cong with well aimed hand-grenades. S/Sgt. Lambers maintained command of the platoon elements by moving from position to position under the hail of enemy fire, providing assistance where the assault was the heaviest and by his outstanding example inspiring his men to the utmost efforts of courage. He displayed great skill and valor throughout the five-hour battle by personally directing artillery and helicopter fire, placing them at times within five meters of the defensive position. He repeatedly exposed himself to the hostile fire at great risk to his own life in order to redistribute ammunition and care for seriously wounded comrades and to move them to sheltered positions. S/Sgt. Lambers' superb leadership, professional skill and mag-

nificent courage saved the lives of his comrades, resulted in the virtual annihilation of a vastly superior enemy force and were largely instrumental in thwarting an enemy offensive against Tay Ninh City. His gallantry at the risk of his life is in keeping with the highest traditions of the military service and reflects great credit upon himself, his unit, and the U.S. Army.

†YOUNG, MARVIN R.

Rank and Organization: Staff Sergeant, U.S. Army, Company C, 1st Battalion (Mechanized), 5th Infantry, 25th Infantry Division.
Born: May 11, 1947, Alpine, Texas.
Entered Service At: Odessa, Texas
Place and Date: Near Ben Cui, Republic of Vietnam, August 21, 1968.
Citation: For conspicuous gallantry and intrepidity in action at the risk of his life above and beyond the call of duty. S/Sgt. Young distinguished himself at the cost of his life while serving as a squad leader with Company C. While conducting a reconnaissance mission in the vicinity of Ben Cui, Company C was suddenly engaged by an estimated regimental-size force of the North Vietnamese Army. During the initial volley of fire the point the point element of the first platoon was pinned down, sustaining several casualties, and the acting platoon leader was killed. S/Sgt. Young unhesitatingly assumed command of the platoon and immediately began to organize and deploy his men into a defensive position in order to repel the attacking force. As a human wave attack advanced on S/Sgt. Young's platoon, he moved from position to position, encouraging and directing fire on the hostile insurgents while exposing himself to the hail of enemy bullets. After receiving orders to withdraw to a better defensive position, he remained behind to provide covering fire for the withdrawal. Observing that a small element of the point squad was unable to extract itself form its position, and completely disregarding his personal safety, S/Sgt. Young began moving toward their position, firing as he maneuvered. When he was halfway to their position he sustained a critical head injury, yet he continued his mission and ordered the element to withdraw. Remaining with the squad as it fought its way to the rear, he was twice seriously wounded in the arm and leg. Although his leg was badly shattered, S/Sgt. Young refused assistance that would have slowed the retreat of his comrades, and he ordered them to continue their withdrawal while he provided protective covering fire. With indomitable courage and heroic self-sacrifice, he continued his self-assigned mission until the enemy force engulfed his position. S/Sgt. Young's gallantry at the cost of his life was in keeping with the highest traditions of the military service and reflect great credit upon himself, his unit, and the U.S. Army.

Note: The following is a newspaper account of the preceding battle in which both S/Sgt. Lambers and S/Sgt. Young were awarded the Medal of Honor:

Allied Soldiers Pursue Viet Cong South Of Tay Ninh Repulse Enemy Assault On City

TAY NINH, South Vietnam, Aug. 20 - United States and South Vietnamese troops pursued enemy soldiers through rice paddies and manioc fields south of Tay Ninh today after crushing an attack on the provincial capitol in a night of savage fighting.

As the troops and helicopter gun-ships prowled the lush sun-dappled flatlands, the enemy countered with sporadic and brief fire tonight around Tay Ninh. Troops there remained on full alert.

[An American armored column fought a three-hour battle with an enemy regiment outside Tay Ninh Monday night in a new surge of fighting. The Associated Press reported.]

The tempo of the fighting however, had decreased markedly in the Tay Ninh area as well as the other 18 areas around the country where the Viet Cong and North Vietnamese staged assaults yesterday. This assault broke the lull in fighting in recent weeks.

Night Of Bitter Fighting

After a night of fires and bitter fighting, this pleasant city of wide banyan-shaded streets appeared suddenly and uneasily quiet. "We know that Charlie has left the town now," said an American officer at the French-built tactical operations center in the heart of Tay Ninh.

Last night about two Viet Cong battalions, comprising about 600 men and dozens of women, slipped into the southeastern part of the city, moving into scores of homes and using a government dispensary as a command post. Hundreds of American soldiers of the 25th Infantry Division were rushed into the city to reinforce South Vietnamese units.

Late official reports indicate that 15 to 20 American soldiers were killed last night and 86 were wounded. A total of 43 Viet Cong were killed according to reliable informants.

Two wounded American soldiers endured a particularly frightening night. They were apparently wounded in their armored personnel carrier, which was overrun by the Viet Cong.

They pretended to be dead, according to military officials, as the Viet Cong climbed into the personnel carrier and removed their rings, wallets and watches. At dawn several Vietnamese of the popular Cao Dai sect found the wounded soldiers and treated them until American medical corpsmen arrived.

†SEAY, WILLIAM W.

Rank and Organization: Sergeant, U.S. Army, 62d Transportation Company (Medium Truck), 7th Transportation Battalion, 48th Transportation Group.
Born: October 24, 1948, Brewton, Alabama
Entered Service At: Montgomery, Alabama
Place and Date: Near Ap Nhi, Republic of Vietnam, August 25, 1968
Citation: For conspicuous gallantry and intrepidity in action at the risk of his life above and beyond the call of duty. Sgt. Seay distinguished himself while serving as a driver with the 62d Transportation Company, on a resupply mission. The convoy with which he was traveling, carrying critically needed ammunition and supplied from Long Binh to Tay Ninh, was ambushed by a reinforced battalion of the North Vietnamese Army. As the main elements of the convoy entered the ambush killing zone, they were struck by intense rocket, machine-gun and automatic weapon fire from the well concealed and entrenched enemy force. When his convoy was forced to stop, Sgt. Seay immediately dismounted and took a defensive position behind the wheels of a vehicle loaded with high-explosive ammunition. As the violent North Vietnamese assault approached to within 10 meters of the road, Sgt. Seay opened fire, killing two of the enemy. He then spotted a sniper in a tree approximately 75 meters to his front and killed him. When an enemy grenade was thrown under an ammunition trailer near his position, without regard for his own safety he left his protective cover, exposing himself to intense enemy fire, picked up the grenade, and threw it back to the North Vietnamese position, killing four more of the enemy and saving the lives of the men around him. Another enemy grenade landed approximately three meters from Sgt. Seay's position. Again Sgt. Seay left his covered position and threw the armed grenade back upon the assaulting enemy. After returning to his position he was painfully wounded in the right wrist; however, Sgt. Seay continued to give encouragement and direction to his fellow soldiers. After moving to the relative cover of a shallow ditch, he detected three enemy soldiers who had penetrated the position and were preparing to fire on his comrades. Although weak from loss of blood and with his right hand immobilized, Sgt. Seay stood up and fired his rifle with his lift hand, killing all three and saving the lives of the other men in his location. As a

result of his heroic action, Sgt. Seay was mortally wounded by a sniper's bullet. Sgt. Seay, by his gallantry in action at the cost of his life, has reflected great credit upon himself, his unit, and the U.S. Army.

Note: The following is a newspaper account of the battle for which Sgt. Seay was awarded the Medal of Honor:

6 Killed In Ambush

SAIGON, South Vietnam, Monday, Aug. 26 - A United States convoy moving toward Tay Ninh was ambushed today by dug-in enemy troops who lobbed mortars and fired machine-guns from both sides of the road. Six Americans were killed and 51 wounded in the attack.

The United States command said this morning that a reaction force of gunships, tactical aircraft and tanks repulsed the enemy force, but only after an all day fight. Spokesmen said that 96 enemy soldiers were killed.

BACON, NICKY DANIEL

Rank and Organization: Staff Sergeant, U.S. Army, Company B, 4th Battalion, 21st Infantry, 11th Infantry Brigade, Americal Division.

Born: November 25, 1945, Caraway, Arkansas

Entered Service At: Phoenix, Arizona

Place and Date: West of Tam Ky, Republic of Vietnam, August 26, 1968

Citation: For conspicuous gallantry and intrepidity in action at the risk of his life above and beyond the call of duty. S/Sgt. Bacon distinguished himself while serving as a squad leader with the 1st Platoon, Company B, during an operation west of Tam Ky. When Company B came under fire from an enemy bunker line to the front, S/Sgt. Bacon quickly organized his men and led them forward in an assault. He advanced on a hostile bunker and destroyed it with grenades. As he did so, several fellow soldiers including the 1st Platoon leader, were struck by machine-gun fire and fell wounded in an exposed position forward of the rest of the platoon. S/Sgt. Bacon immediately assumed command of the platoon and assaulted the hostile gun position, finally killing the enemy guncrew in a single-handed effort. When the 3d Platoon moved to S/Sgt. Bacon's location, its leader was also wounded. Without hesitation S/Sgt. Bacon took charge of the additional platoon and continued the fight. In the ensuing action he personally killed four more enemy soldiers and silenced an antitank weapon. Under his leadership and example, the members of both platoons accepted his authority without question. Continuing to ignore the intense hostile fire, he climbed up on the exposed deck of a tank and directed fire into the enemy position while several wounded men were evacuated. As a result of S/Sgt. Bacon's extraordinary efforts, his company was able to move forward, eliminate the enemy positions, and rescue the men trapped to the front. S/Sgt. Bacon's bravery at the risk of his life was in the highest traditions of the military service and reflects great credit upon himself, his unit, and the U.S. Army.

†JONES, WILLIAM A., III

Rank and Organization: Colonel, U.S. Air Force, 602d Special Operations Squadron, Nakon Phanom Royal Thai Air Force Base, Thailand
Born: May 31, 1922, Norfolk, Virginia
Entered Service At: Charlottesville, Virginia
Place and Date: Near Dong Hoi, North Vietnam, September 1, 1968
Citation: For conspicuous gallantry and intrepidity in action at the risk of his life above and beyond the call of duty. Col. Jones distinguished himself as the pilot of an A-1H Skyraider aircraft near Dong Hoi, North Vietnam. On that day, as the on-scene commander in the attempted rescue of a downed U.S. pilot, Col. Jones' aircraft was repeatedly hit by heavy and accurate antiaircraft fire. On one of his low passes, Col. Jones felt an explosion beneath his aircraft and his cockpit rapidly filled with smoke. With complete disregard of the possibility that his aircraft might still be burning, he unhesitatingly continued his search for the downed pilot. On this pass, he sighted the survivor and a multiple-barrel gun position firing at him from near the top of a karst formation. He could not attack the gun position on that pass for fear he would endanger the downed pilot. Leaving himself exposed to the gun position, Col. Jones attacked the position with cannon and rocket fire on two successive passes. On his second pass, the aircraft was hit with multiple rounds of automatic weapons fire. One round impacted the Yankee Extraction System rocket mounted directly behind the headrest, igniting the rocket. His aircraft was observed to burst into flames in the center fuselage section, with flames engulfing the cockpit area. He pulled the extraction handle, jettisoning the canopy. The influx of fresh air made the fire burn with greater intensity for a few moments, but since the rocket motor had already burned, the extraction system did not pull Col. Jones from the aircraft. Despite searing pains from severe burns sustained on his arms, hands, neck, shoulders, and face, Col. Jones pulled his aircraft into a climb and attempted to transmit the location of the downed pilot and the enemy gun position to the other aircraft in the area. His calls were blocked by other aircraft transmissions repeatedly directing him to bail out and within seconds his transmitters were disabled and he could receive only on one channel. Completely disregarding his injuries, he elected to fly his crippled aircraft back

to his base and pass on essential information for the rescue rather than bail out. Col. Jones successfully landed his heavily damaged aircraft and passed the information to a debriefing officer while on the operating table. As a result of his heroic actions and complete disregard for his personal safety, the downed pilot was rescued later in the day. Col. Jones' profound concern for his fellow man at the risk of his life, above and beyond the call of duty, are in keeping with the highest traditions of the U.S. Air Force and reflect great credit upon himself and the Armed Forces of his country.

†WILLIAMS, DEWAYNE T.

Rank and Organization: Private First Class, U.S. Marine Corps, Company H, 2d Battalion, 1st Marines, 1st Marine Division.
Born: September 18, 1949, Brown City, Michigan
Entered Service At: Saint Clair, Michigan
Place and Date: Quang Nam Province, Republic of Vietnam, September 18, 1968
Citation: For conspicuous gallantry and intrepidity at the risk of his life above and beyond the call of duty while serving as a rifleman with the 1st Platoon, Company H, in action against communist insurgent forces. Pfc. Williams was a member of a combat patrol sent out from the platoon with the mission of establishing positions in the company's area of operations, from which it could intercept and destroy enemy sniper teams operating in the area. In the night as the patrol was preparing to move from its daylight position to a preselected night position, it was attacked from ambush by a squad of enemy using small arms and hand grenades. Although severely wounded in the back by the close intense fire, Pfc. Williams, recognizing the danger to the patrol, immediately began to crawl forward toward a good firing position. While he was moving under the continuing intense fire, he heard one of the members of the patrol sound the alert that an enemy grenade had landed in their position. Reacting instantly to the alert, he saw that the grenade had landed close to where he was lying and without hesitation, in a valiant act of heroism, rolled on top of the grenade as it exploded, absorbing the full and tremendous impact of the explosion with his body. Through his extraordinary initiative and inspiring valor in the face of certain death, he saved the other members of his patrol from serious injury and possible loss of life, and enabled them to successfully defeat the attackers and hold their position until assistance arrived. His personal heroism and devotion to duty upheld the highest traditions of the Marine Corps and the U.S. Naval Service. He gallantly gave his life for his country.

ROGERS, CHARLES CALVIN

Rank and Organization: Lieutenant Colonel, U.S. Army, 1st Battalion, 5th Artillery, 1st Infantry Division.
Born: September 6, 1929, Claremont, West Virginia
Entered Service At: Institute, West Virginia
Place and Date: Fishhook, near Cambodian border, Republic of Vietnam, November 1, 1968
Citation: For conspicuous gallantry and intrepidity in action at the risk of his life above and beyond the call of duty. Lt. Col. Rogers, Field Artillery, distinguished himself in action while serving as commanding officer, 1st Battalion, during the defense of a forward fire support base. In the early morning hours, the fire support base was subjected to a concentrated bombardment of heavy mortar, rocket and rocket propelled grenade fire. Simultaneously the position was struck by a human wave ground assault, led by sappers who breached the defensive barriers with bangalore torpedoes and penetrated the defensive perimeter. Lt. Col. Rogers with complete disregard for his safety moved through the hail of fragments from bursting enemy rounds to the embattled area. He aggressively rallied the dazed artillery crewmen to man their howitzers and he directed their fire on the assaulting enemy. Although knocked to the ground and wounded by an exploding round, Lt. Col. Rogers sprang to his feet and led a small counterattack force against an enemy element that had penetrated the howitzer positions. Although painfully wounded a second time during the assault, Lt. Col. Rogers pressed the attack killing several of the enemy and driving the remainder from the positions. Refusing medical treatment, Lt. Col. Rogers reestablished and reinforced the defensive positions. As a second human wave attack was launched against another sector of the perimeter, Lt. Col. Rogers directed artillery fire on the assaulting enemy and led a second counterattack against the charging forces. His valorous example rallied the beleaguered defenders to repulse and defeat the enemy onslaught. Lt. Col. Rogers moved from position to position through the heavy enemy fire, giving encouragement and direction to his men. At dawn the determined enemy launched a third assault against the fire base in an attempt to overrun the position. Lt. Col. Rogers moved to the threatened area and directed lethal fire on the enemy forces. Seeing a howitzer inoperative due to casualties, Lt. Col. Rogers joined the surviv-

ing members of the crew to return the howitzer to action. While directing the position defense, Lt. Col. Rogers was seriously wounded by fragments from a heavy mortar round which exploded on the parapet of the gun position. Although too severely wounded to physically lead the defenders, Lt. Col. Rogers continued to give encouragement and direction to his men in the defeating and repelling of the enemy attack. Lt. Col. Rogers' dauntless courage and heroism inspired the defenders of the fire support base to the heights of valor to defeat a determined and numerically superior enemy force. His relentless spirit of aggressiveness in action are in the highest traditions of the military service and reflects great credit upon himself, his unit, and the U.S. Army.

†RABEL, LASZLO

Rank and Organization: Staff Sergeant, U.S. Army, 74th Infantry Detachment (Long Range Patrol), 173d Airborne Brigade.
Born: September 21, 1939, Budapest, Hungary
Entered Service At: Minneapolis, Minnesota
Place and Date: Binh Dinh Province, Republic of Vietnam, November 13, 1968
Citation: For conspicuous gallantry and intrepidity in action at the risk of his life above and beyond the call of duty. S/Sgt. Rebel distinguished himself while serving as leader of Team Delta, 74th Infantry Detachment. At 1000 hours on this date, Team Delta was in a defensive perimeter conducting reconnaissance of enemy trail networks when a member of the team detected enemy movement to the front. As S/Sgt. Rabel and a comrade prepared to clear the area, he heard an incoming grenade as it landed in the midst of the team's perimeter. With complete disregard for his life, S/Sgt. Rabel threw himself on the grenade and, covering it with his body, received the complete impact of the immediate explosion. Through his indomitable courage, complete disregard for his safety and profound concern for his fellow soldiers, S/Sgt. Rabel averted the loss of life and injury to the other members of Team Delta. By his gallantry at the cost of his life in the highest traditions of the military service, S/Sgt. Rabel has reflected great credit upon himself, his unit, and the U.S. Army.

†CRESCENZ, MICHAEL J.

Rank and Organization: Corporal, U.S. Army, Company A, 4th Battalion, 31st Infantry, 196th Infantry Brigade, American Division.
Born: January 14, 1949, Philadelphia, Pennsylvania
Entered Service At: Philadelphia, Pennsylvania
Place and Date: Hiep Duc Valley area, Republic of Vietnam, November 20, 1968
Citation: Cpl. Crescenz distinguished himself by conspicuous gallantry and intrepidity in action while serving as a rifleman with Company A. In the morning his unit engaged a large, well-entrenched force of the North Vietnamese Army whose initial burst of fire pinned down the lead squad and killed the two point men, halting the advance of Company A. Immediately, Cpl. Crescenz left the relative safety of his own position, seized a nearby machine-gun and, with complete disregard for his safety, charged 100 meters up a slope toward the enemy's bunkers which he effectively silenced, killing the two occupants of each. Undaunted by the withering machine-gun fire around him, Cpl. Crescenz courageously moved forward toward a third bunker which he also succeeded in silencing, killing two more of the enemy and momentarily clearing the route of advance for his comrades. Suddenly, intense machine-gun fire erupted from an unseen, camouflaged bunker. Realizing the danger to his fellow soldiers, Cpl. Crescenz disregarded the barrage of hostile fire directed at him and daringly advanced toward the position. Assaulting with his machine-gun, Cpl. Crescenz was within five meters of the bunker when he was mortally wounded by the fire from the enemy machine-gun. As a direct result of he heroic actions, his company was able to maneuver freely with minimal danger and to complete its mission, defeating the enemy. Cpl. Crescenz's bravery and extraordinary heroism at the cost of his life are in the highest traditions of the military service and reflect great credit on himself, his unit, and the U.S. Army.

FLEMING, JAMES P.

Rank and Organization: Captain, U.S. Air Force, 20th Special Operations Squadron.

Born: March 12, 1943, Sedalia, Missouri

Entered Service At: Pullman, Washington

Place and Date: Near Duc Co, Republic of Vietnam, November 26, 1968

Citation: For conspicuous gallantry and intrepidity in action at the risk of his life above and beyond the call of duty. Capt. Fleming (then 1st Lt.) distinguished himself as the Aircraft Commander of a UH-1F transport helicopter. Capt. Fleming went to the aid of a six-man special forces long range reconnaissance patrol that was in danger of being overrun by a large, heavily armed hostile force. Despite the knowledge that one helicopter had been downed by intense hostile fire, Capt. Fleming descended, and balanced his helicopter on a river bank with the tail boom hanging over open water. The patrol could not penetrate to the landing site and he was forced to withdraw. Dangerously low on fuel, Capt. Fleming repeated his original landing maneuver. Disregarding his own safety, he remained in this exposed position. Hostile fire crashed through his windscreen as the patrol boarded his helicopter. Capt. Fleming made a successful takeoff through a barrage of hostile fire and recovered safely at a forward base. Capt. Fleming's profound concern for his fellowmen, and at the risk of his life above and beyond the call of duty are in keeping with the highest traditions of the U.S. Air Force and reflect great credit upon himself and the Armed Forces of his country.

†HOLCOMB, JOHN NOBLE

Rank and Organization: Sergeant, U.S. Army, Company D, 2d Battalion, 7th Cavalry, 1st Cavalry Division.

Born: June 11, 1946, Baker, Oregon

Entered Service At: Corvallis, Oregon

Place and Date: Near Quan Loi, Republic of Vietnam, December 3, 1968

Citation: For conspicuous gallantry and intrepidity in action at the risk of his life above and beyond the call of duty. Sgt. Holcomb distinguished himself while serving as a squad leader in Company D during a combat assault mission. Sgt. Holcomb's company assault had landed by helicopter and deployed into a hasty defensive position to organize for a reconnaissance-in-force mission when it was attacked from three sides by an estimated battalion-size enemy force. Sgt. Holcomb's squad was directly in the path of the main enemy attack. With complete disregard for the heavy fire, Sgt. Holcomb moved among his men giving encouragement and directing fire on the assaulting enemy. When his machine gunner was knocked out, Sgt. Holcomb seized the weapon, ran to a forward edge of the position, and placed withering fire on the enemy. His gallant actions caused the enemy to withdraw. Sgt. Holcomb treated and carried his wounded to a position of safety and reorganized his defensive sector despite a raging grass fire ignited by the incoming enemy mortar and rocket rounds. When the enemy assaulted the position a second time, Sgt. Holcomb again manned the forward machine-gun, devastating the enemy attack and forcing the enemy to again break contact and withdraw. During the enemy withdrawal an enemy rocket hit Sgt. Holcomb's position, destroying his machine-gun and severely wounding him. Despite his painful wounds, Sgt. Holcomb crawled through the grass fire and exploding mortar and rocket rounds to move the members of his squad, everyone of whom had been wounded, to more secure positions. Although grievously wounded and sustained solely by his indomitable will and courage, Sgt. Holcomb as the last surviving leader of his platoon organized his men to repel the enemy, crawled to the platoon radio and reported the third enemy assault on his position. His report brought friendly supporting fires on the charging enemy and broke the enemy attack. Sgt. Holcomb's inspiring leadership, fighting spirit, in action at the cost of his life were in keeping with the highest traditions of the military service and reflect great credit on himself, his unit, and the U.S. Army.

†McKIBBEN, RAY

Rank and Organization: Sergeant, U.S. Army, Troop B, 7th Squadron (Airmobile), 17th Cavalry.
Born: October 27, 1945, Felton, Georgia
Entered Service At: Atlanta, Georgia
Place and Date: Near Song Mao, Republic of Vietnam, December 8, 1968
Citation: For conspicuous gallantry and intrepidity in action at the risk of his life above and beyond the call of duty, Sgt. McKibben distinguished himself in action while serving as team leader of the point element of a reconnaissance patrol of Troop B, operating in enemy territory. Sgt. McKibben was leading his point element in a movement to contact along a well-traveled trail when the lead element came under heavy automatic weapons fire from a fortified bunker position, forcing the patrol to take cover. Sgt. McKibben, appraising the situation and without regard for his own safety, charged through bamboo and heavy brush to the fortified position, killed the enemy gunner, secured the weapon and directed his patrol element forward. As the patrol moved out, Sgt. McKibben observed enemy movement to the flank of the patrol. Fire support from helicopter gunships was requested and the area was effectively neutralized. The patrol again continued its mission and as the lead element rounded the bend of a river it came under heavy automatic weapons fire from camouflaged bunkers. As Sgt. McKibben was deploying his men to covered position, he observed one of his men fall wounded. Although bullets were hitting all around the wounded man, Sgt. McKibben, with complete disregard for his safety, sprang to his comrade's side and under heavy enemy fire pulled him to safety behind the cover of a rock emplacement where he administered hasty first aid. Sgt. McKibben, seeing that his comrades were pinned down and were unable to deliver effective fire against the enemy bunkers, again undertook a single-handed assault of the enemy defenses. He charged through the brush and hail of automatic weapons fire closing on the first bunker, killing the enemy with accurate rifle fire and securing the enemy's weapon. He continued his assault against the next bunker, firing his rifle as he charged. As he approached the second bunker his rifle ran out of ammunition; however, he used the captured enemy weapon until it too was empty, at this time he silenced the bunker with well placed hand grenades. He reloaded his weapon and

covered the advance of his men as they moved forward. Observing the fire of another bunker impeding the patrol's advance, Sgt. McKibben again single-handedly assaulted the new position. As he neared the bunker he was mortally wounded but was able to fire a final burst from his weapon killing the enemy and enabling the patrol to continue the assault. Sgt. McKibben's indomitable courage, extraordinary heroism, profound concern for the welfare of his fellow soldiers and disregard for his personal safety saved the lives of his comrades and enabled the patrol to accomplish its mission. Sgt. McKibben's gallantry in action at the cost of his life above and beyond the call of duty are in the highest traditions of the military service and reflect great credit upon himself, his unit, and the U.S. Army.

†TAYLOR, KARL G., SR.

Rank and Organization: Staff Sergeant, U.S. Marine Corps, Company I, 3d Battalion, 26th Marine Regiment, 3d Marine Division (Rein), FMF.
Born: July 14, 1939, Laurel, Maryland
Entered Service At: Baltimore, Maryland
Place and Date: Republic of Vietnam, December 8, 1968
Citation: For conspicuous gallantry and intrepidity at the risk of his life above and beyond the call of duty while serving at night as a company gunnery sergeant during Operation MEADE RIVER. Informed that the commander of the lead platoon had been mortally wounded when his unit was pinned down by a heavy volume of enemy fire, S/Sgt. Taylor along with another marine, crawled forward to the beleaguered unit through a hail of hostile fire, shouted encouragement and instructions to the men, and deployed them to covered positions. With his companion, he then repeatedly maneuvered across an open area to rescue those marines who were too seriously wounded to move by themselves. Upon learning that there were still other seriously wounded men lying in another open area, in proximity to an enemy machine-gun position, S/Sgt. Taylor, accompanied by four comrades, led his men forward across the fire-swept terrain in an attempt to rescue the marines. When his group was halted by devastating fire, he directed his companions to return to the company command post, whereupon he took his grenade launcher and in full view of the enemy, charged across the open rice paddy toward the machine-gun position, firing his weapon as he ran. Although wounded several times, he succeeded in reaching the machine-gun bunker and silencing the fire from that sector, moments before he was mortally wounded. Directly instrumental in saving the lives of several of his fellow marines, S/Sgt. Taylor, by his indomitable courage, inspiring leadership, and selfless dedication, upheld the highest traditions of the Marine Corps and of the U.S. Naval Service.

†NASH, DAVID P.

Rank and Organization: Private First Class, U.S. Army, Company B, 2d Battalion, 39th Infantry, 9th Infantry Division.
Born: November 3, 1947, Whitesville, Kentucky
Entered Service At: Louisville, Kentucky
Place and Date: Giao Duc District, Dinh Tuong Province, Republic of Vietnam, December 29, 1968
Citation: For conspicuous gallantry and intrepidity in action at the risk of his life above and beyond the call of duty. Pfc. Nash distinguished himself while serving as a grenadier with Company B, in Giao Duc District. When an ambush patrol of which he was a member suddenly came under intense attack before reaching its destination, he was the first to return the enemy fire. Taking an exposed location, Pfc Nash suppressed the hostile fusillade with a rapid series of rounds from his grenade launcher, enabling artillery fire to be adjusted on the enemy. After the foe had been routed, his small element continued to the ambush site where he established a position with three fellow soldiers on a narrow dike. Shortly past midnight, while Pfc. Nash and a comrade kept watch and the two other men took their turn sleeping, an enemy grenade wounded two soldiers in the adjacent position. Seconds later, Pfc. Nash saw another grenade land only a few feet from his own position. Although he could have escaped harm by rolling down the other side of the dike, he shouted a warning to his comrades and leaped upon the lethal explosive. Absorbing the blast with his body, he saved the lives of the three men in the area at the sacrifice of his life. By his gallantry at the cost of his life are in the highest traditions of the military service, Pfc. Nash has reflected great credit on himself, his unit, and the U.S. Army.

HOWARD, ROBERT L.

Rank and Organization: First Lieutenant, U.S. Army, 5th Special Forces Group (Airborne), 1st Special Forces.
Born: July 11, 1939, Opelika, Alabama
Entered Service At: Montgomery, Alabama
Place and Date: Republic of Vietnam, December 30, 1968
Citation: For conspicuous gallantry and intrepidity in action at the risk of his life above and beyond the call of duty. 1st Lt. Howard (then Sfc.), distinguished himself while serving as platoon sergeant of an American-Vietnamese platoon which was on a mission to rescue a missing American soldier in enemy controlled territory in the Republic of Vietnam. The platoon had left its helicopter landing zone and was moving out on its mission when it was attacked by an estimated two-company force. During the initial engagement, 1st Lt. Howard was wounded and his platoon leader had been wounded seriously and was exposed to fire. Although unable to walk, and weaponless, 1st Lt. Howard unhesitatingly crawled through a hail of fire to retrieve his wounded leader. As 1st Lt. Howard was administering first aid and removing the officer's equipment, an enemy bullet struck one of the ammunition pouches on the lieutenant's belt, detonating several magazines of ammunition. 1st Lt. Howard momentarily sought cover and then realizing that he must rejoin the platoon, which had been disorganized by the enemy attack, he again began dragging the seriously wounded officer toward the platoon area. Through his outstanding example of indomitable courage and bravery, 1st Lt. Howard was able to rally the platoon into an organized defense force. With complete disregard for his safety, 1st Lt. Howard crawled from position to position, administering first aid to the wounded, giving encouragement to the defenders and directing their fire on the encircling enemy. For 3-1/2 hours 1st Lt. Howard's small force and supporting aircraft successfully repulsed enemy attacks and finally were in sufficient control to permit the landing of rescue helicopters. 1st Lt. Howard personally supervised the loading of his men and did not leave the bullet-swept landing zone until all were aboard safely. 1st Lt. Howard's gallantry in action, his complete devotion to the welfare of his men at the risk of his life were in keeping with the highest traditions of the military service and reflect great credit on himself, his unit, and the U.S. Army.

CHAPTER 6

1969

(† - Indicates Posthumous Award)

Note: The following newspaper article concerning Vietnam appeared on page 4 of *The New York Times* on January 1, 1969:

Thieu Sees A Way To Cut U.S. Force In The Coming Year

SAIGON, South Vietnam, Dec. 31 - President Nguyen Van Thieu said tonight that South Vietnam's armed forces should gain enough strength in the coming year to be able to relieve some of the 600,000 allied troops stationed in the country.

Although the plan to start sending some American troops home as they were replaced by Government troops is an old one, Mr. Thieu's statement represents a change in the time of the expected start of the withdrawal of some allied troops. Nine months ago, the target for the start home for any allied soldiers was late 1968. Four months ago the time discussed was 1970.

Mr. Thieu spoke in a nationally televised New Year's address that amounted to a State of the Nation report.

Evidencing a keen sensitivity to American public opinion, he predicted that the rapidly expanding South Vietnamese military machine would "gradually assume more and more of the burden of the war, starting in 1969."

"That is our moral responsibility, our duty toward our allies," he said. "Our armed forces are coming to maturity. 1969 should be the year of peace."

Turning to the Paris talks, Mr. Thieu blamed "Communist bad will and obduracy" for the deadlock.

†YANO, RODNEY J.T.
Rank and Organization: Sergeant First Class, U.S. Army, Air Cavalry Troop, 11th Armored Cavalry Regiment.
Born: December 13, 1943, Kealakekua Kona, Hawaii
Entered Service At: Honolulu, Hawaii
Place and Date: Near Bien Hao, Republic of Vietnam, January 1, 1969
Citation: Sfc. Yano distinguished himself while serving with the Air Cavalry Troop. Sfc. Yano was performing the duties of crew chief aboard the troop's command-and-control helicopter during action against enemy forces entrenched in dense jungle. From an exposed position in the face of intense small arms and antiaircraft fire he delivered suppressive fire upon the enemy forces and marked their positions with smoke and white phosphorous grenades, thus enabling his troop commander to direct accurate and effective artillery fire against the hostile emplacements. A grenade, exploding prematurely, covered him with burning phosphorous, and left him severely wounded. Flaming fragments within the helicopter caused supplies and ammunition to detonate. Dense white smoke filled the aircraft, obscuring the pilot's vision and causing him to lose control. Although having the use of only one arm and being partially blinded by the initial explosion, Sfc. Yano completely disregarded his welfare and began hurling blazing ammunition from the helicopter. In so doing he inflicted additional wounds upon himself, yet he persisted until the danger was past. Sfc. Yano's indomitable courage and profound concern for his comrades averted loss of life and additional injury to the rest of the crew. By his conspicuous gallantry at the cost of his life, in the highest traditions of the military service, Sfc. Yano has reflected great credit on himself, his unit, and the U.S. Army.

JENKINS, DON J.
Rank and Organization: Staff Sergeant, U.S. Army, Company A, 2d Battalion, 39th Infantry, 9th Infantry Division.
Born: April 18, 1948, Quality, Kentucky
Entered Service At: Nashville, Tennessee
Place and Date: Kien Phong Province, Republic of Vietnam, January 6, 1969
Citation: For conspicuous gallantry and intrepidity in action at the risk of his life above and beyond the call of duty. S/Sgt. Jenkins (then Pfc.), Company A, distinguished himself while serving as a machine gunner on a reconnaissance mission. When his company came under heavy crossfire from an enemy complex, S/Sgt. Jenkins unhesitatingly maneuvered forward to a perilously exposed position and began placing suppressive fire on the enemy. When his own machinegun jammed, he immediately obtained a rifle and continued to fire into the enemy bunkers until his machine-gun was made operative by his assistant. He exposed himself to extremely heavy fire when he repeatedly both ran and crawled across open terrain to obtain resupplies of ammunition until he had exhausted all that was available for his machinegun. Displaying tremendous presence of mind, he then armed himself with two antitank weapons and, by himself, maneuvered through the hostile fusillade to within 20 meters of an enemy bunker to destroy that position. After moving back to the friendly defensive perimeter long enough to secure yet another weapon, a grenade launcher, S/Sgt. Jenkins moved forward to a position providing no protection and resumed placing accurate fire on the enemy until his ammunition was again exhausted. During this time he was seriously wounded by shrapnel. Undaunted and displaying great courage, he moved forward 100 meters to aid a friendly element that was pinned down only a few meters from the enemy. This he did with complete disregard for his own wound and despite having been advised that several previous rescue attempts had failed at the cost of the life of one and the wounding of others. Ignoring the continuing intense fire and his painful wounds, and hindered by darkness, he made three trips to the beleaguered unit, each time pulling a wounded comrade back to safety. S/Sgt. Jenkins' extraordinary valor, dedication, and indomitable spirit inspired his fellow soldiers to repulse the determined enemy attack and ultimately to defeat the larger force. S/Sgt. Jenkins risk of his life reflect great credit upon himself, his unit, and the U.S. Army.

FRITZ, HAROLD A.

Rank and Organization: Captain, U.S. Army, Troop A, 1st Squadron, 11th Armored Cavalry Regiment.
Born: February 21, 1944, Chicago, Illinois
Entered Service At: Milwaukee, Wisconsin
Place and Date: Binh Long Province, Republic of Vietnam, January 11, 1969
Citation: For conspicuous gallantry and intrepidity in action at the risk of his life above and beyond the call of duty. Capt. (then 1st Lt.) Fritz, Armor, U.S. Army, distinguished himself while serving as a platoon leader with Troop A, near Quan Loi. Capt. Fritz was leading his seven vehicle armored column along Highway 13 to meet and escort a truck convoy when the column suddenly came under intense crossfire from a reinforced enemy company deployed in ambush positions. In the initial attack, Capt. Fritz' vehicle was hit and he was seriously wounded. Realizing that his platoon was completely surrounded, vastly outnumbered, and in danger of being overrun, Capt. Fritz leaped to the top of his burning vehicle and directed the positioning of his remaining vehicles and men. With complete disregard for his wounds and safety, he ran from vehicle to vehicle in complete view of the enemy gunners in order to reposition his men, to improve the defenses, to assist the wounded, to distribute ammunition, to direct fire, and to provide encouragement to his men. When a strong enemy force assaulted the position and attempted to overrun the platoon, Capt. Fritz manned a machine-gun and through his exemplary action inspired his men to deliver intense and deadly fire which broke the assault and routed the attackers. Moments later a second enemy force advanced to within two meters of the position and threatened to overwhelm the defenders. Capt. Fritz, armed only with a pistol and bayonet, led a small group of his men in a fierce and daring charge which routed the attackers and inflicted heavy casualties. When a relief force arrived, Capt. Fritz saw that it was not deploying effectively against the enemy positions, and he moved through the heavy enemy fire to direct its deployment against the hostile positions. This deployment forced the enemy to abandon the ambush site and withdraw. Despite his wounds, Capt. Fritz returned to his position, assisted his men, and refused medical attention until all of his wounded comrades had been treated and evacuated. The extraordinary courage and selflessness displayed by Capt. Fritz, at the repeated risk of

his own life above and beyond the call of duty, were in keeping with the highest traditions of the U.S. Army and reflect the greatest credit upon himself, his unit, and the Armed Forces.

†WARREN, JOHN E., JR.

Rank and Organization: First Lieutenant, U.S. Army, Company C, 2d Battalion, (Mechanized), 22d Infantry, 25th Infantry Division.

Born: November 16, 1946, Brooklyn, New York

Entered Service At: New York, New York

Place and Date: Tay Ninh Province, Republic of Vietnam, January 14, 1969

Citation: For conspicuous gallantry and intrepidity in action at the risk of his life above and beyond the call of duty. 1st Lt. Warren, distinguished himself at the cost of his life while serving as a platoon leader with Company C. While moving through a rubber plantation to reinforce another friendly unit, Company C came under intense fire from a well-fortified enemy force. Disregarding his safety, 1st Lt. Warren with several of his men began maneuvering through the hail of enemy fire toward the hostile positions. When he had come to within six feet of one of the enemy bunkers and was preparing to toss a hand grenade into it, an enemy grenade was suddenly thrown into the middle of his small group. Thinking only of his men, 1st Lt. Warren fell in the direction of the grenade, thus shielding those around him from the blast. His action, performed at the cost of his life, saved three men from serious or mortal injury. First Lt. Warren's ultimate action of sacrifice to save the lives of his men was in keeping with the highest traditions of the military service and reflects great credit on him, his unit, and the U.S. Army.

Note: The following is a newspaper account of the preceding battle in which Lt. Warren earned the Medal of Honor:

122 Enemy Soldiers Killed
In Ambush of a U.S. Supply Convoy

SAIGON, South Vietnam, Jan. 15 - United States forces killed 122 enemy soldiers yesterday while beating back an attack on an American supply convoy northwest of Saigon. It was the heaviest combat in South Vietnam in several weeks.

A United States military spokesman said today that only two of the 50 trucks in the convoy had been damaged in the ambush.

But 7 Americans were killed and 10 wounded in nearly seven hours of fighting.

The spokesman said the enemy opened fire on the convoy with automatic rifles, machine guns and rocket-propelled grenades as it approached the town of Tayninh about 58 miles northwest of Saigon.

Troops escorting the convoy counterattacked and within a few minutes armed helicopters and fighter-bombers were strafing and bombing the attackers. Later, reinforcements in armored cars and tanks arrived and battled enemy soldiers at both ends of the supply column until shortly before sundown.

†LANGHORN, GARFIELD M.

Rank and Organization: Private First Class, U.S. Army, Troop C, 7th Squadron (Airmobile), 17th Cavalry, 1st Aviation Brigade.
Born: September 10, 1948, Cumberland, Virginia
Entered Service At: Brooklyn, New York
Place and Date: Pleiku Province, Republic of Vietnam, January 15, 1969
Citation: For conspicuous gallantry and intrepidity in action at the risk of his life above and beyond the call of duty. Pfc. Langhorn distinguished himself while serving as a radio operator with Troop C, near Plei Djereng in Pleiku Province. Pfc. Langhorn's platoon was inserted into a landing zone to rescue two pilots of a Cobra helicopter shot down by enemy fire on a heavily timbered slope. He provided radio coordination with the command-and-control aircraft overhead while the troops hacked their way through dense undergrowth to the wreckage, where both aviators were found dead. As the men were taking the bodies to a pickup site, they suddenly came under intense fire from North Vietnamese soldiers in camouflaged bunkers to the front and right flank, and within minutes they were surrounded. Pfc. Langhorn immediately radioed for help from the orbiting gunships, which began to place minigun and rocket fire on the aggressors. he then lay between the platoon leader and another man, operating the radio and providing covering fire for the wounded who had been moved to the center of the small perimeter. Darkness soon fell, making it impossible for the gunships to give accurate support, and the aggressors began to probe the perimeter. An enemy hand grenade landed in front of Pfc. Langhorn and a few feet from personnel who had become casualties. Choosing to protect these wounded, he unhesitatingly threw himself on the grenade, scooped it beneath his body and absorbed the blast. By sacrificing himself, he saved the lives of his comrades. Pfc. Langhorn's extraordinary heroism at the cost of his life was in keeping with the highest traditions of the military service and reflect great credit on himself, his unit, and the U.S. Army.

†NOONAN, THOMAS P., JR.

Rank and Organization: Lance Corporal, U.S. Marine Corps, Company G, 2d Battalion, 9th Marines, 3d Marine Division.
Born: November 18, 1943, Brooklyn, New York
Entered Service At: Brooklyn, New York
Place and Date: Near Vandergrift Combat Base, A Shau Valley, Republic of Vietnam, February 5, 1969
Citation: For conspicuous gallantry and intrepidity at the risk of his life above and beyond the call of duty while serving as a fire team leader with Company G, in operations against the enemy in Quang Tri Province. Company G was directed to move from a position which they had been holding southeast of the Vandergrift Combat Base to an alternate location. As the marines commenced a slow and difficult descent down the side of the hill made extremely slippery by the heavy rains, the leading element came under a heavy fire from a North Vietnamese Army unit occupying well concealed positions in the rocky terrain. Four men were wounded, and repeated attempts to recover them failed because of the intense hostile fire. L/Cpl. Noonan moved from his position of relative security and, maneuvering down the treacherous slope to a location near the injured men, took cover behind some rocks. Shouting words of encouragement to the wounded men to restore their confidence, he dashed across the hazardous terrain and commenced dragging the most seriously wounded man away from the fire-swept area. Although wounded and knocked to the ground by an enemy round, L/Cpl. Noonan recovered rapidly and resumed dragging the man toward the marginal security of a rock. He was, however, mortally wounded before he could reach his destination. His heroic actions inspired his fellow marines to such aggressiveness that they initiated a spirited assault which forced the enemy soldiers to withdraw. L/Cpl. Noonan's indomitable courage, inspiring initiative, and selfless devotion to duty upheld the highest traditions of the Marine Corps and the U.S. Naval Service. He gallantly gave his life for his country.

†BENNETT, THOMAS W.

Rank and Organization: Corporal, U.S. Army, 2d Platoon, Company B, 1st Battalion, 14th Infantry.
Born: April 7, 1947, Morgantown, West Virginia
Entered Service At: Fairmont, West Virginia
Place and Date: Chu Pa Region, Pleiku Province, Republic of Vietnam, February 9-11, 1969
Citation: For conspicuous gallantry and intrepidity in action at the risk of his life above and beyond the call of duty. Cpl. Bennett distinguished himself while serving as a platoon medical aidman with the 2d Platoon, Company B, during a reconnaissance-in-force mission. On February 9, the platoon was moving to assist the 1st Platoon of Company D which had run into a North Vietnamese ambush when it became heavily engaged by the intense small arms, automatic weapons, mortar and rocket fire from a well fortified and numerically superior enemy unit. In the initial barrage of fire, three of the point members of the platoon fell wounded. Cpl. Bennett, with complete disregard for his safety, ran through the heavy fire to his fallen comrades, administered life-saving first aid under fire and then made repeated trips carrying the wounded men to positions of relative safety from which they would be medically evacuated from the battle position. Cpl. Bennett repeatedly braved the intense enemy fire moving across open areas to give aid and comfort to his wounded comrades. He valiantly exposed himself to the heavy fire in order to retrieve the bodies of several fallen personnel. Throughout the night and following day, Cpl. Bennett moved from position to position treating and comforting the several personnel who had suffered shrapnel and gunshot wounds. On February 11, Company B again moved in an assault on the well fortified enemy positions and became heavily engaged with the numerically superior enemy force. Five members of the company fell wounded in the initial assault. Cpl. Bennett ran to their aid without regard to the heavy fire. He treated one wounded comrade and began running toward another seriously wounded man. Although the wounded man was located forward of the company position covered by heavy enemy grazing fire and Cpl. Bennett was warned that it was impossible to reach the position, he leaped forward with complete disregard for his safety to save his comrade's life. In attempting to save his fellow soldier, he was mortally wounded.

Cpl. Bennett's undaunted concern for his comrades at the cost of his life above and beyond the call of duty are in keeping with the highest traditions of the military service and reflect great credit upon himself, his unit, and the U.S. Army.

†PROM, WILLIAM R.

Rank and Organization: Lance Corporal, U.S. Marine Corps, Company 1, 3d Battalion, 3d Marines, 3d Marine Division (Rein), FMF.
Born: November 17, 1948, Pittsburgh, Pennsylvania
Entered Service At: Pittsburgh, Pennsylvania
Place and Date: Near An Hoa, Republic of Vietnam, February 9, 1969
Citation: For conspicuous gallantry and intrepidity at the risk of his life above and beyond the call of duty while serving as a machine-gun squad leader with Company I, in action against the enemy. While returning from a reconnaissance operation during Operation TAYLOR COMMON, two platoons of Company I came under an intense automatic weapons fire and grenade attack from a well concealed North Vietnamese Army force in fortified positions. The leading element of the platoon was isolated and several marines were wounded. L/Cpl. prom immediately assumed control of one of his machine-guns and began to deliver return fire. Disregarding his safety he advanced to a position from which he could more effectively deliver covering fire while first aid was administered to the wounded men. Realizing that the enemy would have to be destroyed before the injured marines could be evacuated, L/Cpl. Prom again moved forward and delivered a heavy volume of fire with such accuracy that he was instrumental in routing the enemy, thus permitting his men to regroup and resume their march. Shortly thereafter, the platoon again came under heavy fire in which one man was critically wounded. Reacting instantly, L/Cpl. prom moved forward to protect his injured comrade. Unable to continue his fire because of his severe wounds, he continued to advance to within a few yards to the enemy positions. There, standing in full view of the enemy, he accurately directed the fire of his support elements until he was mortally wounded. Inspired by his heroic actions, the marines launched an assault that destroyed the enemy. L/Cpl. Prom's indomitable courage, inspiring initiative and selfless devotion to duty upheld the highest traditions of the Marine Corps and the U.S. Naval Service. He gallantly gave his life for his country.

†CREEK, THOMAS E.

Rank and Organization: Lance Corporal, U.S. Marine Corps, Company I, 3d Battalion, 9th Marines, 3d Marine Division (Rein), FMF.
Born: April 7, 1950, Joplin, Missouri
Entered Service At: Amarillo, Texas
Place and Date: Near Cam Lo, Republic of Vietnam, February 13, 1969
Citation: For conspicuous gallantry and intrepidity at the risk of his life above and beyond the call of duty while serving as a rifleman with Company I, in action against enemy forces. L/Cpl. Creek's squad was providing security for a convoy moving to resupply the Vandegrift Command Base when an enemy command detonated mine destroyed on of the vehicles and halted the convoy near the Cam Lo Resettlement Village. Almost immediately, the marines came under a heavy volume of hostile mortar fire followed by intense small-arms fire from a well-concealed enemy force. As his squad deployed to engage the enemy, L/Cpl. Creek quickly moved to a fighting position and aggressively engaged in the fire fight. Observing a position from which he could more effectively deliver fire against the hostile forces, he completely disregarded his own safety as he fearlessly dashed across the fire-swept terrain and was seriously wounded by enemy fire. At the same time, an enemy grenade was thrown into the gully where he had fallen, landing between him and several companions. Fully realizing the inevitable results of his action, L/Cpl. Creek rolled on the grenade and absorbed the full force of the explosion with his body, thereby saving the lives of five of his fellow marines. As a result of his heroic action, his men were inspired to such aggressive action that the enemy was defeated and the convoy was able to continue its vital mission. L/Cpl. Creek's indomitable courage, inspired the Marine Corps and the U.S. Naval Service. he gallantly gave his life for his country.

Note: The following is a newspaper account of the preceding battle in which L/Cpl. Creek earned the Medal of Honor:

FOE ON OFFENSIVE IN SHARP CLASHES

U.S. Marines Are Attacked In Sweep Near Quangtri

Saigon, South Vietnam, Feb. 13 - Fighting in South Vietnam flared during the last 24 hours as Vietcong and North Vietnamese soldiers took the offensive in several sharp engagements in the north and in the area around Saigon according to allied communiques.

An undetermined number of enemy soldiers attacked a United States Marine force early yesterday 27 miles southwest of the city of Quangtri in the northernmost province.

Seven Americans were killed in the clash and five were wounded. A sweep of the battle area in daylight disclosed the bodies of 13 enemy soldiers.

The Marine force was part of the search-and-clear operation that involves several battalions of American troops and has been under way along the Laotian border in Quangtri Province since Jan. 22.

†**MILLER, GARY L.**
Rank and Organization: First Lieutenant, U.S. Army, Company A, 1st Battalion, 28th Infantry, 1st Infantry Division.
Born: March 19, 1947, Covington, Virginia
Entered Service At: Roanoke, Virginia
Place and Date: Binh Duong Province, Republic of Vietnam, February 16, 1969
Citation: For conspicuous intrepidity and gallantry in action at the risk of his life above and beyond the call of duty. First Lt. Miller, Infantry, Company A, was serving as a platoon leader at night when his company ambushed a hostile force infiltrating from Cambodian sanctuaries. After contact with the enemy was broken, 1st Lt. Miller led a reconnaissance patrol from their prepared positions through the early evening darkness and dense tropical growth to search the area for enemy casualties. As the group advanced they were suddenly attacked. First Lt. Miller was seriously wounded. However, the group fought back with telling effect on the hostile force. An enemy grenade was thrown into the midst of the friendly patrol group and all took cover except 1st Lt. Miller, who in the dim light located the grenade and threw himself on it, absorbing the force of the explosion with his body. His action saved nearby members of his patrol from almost certain serious injury. The extraordinary courage and selflessness displayed by this officer were an inspiration to his comrades and are in the highest traditions of the U.S. Army.

FOX, WESLEY L.

Rank and Organization: Captain, U.S. Marine Corps, Company A, 1st Battalion, 9th Marines, 3d Marine Division..
Born: September 30, 1931, Herndon, Virginia
Entered Service At: Leesburg, Virginia
Place and Date: Quang Tri Province, Republic of Vietnam, February 22, 1969
Citation: For conspicuous gallantry and intrepidity at the risk of his life above and beyond the call of duty while serving as commanding officer of Company A, in action against the enemy in the northern A Shau Valley. Capt. (then 1st Lt.) Fox's company came under intense fire from a large well concealed enemy force. Capt. Fox maneuvered to a position from which he could assess the situation and confer with his platoon leaders. As they departed to execute the plan he had devised, the enemy attacked and Capt. Fox was wounded along with all of the other members of the command group, except the executive officer. Capt. Fox continued to direct the activity of his company. Advancing through heavy enemy fire, he personally neutralized one enemy position and calmly ordered an assault against the hostile emplacements. he then moved through the hazardous area coordinating aircraft support with the activities of his men. When his executive officer was mortally wounded, Capt. Fox reorganized the company and directed the fire of his men as they hurled grenades against the enemy and drove the hostile forces into retreat. Wounded again in the final assault, Capt. Fox refused medical attention, established a defensive posture, and supervised the preparation of casualties for medical evacuation. His indomitable courage, inspiring initiative, and unwavering devotion to duty in the face of grave personal danger inspired his marines to such aggressive action that they overcame all enemy resistance and destroyed a large bunker complex. Capt. Fox's heroic actions reflect great credit upon himself and the Marine Corps. and uphold the highest traditions of the U.S. Naval Service.

LANG, GEORGE C.

Rank and Organization: Specialist Fourth Class, U.S. Army, Company A, 4th Battalion, 47th Infantry, 9th Infantry Division.
Born: April 20, 1947, Flushing, New York
Entered Service At: Brooklyn, New York
Place and Date: Kien Hoa Province, Republic of Vietnam, February 22, 1969
Citation: For conspicuous gallantry and intrepidity in action at the risk of his life above and beyond the call of duty. Sp4c. Lang, Company A, was serving as a squad leader when his unit, on a reconnaissance-in-force mission, encountered intense fire from a well fortified enemy bunker complex. Sp4c. Lang observed an emplacement from which heavy fire was coming. Unhesitatingly, he assaulted the position and destroyed it with hand grenades and rifle fire. Observing another emplacement approximately 15 meters to his front, Sp4c. Lang jumped across a canal, moved through heavy enemy fire to within a few feet of the position, and eliminated it, again using hand grenades and rifle fire. nearby, he discovered a large cache of enemy ammunition. As he maneuvered his squad forward to secure the cache, they came under fire from yet a third bunker. Sp4c. Lang immediately reacted, assaulted his position, and destroyed it with the remainder of his grenades. After returning to the area of the arms cache, his squad again came under heavy enemy rocket and automatic weapons fire from three sides and suffered six casualties. Sp4c. Lang was one of those seriously wounded. Although immobilized and in great pain, he continued to direct his men until his evacuation was ordered over his protests. The sustained extraordinary courage and selflessness exhibited by this soldier over an extended period of time were an inspiration to his comrades and are in keeping with the highest traditions of the U.S. Army.

†**LAW, ROBERT D.**

Rank and Organization: Specialist Fourth Class, U.S. Army, Company I (Ranger), 75th Infantry, 1st Infantry Division.
Born: September 15, 1944, Fort Worth, Texas
Entered Service At: Dallas, Texas
Place and Date: Tinh Phuoc Thanh Province, Republic of Vietnam, February 22, 1969
Citation: For conspicuous gallantry and intrepidity in action at the risk of his life above and beyond the call of duty. Sp4c. Law distinguished himself while serving with Company I. While on a long-range reconnaissance patrol in Tinh Phuoc Thanh Province, Sp4c. Law and five comrades made contact with a small enemy patrol. As the opposing elements exchanged intense fire, he maneuvered to a perilously exposed position flanking his comrades and began placing suppressive fire on the hostile troops. Although his team was hindered by a low supply of ammunition and suffered from an unidentified irritating gas in the air, Sp4c. Law's spirited defense and challenging counter-assault rallied his fellow soldiers against the well-equipped hostile troops. When an enemy grenade landed in his team's position, Sp4c. Law, instead of diving into the safety of a stream behind him threw himself on the grenade to save the lives of his comrades. Sp4c. Law's extraordinary courage and profound concern for his fellow soldiers were in keeping with the highest traditions of the military service and reflect great credit on himself, his unit, and the U.S. Army.

†AUSTIN, OSCAR P.

Rank and Organization: Private First Class, U.S. Marine Corps, Company E, 2d Battalion, 7th Marines, 1st Marine Division, (Rein), FMF.

Born: January 15, 1948, Nacogdoches, Texas

Entered Service At: Phoenix, Arizona

Place and Date: West of Da Nang, Republic of Vietnam, February 23, 1969

Citation: For conspicuous gallantry and intrepidity at the risk of his life above and beyond the call of duty while serving as an assistant machine gunner with Company E, in connection with operations against enemy forces. During the early morning hours Pfc. Austin's observation post was subjected to a fierce ground attack by a large North Vietnamese Army force supported by a heavy volume of hand grenades, satchel charges, and small arms fire. Observing that one of his wounded companions had fallen unconscious in a position dangerously exposed to the hostile fire, Pfc. Austin unhesitatingly left the relative security of his fighting hole and, with complete disregard for his safety, raced across the fire-swept terrain to assist the marine to a covered location. As he neared the casualty, he observed an enemy grenade land nearby and, reacting instantly, leaped between the injured marine and the lethal object, absorbing the effects of its detonation. As he ignored his painful injuries and turned to examine the wounded man, he saw a North Vietnamese Army soldier aiming a weapon at his unconscious companion. With full knowledge of the probable consequences and thinking only to protect the marine, Pfc. Austin resolutely threw himself between the casualty and the hostile soldier, and, in doing, was mortally wounded. Pfc. Austin's indomitable courage, inspiring initiative and selfless devotion to duty upheld the highest traditions of the Marine Corps and the U.S. Naval Service. He gallantly gave his life for his country.

†HARTSOCK, ROBERT W.
Rank and Organization: Staff Sergeant, U.S. Army, 44th Infantry Platoon, 3d Brigade, 25th Infantry Division.
Born: January 24, 1945, Cumberland, Maryland
Entered Service At: Fairmont, West Virginia
Place and Date: Hau Nghia, Province, Republic of Vietnam, February 23, 1969
Citation: For conspicuous gallantry and intrepidity in action at the risk of his life above and beyond the call of duty. S/Sgt. Hartsock, distinguished himself in action while serving as section leader with the 44th Infantry Platoon. When the Dau Tieng Base Camp came under a heavy enemy rocket and mortar attack, S/Sgt. Hartsock and his platoon commander spotted an enemy sapper squad which had infiltrated the camp undetected. Realizing the enemy squad was heading for the brigade tactical operations center and nearby prisoner compound, they concealed themselves and, although heavily outnumbered, awaited the approach of the hostile soldiers. When the enemy was almost upon them, S/Sgt. Hartsock and his platoon commander opened fire on the squad. As a wounded enemy soldier fell, he managed to detonate a satchel charge he was carrying. S/Sgt. Hartsock, with complete disregard for his life, threw himself on the charge and was gravely wounded. In spite of his wounds, S/Sgt. Hartsock crawled about five meters to a ditch and provided heavy suppressive fire, completely pinning down the enemy and allowing his commander to seek shelter. S/Sgt. Hartsock continued his deadly stream of fire until he succumbed to his wounds. S/Sgt. Hartsock's extraordinary heroism and profound concern for the lives of his fellow soldiers were in keeping with the highest traditions of the military service and reflect great credit on him, his unit, and the U.S. Army.

Note: The following is a newspaper account of the battle for which S/Sgt. Hartsock was awarded the Medal of Honor:

Allies Say Foe Has Begun
Long-Expected Offensive

SAIGON, South Vietnam, Mon. Feb. 24 - Enemy troops, striking simultaneously at Saigon and about 105 other towns and military targets throughout the country, have launched what the allied command considers the long-predicted general offensive.

The enemy troops poured rockets and mortar shells into 17 provincial capitals, 28 towns and about 60 military installations. In most places the attackers confined themselves to shelling and held their ground assaults to a minimum.

Two Battalions Attack

An exception was the base camp of the Third Brigade of the 25th Infantry Division at Dautieng in Binh Doung Province, where two enemy battalions - about 1,000 men - charged the position under the covering fire of mortar rounds.

The enemy troops briefly broke through the defensive perimeter, but were repulsed by the infantrymen, who were supported by Army helicopter gun-ships, artillery and tactical air strikes.

A high American military source said last night that the allied command considered the day's attacks to be the beginning of a general offensive that would probably last most of the week.

†WEBER, LESTER W.

Rank and Organization: Lance Corporal, U.S. marine Corps, Company M, 3d Battalion, 7th Marines, 1st Marine Division.
Born: July 30, 1948, Aurora, Illinois
Entered Service At: Chicago, Illinois
Place and Date: Quang Nam province, Republic of Vietnam, February 23, 1969
Citation: For conspicuous gallantry and intrepidity at the risk of his life above and beyond the call of duty while serving as a machine-gun squad leader with Company M, in action against the enemy. The 2d Platoon of Company M was dispatched to the Bo Ban area of Hieu Duc District to assist a squad from another platoon which had become heavily engaged with a well entrenched enemy battalion. While moving through a rice paddy covered with tall grass L/Cpl. Weber's platoon came under heavy attack from concealed hostile soldiers. he reacted by plunging into the tall grass, successfully attacking one enemy and forcing 11 others to break contact. Upon encountering a second North Vietnamese Army soldier he overwhelmed him in fierce hand-to-hand combat. Observing two other soldiers firing upon his comrades from behind a dike, L/Cpl. Weber ignored the frenzied firing of the enemy and racing across the hazardous area, dived into their position. he neutralized the position by wrestling weapons from the hands of the two soldiers and overcoming them. Although by now the target for concentrated fire from hostile riflemen, L/Cpl. Weber remained in a dangerously exposed position to shout words of encouragement to his emboldened companions. As he moved forward to attack a fifth enemy soldier, he was mortally wounded. L/Cpl. Weber's indomitable courage, aggressive fighting spirit and unwavering devotion to duty upheld the highest traditions of the Marine Corps and of the U.S. Naval Service. He gallantly gave his life for his country.

LEVITOW, JOHN L.

Rank and Organization: Sergeant, U.S. Air Force, 3d Special Operations Squadron.

Born: November 1, 1945, Hartford, Connecticut

Entered Service At: New Haven, Connecticut

Place and Date: Long Binh Army Post, Republic of Vietnam, February 24, 1969

Citation: For conspicuous gallantry and intrepidity in action at the risk of his life above and beyond the call of duty. Sgt. Levitow (then A1c.), U.S. Air Force, distinguished himself by exceptional heroism while assigned as a loadmaster aboard an AC-47 aircraft flying a night mission in support of Long Binh Army Post. Sgt. Levitow's aircraft was struck by a hostile mortar round. The resulting explosion ripped a hole two feet in diameter through the wing and fragments made over 3,500 holes in the fuselage. All occupants of the cargo compartment were wounded and helplessly slammed against the floor and fuselage. The explosion tore an activated flare from the grasp of a crewmember who had been launching flares to provide illumination for Army ground troops engaged in combat. Sgt. Levitow, though stunned by the concussion of the blast and suffering from over 40 fragment wounds in the back and legs, staggered to his feet and turned to assist the man nearest to him who had been knocked down and was bleeding heavily. As he was moving his wounded comrade forward and away from the opened cargo compartment door, he saw the smoking flare ahead of him in the aisle. Realizing the danger involved and completely disregarding his own wounds, Sgt. Levitow started toward the burning flare. The aircraft was partially out of control and the flare was rolling wildly from side to side. Sgt. Levitow struggled forward despite the loss of blood from his many wounds and the partial loss of feeling in his right leg. Unable to grasp the rolling flare with his hands, he threw himself bodily upon the burning flare. Hugging the deadly device to his body, he dragged himself back to the rear of the aircraft and hurled the flare through the open cargo door. At that instant the flare separated and ignited in the air, but clear of the aircraft. Sgt. Levitow, by his selfless and heroic actions, saved the aircraft and its entire crew from certain death and destruction. Sgt. Levitow's gallantry, his profound concern for his fellowmen, at the risk of his life above and beyond the call of duty are in keeping with the highest traditions of the U.S. Air Force and reflect great credit upon himself and the Armed Forces of his country.

†MORGAN, WILLIAM D.

Rank and Organization: Corporal, U.S. Marine Corps, Company H, 2d Battalion, 9th Marines, 3d Marine Division.
Born: September 17, 1947, Pittsburgh, Pennsylvania
Entered Service At: Pittsburgh, Pennsylvania
Place and Date: Quang Tri Province, Republic of Vietnam, February 25, 1969
Citation: For conspicuous gallantry and intrepidity at the risk of his life above and beyond the call of duty while serving as a squad leader with Company H, in operations against the enemy. While participating in Operation DEWEY CANYON southeast of Vandergrift Combat Base, one of the squads of Cpl. Morgan's platoon was temporarily pinned down and sustained several casualties while attacking a North Vietnamese Army force occupying a heavily fortified bunker complex. Observing that two of the wounded marines had fallen in a position dangerously exposed to the enemy fire and that all attempts to evacuate them were halted by a heavy volume of automatic weapons fire and rocket-propelled grenades. Cpl. Morgan unhesitatingly maneuvered through the dense jungle undergrowth to a road that passed in front of a hostile emplacement which was the principal source of enemy fire. Fully aware of the possible consequences of his valiant action, but thinking only of the welfare of his injured companions, Cpl. Morgan shouted words of encouragement to them as he initiated an aggressive assault against the hostile bunker. While charging across the open road, he was clearly visible to the hostile soldiers who turned their fire in his direction and mortally wounded him, but his diversionary tactic enabled the remainder of his squad to retrieve their casualties and overrun the North Vietnamese Army position. His heroic and determined actions saved the lives of two fellow marines and were instrumental in the subsequent defeat of the enemy. Cpl. Morgan's indomitable courage, inspiring initiative and selfless devotion to duty upheld the highest traditions of the Marine Corps and of the U.S. Naval Services. He gallantly gave his life for his country.

Note: The following is a newspaper account of the preceding battle in which Cpl. Morgan earned the Medal of Honor:

VIETCONG ATTACK MARINE POSITIONS NEAR BUFFER ZONE

Suicide Troops Carrying Explosives Breach Wire-36 Americans Killed

SAIGON, South Vietnam, Feb. 25 - North Vietnamese troops mounted two attacks on United States Marines dug in just south of the demilitarized zone today while enemy gunners continued to shell targets throughout the country.

[Thirty-six Marines were killed in one of the attacks by enemy suicide troops with explosives tied to their backs, a military spokesman at Danang reported. The report said that the suicide troops had blown holes in the barbed wire of the camp's perimeter.]

Although United States military authorities were unsure they conceded that the enemy troops might have passed through the demilitarized zone to strike at the marines. They were deployed just south of the six-mile-deep strip lying on both sides of the border between North and South Vietnam.

Perimeter Is Pierced

The United States halted the bombing of North Vietnam last Nov. 1 with the understanding that the zone would not be used for infiltration into the South.

The two attacks occurred shortly before dawn within a few miles of each other in an area northwest of a sprawling artillery base known as the Rockpile. American losses after three hours of fighting were termed the highest in a single battle in South Vietnam in nearly six months.

The North Vietnamese troops broke through the perimeter of the fire base's position less than two miles south of the demilitarized zone. They were driven out of the area after almost an hour of hand-to-hand fighting.

Suicide Attack Described

Thirty-six American Marines were killed today when North Vietnamese suicide troops with explosives lashed to their backs attacked an artillery base near the demilitarized zone, a spokesman at this northern military base said.

Reports from the base said that one marine had beaten a North Vietnamese to death with his hands after his weapon failed to fire. Another marine was said to have killed five North Vietnamese with his 12-inch-long knife.

"At times, marine artillery men fired at point-blank range into the fanatic suicide troops as they threw themselves at the camp perimeter to blow holes in the barbed wire," the base commander said in a report.

†BRUCE, DANIEL D.

Rank and Organization: Private First Class, U.S. Marine Corps, Headquarters and Service Company, 3d Battalion, 5th Marines, 1st Marine Division.
Born: May 18, 1950, Michigan City, Indiana
Entered Service At: Chicago, Illinois
Place and Date: Fire Support Base Tomahawk, Quang Nam Province, Republic of Vietnam, March 1, 1969
Citation: For conspicuous gallantry and intrepidity at the risk of his life above and beyond the call of duty while serving as a mortar man with Headquarters and Service Company, 3d Battalion, against the enemy. Early in the morning Pfc. Bruce was on watch in his night defensive position at fire support base tomahawk when he heard movements ahead of him. An enemy explosive charge was thrown toward his position and he reacted instantly, catching the device and shouting to alert his companions. Realizing the danger to the adjacent position with its two occupants, Pfc. Bruce held the device to his body and attempted to carry it from the vicinity of the entrenched marines. As he moved away, the charge detonated and he absorbed the full force of the explosion. Pfc. Bruce's indomitable courage, inspiring valor and selfless devotion to duty saved the lives of three of his fellow marines and upheld the highest traditions of the Marine Corps and the U.S. Naval Service. He gallantly gave his life for his country.

†STONE, LESTER R., JR.

Rank and Organization: Sergeant, U.S. Army, 1st Platoon, Company B, 1st Battalion, 20th Infantry, 11th Infantry Brigade, 23d Infantry Division (Americal).

Born: June 4, 1947, Binghamton, New York

Entered Service At: Syracuse, New York

Place and Date: West of Landing Zone Liz, Republic of Vietnam, March 3, 1969

Citation: For conspicuous gallantry and intrepidity in action at the risk of his life above and beyond the call of duty. Sgt. Stone, distinguished himself while serving as squad leader of the 1st Platoon. The 1st Platoon was on a combat patrol mission just west of Landing Zone Liz when it came under intense automatic weapons and grenade fire from a well concealed company-size force of North Vietnamese regulars. Observing the platoon machine-gunner fall critically wounded, Sgt. Stone remained in the exposed area to provide cover fire for the wounded soldier who was being pulled to safety by another member of the platoon. With enemy fire impacting all around him, Sgt. Stone had a malfunction in the machine-gun, preventing him from firing the weapon automatically. Displaying extraordinary courage under the most adverse conditions, Sgt. Stone repaired the weapon and continued to place on the enemy positions effective suppressive fire which enabled the rescue to be completed. In a desperate attempt to overrun his position, an enemy force left its cover and charged Sgt. Stone. Disregarding the danger involved, Sgt. Stone rose to his knees and began placing intense fire on the enemy at pointblank range, killing six of the enemy before falling mortally wounded. His actions of unsurpassed valor were a source of inspiration to his entire unit, and he was responsible for saving the lives of a number of he fellow soldiers. His actions were in keeping with the highest traditions of the military profession and reflect great credit on him, his unit, and the U.S. Army.

†WILSON, ALFRED M.

Rank and Organization: Private First Class, U.S. Marine Corps, Company M, 3d Battalion, 9th Marines, 3d Marine Division.
Born: January 13, 1948, Olney, Illinois
Entered Service At: Abilene, Texas
Place and Date: Quang Tri Province, Republic of Vietnam, March 3, 1969.
Citation: For conspicuous gallantry and intrepidity at the risk of his life above and beyond the call of duty while serving as a rifleman with Company M, in action against hostile forces. While returning from a reconnaissance-in-force mission in the vicinity of Fire Support Base Cunningham, the 1st Platoon of Company M came under intense automatic weapons fire and a grenade attack from a well concealed enemy force. As the center of the column was pinned down, the leading squad moved to outflank the enemy. Pfc. Wilson, acting as squad leader of the rear squad, skillfully maneuvered his men to form a base of fire and act as a blocking force. In the ensuing fire fight, both his machine gunner and assistant machine gunner were seriously wounded and unable to operate their weapons. Realizing the urgent need to bring the weapon into operation again, Pfc. Wilson, followed by another marine and with complete disregard for his safety, fearlessly dashed across the fire-swept terrain to recover the weapon. As they reached the machine-gun, an enemy soldier stepped from behind a tree and threw a grenade toward the two marines. Observing the grenade fall between himself and the other marine, Pfc. Wilson, fully realizing the inevitable result of his actions, shouted to his companion and unhesitating threw himself on the grenade, absorbing the full force of the explosion with his own body. His heroic actions inspired his platoon members to maximum effort as they aggressively attacked and defeated the enemy. Pfc. Wilson's indomitable courage, inspiring valor and selfless devotion to duty upheld the highest traditions of the Marine Corps and the U.S. naval Service. He gallantly gave his life for his country.

Note: The following is a newspaper account of the battle for which Pfc. Wilson was awarded the Medal of Honor:

Marines Beat Back Assault On Base Near DMZ

SAIGON, South Vietnam, March 3 - About 500 United States Marines fought off a strong North Vietnamese attack today on an artillery base three miles south of the demilitarized zone.

The enemy's drive was the fourth in that area since the spring offensive of the foe opened Feb. 23.

Thirteen marines were killed and 22 were wounded in the defense of the artillery base against repeated charges by scores of North Vietnamese infantrymen. The bodies of 20 North Vietnamese were found on the field, about 15 miles west of Dongha, after the fighting ended in the late afternoon, the United States command said.

Enemy Struck Early

The North Vietnamese force struck in the early morning hours with machine-gun and small-arms fire, and the marines fought back with machine-guns, rifles and artillery.

Reports from Danang said that a marine patrol operating outside the base became involved in the initial fighting and apparently suffered many of the casualties. These reports said that there had been no penetration of the base itself. Officers at Marine headquarters in Danang declined to speculate whether the attacks on the bases near the DMZ signaled a new outburst of sustained fighting along the once neutral buffer zone.

†JENKINS, ROBERT H., JR.

Rank and Organization: Private First Class, U.S. marine Corps, 3d Reconnaissance Battalion, 3d Marine Division (Rein), FMF.

Born: June 1, 1948, Interlachen, Florida

Entered Service At: Jacksonville, Florida

Place and Date: Fire Support Base Argonne, Republic of Vietnam, March 5, 1969

Citation: For conspicuous gallantry and intrepidity at the risk of his life above and beyond the call of duty while serving as a machine gunner with Company C, 3d Reconnaissance Battalion, in connection with operations against enemy forces. Early in the morning Pfc. Jenkins' 12-man reconnaissance team was occupying a defensive position at Fire Support Base Argonne south of the Demilitarized Zone. Suddenly, the marines were assaulted by a North Vietnamese Army platoon employing mortars, automatic weapons, and hand grenades. Reacting instantly, Pfc. Jenkins and another marine quickly moved into a two-man fighting emplacement, and as they boldly delivered accurate machine-gun fire against the enemy, a North Vietnamese soldier threw a hand grenade into a friendly emplacement. Fully realizing the inevitable results of his actions, Pfc. Jenkins quickly seized his comrade, and pushing the man to the ground, he leaped on top of the marine to shield him from the explosion. Absorbing the full impact of the detonation, Pfc. Jenkins was seriously injured and subsequently succumbed to his wounds. His courage, inspiring valor and selfless devotion to duty saved a fellow marine from serious injury or possible death and upheld the highest traditions of the Marine Corps and the U.S. Naval Service. He gallantly gave his life for his country.

KERREY, JOSEPH R.

Rank and Organization: Lieutenant, Junior Grade, U.S. Naval Reserve, Sea, Air, and Land Team (SEAL).
Born: August 27, 1943, Lincoln, Nebraska
Entered Service At: Omaha, Nebraska
Place and Date: Near Nha Trang Bay, Republic of Vietnam, March 14, 1969
Citation: For conspicuous gallantry and intrepidity at the risk of his life above and beyond the call of duty while serving as a SEAL team leader during action against enemy aggressor (Viet Cong) forces. Acting in response to reliable intelligence, Lt. (jg.) Kerrey led his SEAL team on a mission to capture important members of the enemy's area political cadre known to be located on an island in the bay of Nha Trang. In order to surprise the enemy, he and his team scaled a 350 foot sheer cliff to place themselves above the ledge on which the enemy was located. Splitting his team in two elements and coordinating both, Lt. (jg.) Kerrey led his men in the treacherous downward descent to the enemy's camp. Just as they neared the end of their descent, intense enemy fire was directed at them, and Lt. (jg.) Kerrey received massive injuries from a grenade which exploded at his feet and threw him backward onto the jagged rocks. Although bleeding profusely and suffering great pain, he displayed outstanding courage and presence of mind in immediately directing his element's fire into the heart of the enemy camp. Utilizing his radioman, Lt. (jg.) Kerrey called in the second element's fire support which caught the confused Viet Cong in a devastating crossfire. After successfully suppressing the enemy's fire, and although immobilized by his multiple wounds, he continued to maintain calm, superlative control as he ordered his team to secure and defend an extraction site. Lt. (jg.) Kerrey resolutely directed his men, despite his near unconscious state, until he was eventually evacuated by helicopter. The havoc brought to the enemy by this very successful mission cannot be over-estimated. The enemy soldiers who were captured provided critical intelligence to the allied effort. Lt. (jg.) Kerrey's courageous and inspiring leadership, valiant fighting spirit, and tenacious devotion to duty in the face of almost overwhelming opposition sustain and enhance the finest traditions of the U.S. Naval Service.

Note: Lt. Kerrey is now a United States Senator from Nebraska.

†McMAHON, THOMAS J.

Rank and Organization: Specialist Fourth Class, U.S. Army, Company A, 2d Battalion, 1st Infantry, 196th Infantry Brigade, Americal Division.

Born: June 24, 1948, Washington, D.C.

Entered Service At: Portland, Maine

Place and Date: Quang Tin Province, Republic of Vietnam, March 19, 1969

Citation: For conspicuous gallantry and intrepidity in action at the risk of his life above and beyond the call of duty. Sp4c. McMahon distinguished himself while serving as medical aid man with Company A. When the lead elements of his company came under heavy fire from well-fortified enemy positions, three soldiers fell seriously wounded. Sp4c. McMahon, with complete disregard for his safety, left his covered position and ran through intense enemy fire to the side of one of the wounded, administered first aid and then carried him to safety. He returned through the hail of fire to the side of a second wounded man. Although painfully wounded by an exploding mortar round while returning the wounded man to a secure position, Sp4c. McMahon refused medical attention and heroically ran back through the heavy enemy fire toward his remaining wounded comrade. he fell mortally wounded before he could rescue the last man. Sp4c. McMahon's undaunted concern for the welfare of his comrades at the cost of his life are in keeping with the highest traditions of the military service and reflect great credit on himself, his unit, and the U.S. Army.

†RAY, DAVID ROBERT

Rank and Organization: Hospital Corpsman Second Class, U.S. Navy, 2d Battalion, 11th Marines, 1st Marine Division (Rein), FMF.
Born: February 14, 1945, McMinnville, Tennessee
Entered Service At: Nashville, Tennessee
Place and Date: Quang Nam Province, Republic of Vietnam, March 19, 1969
Citation: For conspicuous gallantry and intrepidity at the risk of his life above and beyond the call of duty while serving as a HC2c. with Battery D, 2d Battalion, at Phu Loc 6, near An Hoa. During the early morning hours, an estimated battalion-sized enemy force launched a determined assault against the battery's position, and succeeded in effecting a penetration of the barbed-wire perimeter. The initial burst of enemy fire caused numerous casualties among the marines who had immediately manned their howitzers during the rocket and mortar attack. Undaunted by the intense hostile fire, HC2c. Ray moved from parapet to parapet, rendering emergency medical treatment to the wounded. Although seriously wounded himself while administering first aid to a marine casualty, he refused medical aid and continued his lifesaving efforts. While he was bandaging and attempting to comfort another wounded marine, HC2c. Ray was forced to battle two enemy soldiers who attacked his position, personally killing one and wounding the other. Rapidly losing his strength as a result of his severe wounds, he nonetheless managed to move through the hail of enemy fire to other casualties. Once again, he was faced with the intense fire of oncoming enemy troops and, despite the grave personal danger and insurmountable odds, succeeded in treating the wounded and holding off the enemy until he ran out of ammunition, at which time he sustained fatal wounds. HC2c. Ray's final act of heroism was to protect the patient he was treating. He threw himself upon the wounded marine, thus saving the man's life when an enemy grenade exploded nearby. By his determined and persevering actions, courageous spirit, and selfless devotion to the welfare of his marine comrades, HC2c. Ray served to inspire the men of Battery D to heroic efforts in defeating the enemy. His conduct throughout was in keeping with the finest traditions of the U.S. Naval Service.

†KAWAMURA, TERRY TERUO

Rank and Organization: Corporal, U.S. Army, 173d Engineer Company, 173d Airborne Brigade, Republic of Vietnam.
Born: December 10, 1949, Wahaiwa, Oahu, Hawaii
Entered Service At: Oahu, Hawaii
Place and Date: Camp Radcliff, Republic of Vietnam, March 20, 1969
Citation: For conspicuous gallantry and intrepidity in action at the risk of his life above and beyond the call of duty. Cpl. Kawamura distinguished himself by heroic action while serving as a member of the 173d Engineer Company. An enemy demolition team infiltrated the unit quarters area and opened fire with automatic weapons. Disregarding the intense fire, Cpl. Kawamura ran for his weapon. At that moment, a violent explosion tore a hole in the roof and stunned the occupants of the room. Cpl. Kawamura jumped to his feet, secured his weapon and, as he ran toward the door to return the enemy fire, he observed that another explosive charge had been thrown through the hole in the roof to the floor. He immediately realized that two stunned fellow soldiers were in great peril and shouted a warning. Although in a position to escape, Cpl. Kawamura unhesitatingly wheeled around and threw himself on the charge. In completely disregarding his safety, Cpl. Kawamura prevented serious injury or death to several members of his unit. The extraordinary courage and selflessness displayed by Cpl. Kawamura are in the highest traditions of the military service and reflect great credit upon himself, his unit, and the U.S. Army.

†JOHNSTON, DONALD R.
Rank and Organization: Specialist Fourth Class, U.S. Army, Company D, 1st Battalion, 8th Cavalry, 1st Cavalry Division.
Born: November 19, 1947, Columbus, Georgia
Entered Service At: Columbus, Georgia
Place and Date: Tay Ninh Province, Republic of Vietnam, March 21, 1969
Citation: For conspicuous gallantry and intrepidity in action at the risk of his life above and beyond the call of duty. Sp4c. Johnston distinguished himself while serving as a mortarman with Company D, at a fire support base in Tay Ninh Province. Sp4c. Johnston's company was in defensive positions when it came under a devastating rocket and mortar attack. Under cover of the bombardment, enemy sappers broke through the defensive perimeter and began hurling explosive charges into the main defensive bunkers. Sp4c. Johnston and six of his comrades had moved from their exposed positions to one of the bunkers to continue their fight against the enemy attackers. As they were firing from the bunker, an enemy soldier threw three explosive charges into their position. Sensing the danger to his comrades, Sp4c. Johnston, with complete disregard for his safety, hurled himself onto the explosive charges, smothering the detonations with his body and shielding his fellow soldiers from the blast. His heroic action saved the lives of six of his comrades. Sp4c. Johnston's concern for his fellow men at the cost of his life were in the highest traditions of the military service and reflect great credit upon himself, his unit, and the U.S. Army.

Note: The following is a newspaper account of the battle for which Sp4c. Johnston was awarded the Medal of Honor:

Artillery Post Assaulted

SAIGON, Fri. March 21 (AP) - Enemy forces heavily bombarded an American artillery base northwest of Saigon today with mortars and rocket-propelled grenades, then followed up with an infantry assault using tear gas, a military spokesman reported.

According to reports from the field, 18 Americans were killed and 12 were wounded in the night-long assault on the post, a fire base of the First Cavalry Division (Airmobile) about 45 miles northwest of Saigon. It is one of a string of patrol bases blocking infiltration routes to the capital.

The bodies of three enemy soldiers were found along the base's barbed-wire perimeter.

The enemy opened up first with mortar and rocket-grenade barrages, the spokesman said. Most of the American casualties were inflicted by mortar rounds, which ripped into exposed artillery pits from which the Americans were firing at the enemy positions.

Then, according to the account, the enemy charged the base, manned by about 250 Americans, and threw tear-gas grenades over the barbed wire. They were thrown back after heavy fighting, having failed to penetrate the base camp, the spokesman said.

†BRYANT, WILLIAM MAUD

Rank and Organization: Sergeant First Class, U.S. Army, Company A, 5th Special Forces Group, 1st Special Forces.

Born: February 16, 1933, Cochran, Georgia

Entered Service At: Detroit, Michigan

Place and Date: Long Khanh Province, Republic of Vietnam, March 24, 1969

Citation: For conspicuous gallantry and intrepidity in action at the risk of his life above and beyond the call of duty. Sfc. Bryant, assigned to Company A, distinguished himself while serving as commanding officer of Civilian Irregular Defense Group Company 321, 2d Battalion, 3d Mobile Strike Force Command, during combat operations. The battalion came under heavy fire and became surrounded by the elements of three enemy regiments. Sfc. Bryant displayed extraordinary heroism throughout the succeeding 34 hours of incessant attack as he moved throughout the company position heedless of the intense hostile fire while establishing and improving the defensive perimeter, directing fire during critical phases of the battle, distributing ammunition, assisting the wounded, and providing the leadership and inspirational example of courage to his men. When a helicopter drop of ammunition was made to resupply the beleaguered force, Sfc. Bryant with complete disregard for his safety ran through the heavy enemy fire to retrieve the scattered ammunition boxes and distributed needed ammunition to his men. During a lull in the intense fighting, Sfc. Bryant led a patrol outside the perimeter to obtain information of the enemy. The patrol came under intense automatic weapons fire and was pinned down. Sfc. Bryant singlehandedly repulsed one enemy attack on his small force and by his heroic action inspired his men to fight off other assaults. Seeing a wounded enemy soldier some distance from the patrol location, Sfc. Bryant crawled forward alone under heavy fire to retrieve the soldier for intelligence purposes. Finding that the enemy soldier had expired, Sfc. Bryant crawled back to his patrol and led his men back to the company position where he again took command of the defense. As the siege continued, Sfc. Bryant organized and led a patrol in a daring attempt to break through the enemy encirclement. The patrol had advanced some 200 meters by heavy fighting when it was pinned down by the intense automatic weapons fire from heavily fortified bunkers and Sfc. Bryant was severely wounded. Despite his wounds he rallied his men, called for helicopter gunship support, and directed heavy suppressive fire upon the enemy positions. Following the last gunship attack, Sfc. Bryant fearlessly charged an enemy automatic weapons position, overrunning it, and singlehandedly destroying its three defenders. Inspired by his heroic example, his men renewed their attack on the entrenched enemy. While regrouping his small force for the final assault against the enemy, Sfc. Bryant fell mortally wounded by an enemy rocket. Sfc. Bryant's selfless concern for his comrades, at the cost of his life above and beyond the call of duty are in keeping with the highest traditions of the military service and reflect great credit upon himself, his unit, and the U.S. Army.

†COKER, RONALD L.

Rank and Organization: Private First Class, U.S. Marine Corps, Company M, 3d Battalion, 3d Marine Division (Rein), FMF
Born: August 9, 1947, Alliance, Colorado
Entered Service At: Denver, Colorado
Place and Date: Quang Tri Province, Republic of Vietnam, March 24, 1969
Citation: For conspicuous gallantry and intrepidity at the risk of his life above and beyond the call of duty while serving as a rifleman with Company M in action against enemy forces. While serving as point man for the 2d Platoon, Pfc. Coker was leading his patrol when he encountered five enemy soldiers on a narrow jungle trail. Pfc. Coker's squad aggressively pursued them to a cave. As the squad neared the cave, it came under intense hostile fire, seriously wounding one marine and forcing the others to take cover. Observing the wounded man lying exposed to continuous enemy fire, Pfc. Coker disregarded his safety and moved across the fire-swept terrain toward his companion. Although wounded by enemy small-arms fire, he continued to crawl across the hazardous area and skillfully threw a hand grenade into the enemy positions, suppressing the hostile fire sufficiently to enable him to reach the wounded man. As he began to drag his injured comrade toward safety, a grenade landed on the wounded marine. Unhesitatingly, Pfc. Coker grasped it with both hands and turned away from his wounded companion, but before he could dispose of the grenade it exploded. Severely wounded, but undaunted, he refused to abandon his comrade. As he moved toward friendly lines, two more enemy grenades exploded near him, inflicting still further injuries. Concerned only for the safety of his comrade, Pfc. Coker, with supreme effort continued to crawl and pull the wounded marine with him. His heroic deeds inspired his fellow marines to such aggressive action that the enemy fire was suppressed sufficiently to enable others to reach him and carry him to a relatively safe area where he succumbed to his extensive wounds. Pfc. Coker's indomitable courage, inspiring initiative and selfless devotion to duty upheld the highest traditions of the Marine Corps and of the U.S. Naval Service. He gallantly gave his life for his country.

†DOANE, STEPHEN HOLDEN

Rank and Organization: First Lieutenant, U.S. Army, Company B, 1st Battalion, 5th Infantry, 25th Infantry Division.
Born: October 13, 1947, Beverly, Massachusetts
Entered Service At: Albany, New York
Place and Date: Hau Nghia Province, Republic of Vietnam, March 25, 1969
Citation: For conspicuous gallantry and intrepidity in action at the risk of his life above and beyond the call of duty. First Lt. Doane was serving as a platoon leader when his company, engaged in a tactical operation, abruptly contacted an enemy force concealed in protected bunkers and trenches. Three of the leading soldiers were pinned down by enemy crossfire. One was seriously wounded. After efforts of one platoon to rescue these men has failed, it become obvious that only a small group could successfully move close enough to destroy the enemy position and rescue or relieve the trapped soldiers. First Lt. Doane, although fully aware of the danger of such an action, crawled to the nearest enemy bunker and silenced it. He was wounded but continued to advance to a second enemy bunker. As he prepared to throw a grenade, he was again wounded. Undaunted, he deliberately pulled the pin on the grenade and lunged with it into the enemy bunker, destroying this final obstacle. First Lt. Doane's supreme act enabled his company to rescue the trapped men without further casualties. The extraordinary courage and selflessness displayed by this officer were an inspiration to his men and are in the highest traditions of the U.S. Army.

DUNAGAN, KERN W.

Rank and Organization: Major, U.S. Army, Company A, 1st Battalion, 46 Infantry, Americal Division.
Born: February 20, 1934, Superior, Arizona
Entered Service At: Los Angeles, California
Place and Date: Quang Tin Province, Republic of Vietnam, May 13, 1969
Citation: For conspicuous gallantry and intrepidity in action at the risk of his life above and beyond the call of duty. Maj. (then Capt.) Dunagan distinguished himself during the period May 13, and 14, 1969, while serving as commanding officer, Company A. On May 13, 1969, Maj. Dunagan was leading an attack to relieve pressure on the battalion's forward support base when his company came under intense fire from a well entrenched enemy battalion. Despite continuous hostile fire from a numerically superior force, Maj. Dunagan repeatedly and fearlessly exposed himself in order to locate enemy positions, direct friendly supporting artillery, and position the men of his company. In the early evening, while directing an element of his unit into perimeter guard, he was seriously wounded during an enemy mortar attack, but he reused to leave the battlefield and continued to supervise the evacuation of dead and wounded and to lead his command in the difficult task of disengaging from an aggressive enemy. In spite of painful wounds and extreme fatigue, Maj. Dunagan risked heavy fire on two occasions to rescue critically wounded men. He was again seriously wounded. Undaunted, he continued to display outstanding courage, professional competence, and leadership and successfully extricated his command from its untenable position on the evening of May 14. Having maneuvered his command into contact with an adjacent friendly unit, he learned that a six-man party from his company was under fire and had not reached the new perimeter. Maj. Dunagan unhesitatingly went back and searched for his men. Finding one soldier critically wounded, Maj. Dunagan, ignoring his wounds, lifted the man to his shoulders and carried him to the comparative safety of the friendly perimeter. Before permitting himself to be evacuated, he insured all of his wounded received emergency treatment and were removed from the area. Throughout the engagement, Maj. Dunagan's actions gave great inspiration to his men and were directly responsible for saving the lives of many of his fellow soldiers. Maj. Dunagan's extraordinary heroism above and beyond the call of duty, are in the highest traditions of the U.S. Army and reflect great credit on him, his unit, and the U.S. Army.

†SHEA, DANIEL JOHN

Rank and Organization: Private First Class, U.S. Army, Headquarters Company, 3d Battalion, 21st Infantry, 196th Infantry Brigade, Americal Division.
Born: January 29, 1947, Norwalk, Connecticut
Entered Service At: New Haven, Connecticut
Place and Date: Quang Tri Province, Republic of Vietnam, May 14, 1969
Citation: For conspicuous gallantry and intrepidity in action at the risk of his life above and beyond the call of duty. Pfc. Shea, Headquarters and Headquarters Company, 3d Battalion, distinguished himself while serving as a medical aidman with Company C, 3d Battalion, during a combat patrol mission. As the lead platoon of the company was crossing a rice paddy, a large enemy force in ambush positions opened fire with mortars, grenades and automatic weapons. Under heavy crossfire from three sides, the platoon withdrew to a small island in the paddy to establish a defensive perimeter. Pfc. Shea, seeing that a number of his comrades had fallen in the initial hail of fire, dashed from the defensive position to assist the wounded. With complete disregard for his safety and braving the intense hostile fire sweeping the open rice paddy, Pfc. Shea made four trips to tend wounded soldiers and to carry them to the safety of the platoon position. Seeing a fifth wounded comrade directly in front of one of the enemy strong-points, Pfc. Shea ran to his assistance. As he reached the wounded man, Pfc. Shea was grievously wounded. Disregarding his welfare, Pfc. Shea tended his wounded comrade and began to move him back to the safety of the defensive perimeter. As he neared the platoon position, Pfc. Shea was mortally wounded by a burst of enemy fire. By his heroic actions Pfc. Shea saved the lives of several of his fellow soldiers. Pfc. Shea's gallantry in action at the cost of his life were in keeping with the highest traditions of the military service and reflect great credit upon himself, his unit, and the U.S. Army.

BONDSTEEL, JAMES LEROY

Rank and Organization: Staff Sergeant, U.S. Army, Company A, 2d Battalion, 2d Infantry, 1st Infantry Division.

Born: July 18, 1947, Jackson, Michigan

Entered Service At: Detroit, Michigan

Place and Date: An Loc Province, Republic of Vietnam, May 24, 1969

Citation: For conspicuous gallantry and intrepidity in action at the risk of his life above and beyond the call of duty. S/Sgt. Bondsteel distinguished himself while serving as a platoon sergeant with Company A, near the village of Lang Sau. Company A was directed to assist a friendly unit which was endangered by intense fire from a North Vietnamese Battalion located in a heavily fortified base camp. S/Sgt. Bondsteel quickly organized the men of his platoon into effective combat teams and spearheaded the attack by destroying four enemy occupied bunkers. he then raced some 200 meters under heavy enemy fire to reach an adjoining platoon which had begun to falter. After rallying this unit and assisting their wounded, S/Sgt. Bondsteel returned to his own sector with critically needed munitions. Without pausing he moved to the forefront and destroyed four enemy occupied bunkers and a machine-gun which had threatened his advancing platoon. Although painfully wounded by an enemy grenade, S/Sgt. Bondsteel refused medical attention and continued his assault by neutralizing two more enemy bunkers nearby. While searching one of these emplacements S/Sgt. Bondsteel narrowly escaped death when an enemy soldier detonated a grenade at close range. Shortly thereafter, he ran to the aid of a severely wounded officer and struck down an enemy soldier who was threatening the officer's life. S/Sgt. Bondsteel then continued to rally his men and led them through the entrenched enemy until his company was relieved. His exemplary leadership and great personal courage throughout the four hour battle ensured the success of his own and nearby units, and resulted n the saving of numerous lives of his fellow soldiers. By individual acts of bravery he destroyed 10 enemy bunkers and accounted for a large toll of the enemy, including two key enemy commanders. His extraordinary heroism at the risk of his life was in the highest traditions of the military service and reflect great credit on him, his unit, and the U.S. Army.

†PHIPPS, JIMMY W.

Rank and Organization: Private First Class, U.S. Marine Corps, Company B, 1st Engineer Battalion, 1st Marine Division (Rein), FMF.
Born: November 1, 1950, Santa Monica, California
Entered Service At: Culver City, California
Place and Date: Near An Hoa, Republic of Vietnam, May 27, 1969
Citation: For conspicuous gallantry and intrepidity at the risk of his life above and beyond the call of duty while serving as a combat engineer with Company B in connection with combat operations against the enemy. Pfc. Phipps was a member of a two man combat engineer demolition team assigned to locate and destroy enemy artillery ordnance and concealed firing devices. After he had expended all of his explosives and blasting caps, Pfc. Phipps discovered a 175mm high explosive artillery round in a rice paddy. Suspecting that the enemy had attached the artillery round to a secondary explosive device, he warned other marines in the area to move to covered positions and prepared to destroy the round with a hand grenade. As he was attaching the hand grenade to a stake beside the artillery round, the fuse of the enemy's secondary explosive device ignited. Realizing that his assistant and the platoon commander were both within a few meters of him and that the imminent explosion could kill all three men, Pfc. Phipps grasped the hand grenade to his chest and dived forward to cover the enemy's explosive and the artillery round with his body, thereby shielding his companions from the detonation while absorbing the full and tremendous impact with his body. Pfc. Phipps' indomitable courage, inspiring initiative, and selfless devotion to duty saved the lived of two marines and upheld the highest traditions of the Marine Corps and the U.S. Naval Service. He gallantly gave his life for his country.

†LaPOINTE, JOSEPH G., JR.

Rank and Organization: Specialist Fourth Class, U.S. Army, 2d Squadron, 17th Cavalry, 101st Airborne Division.
Born: July 2, 1948, Dayton, Ohio
Entered Service At: Cincinnati, Ohio
Place and Date: Quang Tin Province, Republic of Vietnam, June 2, 1969
Citation: For conspicuous gallantry and intrepidity in action at the risk of his life above and beyond the call of duty. Sp4c. LaPointe, Headquarters and Headquarters Troop, 2d Squadron, distinguished himself while serving as a medical aidman during a combat helicopter assault mission. Sp4c. LaPointe's patrol was advancing from the landing zone through an adjoining valley when it suddenly encountered heavy automatic weapons fire from a large enemy force entrenched in well fortified bunker positions. In the initial hail of fire, two soldiers in the formation vanguard were seriously wounded. Hearing a call for aid from one of the wounded, Sp4c. LaPointe ran forward through heavy fire to assist his fallen comrades. To reach the wounded men, he was forced to crawl directly in view of an enemy bunker. As members of his unit attempted to provide covering fire, he administered first aid to one man, shielding the other with his body. He was hit by a burst of fire from the bunker while attending the wounded soldier. In spite of his painful wounds, Sp4c. LaPointe continued his lifesaving duties until he was again wounded and knocked to the ground. making strenuous efforts, he moved back again into a shielding position to continue administering first aid. An exploding enemy grenade mortally wounded all three men. Sp4c. LaPointe's courageous actions at the cost of his life were an inspiration to his comrades. His gallantry and selflessness are in the highest traditions of the military service and reflect great credit on him, his unit, and the U.S. Army.

†POXON, ROBERT LESLIE

Rank and Organization: First Lieutenant, U.S. Army, Troop B, 1st Squadron, 9th Cavalry, 1st Cavalry Division.
Born: January 3, 1947, Detroit, Michigan
Entered Service At: Detroit, Michigan
Place and Date: Tay Ninh Province, Republic of Vietnam, June 2, 1969.
Citation: For conspicuous gallantry and intrepidity in action at the risk of his life above and beyond the call of duty. First Lt. Poxon, Armor, Troop B, distinguished himself while serving as a platoon leader on a reconnaissance mission. Landing by helicopter in an area suspected of being occupied by the enemy, the platoon came under intense fire from enemy soldiers in concealed positions and fortifications around the landing zone. A soldier fell, hit by the first burst of fire. First Lt. Poxon dashed to his aid, drawing the majority of the enemy fire as he crossed 20 meters of open ground. The fallen soldier was beyond help and 1st Lt. Poxon was seriously and painfully wounded. First Lt. Poxon, with indomitable courage, refused medical aid and evacuation and turned his attention to seizing the initiative from the enemy. With sure instinct he marked a central enemy bunker as the key to success. Quickly instructing his men to concentrate their fire on the bunker, and in spite of his wound, 1st. Lt. Poxon crawled toward the bunker, readied a hand grenade and charged. He was hit again but continued his assault. After succeeding in silencing the enemy guns in the bunker he was struck once again by enemy fire and fell, mortally wounded. First Lt. Poxon's comrades followed their leader, pressed the attack and drove the enemy from their positions. First Lt. Poxon's gallantry, indomitable will, and courage are in keeping with the highest traditions of the military service and reflect great credit upon himself, his unit, and the U.S. Army.

KELLEY, THOMAS G.

Rank and Organization: Lieutenant Commander, U.S. Navy, River Assault Division 152.
Born: May 13, 1939, Boston, Massachusetts
Entered Service At: Boston, Massachusetts
Place and Date: Ong Muong Canal, Kien Hoa Province, Republic of Vietnam, June 15, 1969
Citation: For conspicuous gallantry and intrepidity at the risk of his life above and beyond the call of duty in the afternoon while serving as commander of River Assault Division 152 during combat operations against enemy aggressor forces. Lt. Comdr. (then Lt.) Kelley was in charge of a column of eight river assault craft which were extracting one company of U.S. Army infantry troops on the east bank of the Ong Muong Canal in Kien Hoa Province, when one of the armored troop carriers reported a mechanical failure of a loading ramp. At approximately the same time, Viet Cong forces opened fire from the opposite bank of the canal. After issuing orders for the crippled troop carrier to raise its ramp manually, and for the remaining boats to form a protective cordon around the disabled craft, Lt. Comdr. Kelley realizing the extreme danger to his column and its inability to clear the ambush site until the crippled unit was repaired, boldly maneuvered the monitor in which he was embarked to the exposed side of the protective cordon in direct line with the enemy's fire, and ordered the monitor to commence firing. Suddenly, an enemy rocket scored a direct hit on the coxswain's flat, the shell penetrating the thick armor plate, and the explosion spraying shrapnel in all directions. Sustaining serious head wounds from the blast, which hurled him to the deck of the monitor, Lt. Comdr. Kelley disregarded his severe injuries and attempted to continue directing the other boats. Although unable to move from the deck or to speak clearly into the radio, he succeeded in relaying his commands through one of his men until the enemy attack was silenced and the boats were able to move to an area of safety. Lt. Comdr. Kelley's brilliant leadership, bold initiative, and resolute determination served to inspire his men and provide the impetus needed to carry out the mission after he was medically evacuated by helicopter. His extraordinary courage under fire, and his selfless devotion to duty sustain and enhance the finest traditions of the U.S. Naval Service.

†BOWEN, HAMMETT L., JR.
Rank and Organization: Staff Sergeant, U.S. Army, Company C, 2d Battalion, 14th Infantry, 25th Infantry Division.
Born: November 30, 1947, Lagrange, Georgia.
Entered Service At: Jacksonville, Florida
Place and Date: Binh Duong Province, Republic of Vietnam, June 27, 1969
Citation: S/Sgt. Bowen distinguished himself while serving as a platoon sergeant during combat operations in Binh Duong Province, Republic of Vietnam. S/Sgt. Bowen's platoon was advancing on a reconnaissance mission into enemy controlled terrain when it came under the withering crossfire of small arms and grenades from an enemy ambush force. S/Sgt. Bowen placed heavy suppressive fire on the enemy positions and ordered his men to fall back. As the platoon was moving back, an enemy grenade was thrown amid S/Sgt. Bowen and three of his men. Sensing the danger to his comrades, S/Sgt. Bowen shouted a warning to his men and hurled himself on the grenade, absorbing the explosion with his body while saving the lives of his fellow soldiers. S/Sgt. Bowen's extraordinary courage and concern for his men at the cost of his life served as an inspiration to his comrades and are in the highest traditions of the military service and the U.S. Army.

†BLANCHFIELD, MICHAEL R.

Rank and Organization: Specialist Fourth Class, U.S. Army, Company A, 4th Battalion, 503d Infantry, 173d Airborne Brigade.
Born: January 4, 1950, Minneapolis, Minnesota
Entered Service At: Chicago, Illinois
Place and Date: Binh Dinh Province, Republic of Vietnam, July 3, 1969
Citation: For conspicuous gallantry and intrepidity in action at the risk of his life above and beyond the call of duty. Sp4c. Blanchfield distinguished himself while serving as a rifleman in Company A on a combat patrol. The patrol surrounded a group of houses to search for suspects. During the search of one of the huts, a man suddenly ran out toward a nearby tree line. Sp4c. Blanchfield, who was on guard outside the hut, saw the man, shouted for him to halt, and began firing at him as the man ignored the warning and continued to run. The suspect suddenly threw a grenade toward the hut and its occupants. Although the exploding grenade severely wounded Sp4c. Blanchfield and several others, he regained his feet to continue the pursuit of the enemy. The fleeing enemy threw a second grenade which landed near Sp4c. Blanchfield and several members of his patrol. Instantly realizing the danger, he shouted a warning to his comrades. Sp4c. Blanchfield unhesitatingly and with complete disregard for his safety, threw himself on the grenade, absorbing the full and fatal impact of the explosion. By his gallant action and self-sacrifice, he was able to save the lives and prevent injury to four members of the patrol and several Vietnamese civilians in the immediate area. Sp4c. Blanchfield's extraordinary courage and gallantry at the cost of his life above and beyond the call of duty are in keeping with the highest traditions of the military service and reflect great credit upon himself, his unit, and the U.S. Army.

†FOLLAND, MICHAEL FLEMING

Rank and Organization: Corporal, U.S. Army, Company D, 2d Battalion, 3d Infantry, 199th Infantry Brigade.
Born: April 15, 1949, Richmond, Virginia
Entered Service At: Richmond, Virginia
Place and Date: Long Khanh, Providence, Republic of Vietnam, July 3, 1969
Citation: For conspicuous gallantry and intrepidity in action at the risk of his life above and beyond the call of duty. Cpl. Folland distinguished himself while serving as an ammunition bearer with the weapons platoon of Company D, during a reconnaissance patrol mission. As the patrol was moving through a dense jungle area, it was caught in an intense crossfire from heavily fortified and concealed enemy ambush positions. As the patrol reacted to neutralize the ambush, it became evident that the heavy weapons could not be used in the cramped fighting area. Cpl. Folland dropped his recoilless rifle ammunition, and ran forward to join his commander in an assault on the enemy bunkers. The assaulting force moved forward until it was pinned down directly in front of the heavily fortified bunkers by machine-gun fire. Cpl. Folland stood up to draw enemy fire on himself and to place suppressive fire on the enemy positions while his commander attempted to destroy the machine-gun positions with grenades. Before the officer could throw a grenade, an enemy grenade landed in the position. Cpl. Folland alerted his comrades and his commander hurled the grenade from the position. When a second enemy grenade landed in the position, Cpl. Folland again shouted a warning to his fellow soldiers. Seeing that no one could reach the grenade and realizing that it was about to explode, Cpl. Folland, with complete disregard for his safety, threw himself on the grenade. By his dauntless courage, Cpl. Folland saved the lives of his comrades although he was mortally wounded by the explosion. Cpl. Folland's extraordinary heroism, at the cost of his life, was in keeping with the highest traditions of the military service and reflects great credit upon himself, his unit, and the U.S. Army.

ROBERTS, GORDON R.

Rank and Organization: Sergeant (Then Sp4c.), U.S. Army, Company B, 1st Battalion, 506th Infantry, 101st Airborne Division.
Born: June 14, 1950, Middletown, Ohio
Entered Service At: Cincinnati, Ohio
Place and Date: Thua Thien Province, Republic of Vietnam, July 11, 1969
Citation: For conspicuous gallantry and intrepidity in action at the risk of his life above and beyond the call of duty. Sgt. Roberts distinguished himself while serving as a rifleman in Company B, during combat operations. Sgt. Roberts' platoon was maneuvering along a ridge to attack heavily fortified enemy bunker positions which had pinned down an adjoining friendly company. As the platoon approached the enemy positions, it was suddenly pinned down by heavy automatic weapons and grenade fire from camouflaged enemy fortifications atop the overlooking hill. Seeing his platoon immobilized and in danger of failing in its mission. Sgt. Roberts crawled rapidly toward the closest enemy bunker. With complete disregard for his safety, he leaped to his feet and charged the bunker, firing as he ran. Despite the intense enemy fire directed at him, Sgt. Roberts silenced the two man bunker. Without hesitation, Sgt. Roberts continued his one man assault on a second bunker. As he neared the second bunker, a burst of enemy fire knocked his rifle from his hands. Sgt. Roberts picked up a rifle dropped by a comrade and continued his assault, silencing the bunker. He continued his charge against a third bunker and destroyed it with well-thrown hand grenades. Although Sgt. Roberts was now cut off from his platoon, he continued his assault against a fourth enemy emplacement. He fought through a heavy hail of fire to join elements of the adjoining company which had been pinned down by the enemy fire. Although continually exposed to hostile fire, he assisted in moving wounded personnel from exposed positions on the hilltop to an evacuation area before returning to his unit. By his gallant and selfless actions, Sgt. Roberts contributed directly to saving the lives of his comrades and served as an inspiration to his fellow soldiers in the defeat of the enemy force. Sgt. Roberts' extraordinary heroism in action at the risk of his life were in keeping with the highest traditions of the military service and reflect great credit upon himself, his unit, and the U.S. Army.

†GERTSCH, JOHN G.

Rank and Organization: Staff Sergeant, U.S. Army, Company E, 1st Battalion, 327th Infantry, 101st Airborne Division.
Born: September 29, 1944, Jersey City, New Jersey
Entered Service At: Buffalo, New York
Place and Date: A Shau Valley, Republic of Vietnam, July 15, to 19, 1969
Citation: S/Sgt. Gertsch distinguished himself while serving as a platoon sergeant and platoon leader during combat operations in the A Shau Valley. During the initial phase of an operation to seize a strongly defended enemy position, S/Sgt. Gertsch's platoon leader was seriously wounded and lay exposed to intense enemy fire. Forsaking his own safety, without hesitation S/Sgt. Gertsch rushed to aid his fallen leader ad dragged him to a sheltered position. He then assumed command of the heavily engaged platoon and led his men in a fierce counterattack that forced the enemy to withdraw. Later, a small element of S/Sgt. Gertsch's unit was reconnoitering when attacked again by the enemy. S/Sgt. Gertsch moved forward to his besieged element and immediately charged, firing as he advanced. His determined assault forced the enemy troops to withdraw in confusion and made possible the recovery of two wounded men who had been exposed to heavy enemy fire. Sometime later his platoon came under attack by an enemy force employing automatic weapons, grenade, and rocket fire. S/Sgt. Gertsch was severely wounded during the onslaught but continued to command his platoon despite his painful wound. While moving under fire and encouraging his men he sighted an aidman treating a wounded officer from an adjacent unit. Realizing that both men were in imminent danger of being killed, he rushed forward and positioned himself between them and the enemy nearby. While the wounded officer was being moved to safety S/Sgt. Gertsch was mortally wounded by enemy fire. Without S/Sgt. Gertsch's courage, ability to inspire others, and profound concern for the welfare of his men, the loss of life among his fellow soldiers would have been significantly greater. His conspicuous gallantry, extraordinary heroism, and intrepidity at the cost of his life, above and beyond the call of duty, are in the highest traditions of the U.S. Army and reflect great credit on him and the Armed Forces of his country.

†EVANS, RODNEY J.

Rank and Organization: Sergeant, U.S. Army, Company D, 1st Battalion, 12th Cavalry, 1st Cavalry Division.
Born: July 17, 1948, Chelsea, Massachusetts
Entered Service At: Montgomery, Alabama
Place and Date: Tay Ninh Province, Republic of Vietnam, July 18, 1969
Citation: For conspicuous gallantry and intrepidity in action at the risk of his life above and beyond the call of duty. Sgt. Evans distinguished himself by extraordinary heroism while serving as a squad leader in a reconnaissance sweep through heavy vegetation to reconnoiter a strong enemy position. As the force approached a well defined trail, the platoon scout warned that the trail was boobytrapped. Sgt. Evans led his squad on a route parallel to the trail. The force had started to move forward when a nearby squad was hit by the blast of a concealed mine. Looking to his right Sgt. Evans saw a second enemy device. With complete disregard for his safety he shouted a warning to his men, dived to the ground and crawled toward the mine. Just as he reached it an enemy soldier detonated the explosive and Sgt. Evans absorbed the full impact with his body. His gallant and selfless action saved his comrades from probable death or injury and served as an inspiration to his entire unit. Sgt. Evans' gallantry in action at the cost of his life were in keeping with the highest traditions of the military service and reflect great credit upon himself, his unit, and the U.S. Army.

†CARTER, BRUCE W.

Rank and Organization: Private First Class, U.S. Marine Corps, Company H, 2d Battalion, 3d Marines, 3d Marine Division (Rein), FMF.

Born: May 7, 1950, Schenectady, New York

Entered Service At: Jacksonville, Florida

Place and Date: Quang Tri Province, Republic of Vietnam, August 7, 1969

Citation: For conspicuous gallantry and intrepidity at the risk of his life above and beyond the call of duty while serving as grenadier with Company H in connection with combat operations against the enemy. Pfc. Carter's unit was maneuvering against the enemy during Operation Idaho Canyon and came under a heavy volume of fire from a numerically superior hostile force. The lead element soon became separated from the main body of the squad by a brush fire. Pfc. Carter and his fellow marines were pinned down by vicious crossfire when, with complete disregard for his safety, he stood in full view of the North Vietnamese Army soldiers to deliver a devastating volume of fire at their positions. The accuracy and aggressiveness of his attack caused several enemy casualties and forced the remainder of the soldiers to retreat from the immediate area. Shouting directions to the marines around him, Pfc. Carter then commenced leading them from the path of the rapidly approaching brush fire when he observed a hostile grenade land between him and his companions. Fully aware of the probably consequences of his action but determined to protect the men following him, he unhesitatingly threw himself over the grenade, absorbing the full effects of its detonation with his body. Pfc. Carter's indomitable courage, inspiring initiative, and selfless devotion to duty upheld the highest traditions of the Marine Corps and the U.S. Naval Service. He gallantly gave his life in the service of his country.

Note: The following is a newspaper account of the preceding battle in which Pfc. Carter earned the Medal of Honor:

Fighting Steps Up In South Vietnam

SAIGON, South Vietnam, Aug. 8 - In the last 24 hours fighting in South Vietnam rose to its highest pitch in nearly two months.

United States officers said, however, that they were still uncertain whether the enemy had opened a new drive, which had been expected this month.

Since early yesterday, an allied spokesman said, 147 enemy troops and 14 Americans and 17 South Vietnamese soldiers had been killed in significant actions ranging from the demilitarized zone to the Saigon area. In addition, 164 Americans and 51 South Vietnamese were wounded.

The spokesman said that this was the largest 24-hour casualty toll since June 18. Military officers pointed out that these figures did not include casualties from scores of skirmishes that are not reported in daily communiques.

A spokesman for the United States command said that the increased ground fighting "is not necessarily an indication of increased enemy-initiated activity."

"We may be catching him before he gets ready to do something," the spokesman said. "Several of the actions were initiated by allied forces."

About three North Vietnamese companies of more than 100 men each fought troops of the United States Third Marine Division and the Fifth Mechanized Division near the demilitarized zone. By United States count, 82 North Vietnamese were killed and eight Americans were killed and 23 wounded.

Another battle erupted 47 miles south of the big United States base at Danang, after two American observation helicopters were knocked down, wounding three crewmen.

Paratroopers of the 101st Airborne were rushed to the area, touching off a battle that left at least one enemy soldier and one American killed and 11 Americans wounded.

Other sharp clashes were reported in the Central Highlands and northeast of Saigon.

†ANDERSON, RICHARD A.

Rank and Organization: Lance Corporal, U.S. Marine Corps, Company E, 3d Reconnaissance Battalion, 3d Marine Division.
Born: April 16, 1948, Washington, D.C.
Entered Service At: Houston, Texas
Place and Date: Quang Tri Province, Republic of Vietnam, August 24, 1969
Citation: For conspicuous gallantry and intrepidity at the risk of his life above and beyond the call of duty while serving as an assistant team leader with Company E, in connection with combat operations against an armed enemy. While conducting a patrol during the early morning hours L/Cpl. Anderson's reconnaissance team came under a heavy volume of automatic weapons and machine-gun fire from a numerically's superior and well concealed enemy force. Although painfully wounded in both legs and knocked to the ground during the initial moments of the fierce fire fight, L/Cpl. Anderson assumed a prone position and continued to deliver intense suppressive fire in an attempt to repulse the attackers. Moments later he was wounded a second time by an enemy soldier who had approached to within eight feet of the team's position. Undaunted, he continued to pour a relentless stream of fire at the assaulting unit, even while a companion was treating his leg wounds. Observing an enemy grenade land between himself and the other marine, L/Cpl. Anderson immediately rolled over and covered the lethal weapon with his body, absorbing the full effects of the detonation. By his indomitable courage, inspiring initiative, and selfless devotion to duty, L/Cpl. Anderson was instrumental in saving several marines from serious injury or possible death. His actions were in keeping with the highest traditions of the Marine Corps and of the U.S. Naval Service. He gallantly gave his life in the service of his country.

†**JIMENEZ, JOSE FRANCISCO**
Rank and Organization: Lance Corporal, U.S. Marine Corps, Company K, 3d Battalion, 7th Marines, 1st Marine Division.
Born: March 20, 1946, Mexico City, Mexico
Entered Service At: Phoenix, Arizona
Place and Date: Quang Nam Province, Republic of Vietnam, August 28, 1969
Citation: For conspicuous gallantry and intrepidity at the risk of his life above and beyond the call of duty while serving as a fire team leader with Company K, in operation against the enemy. L/Cpl. Jimenez' unit came under heavy attack by North Vietnamese soldiers concealed in well camouflaged emplacements. L/Cpl. Jimenez reacted by seizing the initiative and plunging forward toward the enemy positions. He personally destroyed several enemy personnel and silenced an antiaircraft weapon. Shouting encouragement to his companions, L/Cpl. Jimenez continued his aggressive forward movement. He slowly maneuvered to within 10 feet of hostile soldiers who were firing automatic weapons from a trench and, in the face of vicious enemy fire, destroyed the position. Although he was by now the target of concentrated fire from hostile gunners intent upon halting his assault, L/Cpl. Jimenez continued to press forward. As he moved to attack another enemy soldier, he was mortally wounded. L/Cpl. Jimenez' indomitable courage, aggressive fighting spirit and unfaltering devotion to duty upheld the highest traditions of the Marine Corps and of the U.S. Naval Service.

Note: The following is a newspaper account of the battle for which L/Cpl. Jimenez was awarded the Medal of Honor:

Casualties On Both Sides In Vietnam Drop In Week

SAIGON, South Vietnam, Fri. Aug. 29 (AP) - Casualties for the United States, South Vietnam and the enemy dropped last week as enemy-initiated attacks subsided, according to the United States command.

United States headquarters said that 190 Americans had been killed and 1,367 wounded, compared with 244 killed and 1,409

wounded the week before. That week saw a surge of enemy infantry and rocket attacks.

Sharp fighting erupted again yesterday in the area south of
Danang where United States forces have clashed repeatedly with
strong North Vietnamese forces in the last two weeks.

The heaviest action reported early today involved elements
of the Seventh Marine Regiment, 31 miles south of Danang. Eighteen enemy soldiers were reported killed. Marine losses were put
at 13 dead and 32 wounded.

In combat action, the allies reported 6 clashes and 29 enemy
shellings of towns and bases Wednesday night and early yesterday.

STOCKDALE, JAMES B.

Rank and Organization: Rear Admiral (then Captain), U.S. Navy.
Born: December 23, 1923, Abingdon, Illinois
Entered Service At: Abingdon, Illinois
Place and Date: Hoa Lo Prison, Hanoi, North Vietnam, September 4, 1969
Citation: For conspicuous gallantry and intrepidity at the risk of his life above and beyond the call of duty while senior naval officer in the Prisoner of War camps of North Vietnam. Recognized by his captors as the leader in the Prisoners' of War resistance to interrogation and in their refusal to participate in propaganda exploitation, Rear Adm. Stockdale was singled out for interrogation and attendant torture after he was detected in a covert communications attempt. Sensing the start of another purge, and aware that his earlier efforts at self-disfiguration to dissuade his captors from exploiting him for propaganda purposes had resulted in cruel and agonizing punishment, Rear Adm. Stockdale resolved to make himself a symbol of resistance regardless of personal sacrifice. He deliberately inflicted a near-mortal wound to his person in order to convince his captors of his willingness to give up his life rather than capitulate. He was subsequently discovered and revived by the North Vietnamese who, convinced of his indomitable spirit, abated in their employment of excessive harassment and torture toward all of the Prisoners of War. By his heroic action, at great peril to himself, he earned the everlasting gratitude of his fellow prisoners and of his country. Rear Adm. Stockdale's valiant leadership and extraordinary courage in a hostile environment sustain and enhance the finest traditions of the U.S. Naval Service.

†SKIDGEL, DONALD SIDNEY

Rank and Organization: Sergeant, U.S. Army, Troop D, 1st Squadron, 9th Cavalry, 1st Cavalry Division.

Born: October 13, 1948, Caribou, Maine

Entered Service At: Bangor, Maine

Place and Date: Near Song Be, Republic of Vietnam, September 14, 1969

Citation: For conspicuous gallantry and intrepidity in action at the risk of his life above and beyond the call of duty. Sgt. Skidgel distinguished himself while serving as a reconnaissance section leader in Troop D. On a road near Song Be in Binh Long Province, Sgt. Skidgel and his section with other elements of his troop were acting as a convoy security and screening force when contact occurred with an estimated enemy battalion concealed in tall grass and in bunkers bordering the road. Sgt. Skidgel maneuvered off the road and began placing effective machine-gun fire on the enemy automatic weapons and rocket propelled grenade positions. After silencing at least one position, he ran with his machine-gun across 60 meters of bullet swept ground to another location from which he continued to rake the enemy positions. Running low on ammunition, he returned to his vehicle over the same terrain. Moments later he was alerted that the command element was receiving intense automatic weapons, rocket propelled grenade and mortar fire. Although he knew the road was saturated with enemy fire, Sgt. Skidgel calmly mounted his vehicle and with his driver advanced toward the command group in an effort to draw the enemy fire onto himself. Despite the hostile fire concentrated on him, he succeeded in silencing several enemy positions with his machine-gun. Moments later Sgt. Skidgel was knocked down onto the rear fender by the explosion of an enemy rocket propelled grenade. Ignoring his extremely painful wounds, he staggered back to his feet and placed effective fire on several other enemy positions until he was mortally wounded by hostile small arms fire. His selfless actions enabled the command group to withdraw to a better position without casualties and inspired the rest of his fellow soldiers to gain fire superiority and defeat the enemy. Sgt. Skidgel's gallantry at the cost of his life were in keeping with the highest traditions of the military service and reflect great credit upon himself, his unit, and the U.S. Army.

NOVOSEL, MICHAEL J.
Rank and Organization: Chief Warrant Officer, U.S. Army, 82d Medical Detachment, 45th Medical Company, 68th Medical Group.
Born: September 3, 1922, Etna, Pennsylvania
Entered Service At: Kenner, Louisiana
Place and Date: Kien Tuong Province, Republic of Vietnam, October 2, 1969
Citation: For conspicuous gallantry and intrepidity in action at the risk of his life above and beyond the call of duty. CWO Novosel, 82d Medical Detachment, distinguished himself while serving as commander of a medical evacuation helicopter. he unhesitatingly maneuvered his helicopter into a heavily fortified and defended enemy training area where a group of wounded Vietnamese soldiers were pinned down by a large enemy force. Flying without gunship or other cover and exposed to intense machine-gun fire, CWO Novosel was able to locate and rescue a wounded soldier. Since all communications with the beleaguered troops had been lost, he repeatedly circled the battle area, flying a low level under continuous heavy fire, to attract the attention of the scattered friendly troops. This display of courage visibly raised their morale, as they recognized this as a signal to assemble for evacuation. On six occasions he and his crew were forced out of the battle area by the intense enemy fire, only to circle and return from another direction to land and extract additional troops. Near the end of the mission, a wounded soldier was spotted close to an enemy bunker. Fully realizing that he would attract a hail of enemy fire, CWO Novosel nevertheless attempted the extraction by hovering the helicopter backward. As the man was pulled on aboard, enemy automatic weapons opened fire at close range, damaged the aircraft and wounded CWO Novosel. he momentarily lost control of the aircraft, but quickly recovered and departed under the withering enemy fire. In all, 15 extremely hazardous extractions were performed in order to remove wounded personnel. As a direct result of his selfless conduct, the lives of 29 soldiers were saved. The extraordinary heroism displayed by CWO Novosel was an inspiration to his comrades in arms and reflect great credit on him, his unit, and the U.S. Army.

†**DIAS, RALPH E.**

Rank and Organization: Private First Class, U.S. Marine Corps, 3d Platoon, Company D, 1st Battalion, 7th Marines, 1st Marine Division (Rein) FMF.

Born: July 15, 1950, Shelocta, Indiana County, Pennsylvania

Entered Service At: Pittsburgh, Pennsylvania

Place and Date: Que Son Mountains, Republic of Vietnam, November 12, 1969

Citation: As a member of a reaction force which was pinned down by enemy fire while assisting a platoon in the same circumstance, Pfc. Dias, observing that both units were sustaining casualties, initiated an aggressive assault against an enemy machine-gun bunker which was the principal source of hostile fire. Severely wounded by enemy snipers while charging across the open area, he pulled himself to the shelter of a nearby rock. Braving enemy fire for a second time, Pfc. Dias was again wounded. Unable to walk, he crawled 15 meters to the protection of a rock located near his objective and, repeatedly exposing himself to intense hostile fire, unsuccessfully threw several hand grenades at the machine-gun emplacement. Still determined to destroy the emplacement, Pfc. Dias again moved into the open and was wounded a third time by sniper fire. As he threw a last grenade which destroyed the enemy position, he was mortally wounded by another enemy round. Pfc. Dias' indomitable courage, dynamic initiative, and selfless devotion to duty upheld the highest traditions of the Marine Corps and the U.S. Naval Service. He gallantly gave his life in the service to his country.

†PRUDEN, ROBERT J.

Rank and Organization: Staff Sergeant, U.S. Army, 75th Infantry, Americal Division.

Born: September 9, 1949, St. Paul, Minnesota

Entered Service At: Minneapolis, Minnesota

Place and Date: Quang Ngai Province, Republic of Vietnam, November 29, 1969

Citation: For conspicuous gallantry and intrepidity in action at the risk of his life above and beyond the call of duty. S/Sgt. Pruden, Company G, distinguished himself while serving as a reconnaissance team leader during an ambush mission. The six man team was inserted by helicopter into enemy controlled territory to establish an ambush position and to obtain information concerning enemy movements. As the team moved into the preplanned area, S/Sgt. Pruden deployed his men into two groups on the opposite sides of a well used trail. As the groups were establishing their defensive positions, one member of the team was trapped in the open by the heavy fire from an enemy squad. Realizing that the ambush position had been compromised, S/Sgt. Pruden directed his team to open fire on the enemy force. Immediately, the team came under heavy fire from a second enemy element. S/Sgt. Pruden, with full knowledge of the extreme danger involved, left his concealed position and, firing as he ran, advanced toward the enemy to draw the hostile fire. He was seriously wounded twice but continued his attack until he fell for a third time, in front of the enemy positions. S/Sgt. Pruden's actions resulted in several enemy casualties and withdrawal of the remaining enemy force. Although grievously wounded, he directed his men into defensive positions and called for evacuation helicopters, which safely withdrew the members of the team. S/Sgt. Pruden's outstanding courage, selfless concern for the welfare of his men, and intrepidity in action at the cost of his life were in keeping with the highest traditions of the military service and reflect great credit upon himself, his unit, and the U.S. Army.

†LEISY, ROBERT RONALD

Rank and Organization: Second Lieutenant, U.S. Army, Infantry, Company B, 1st Battalion, 8th Cavalry, 1st Cavalry Division.
Born: March 1, 1945, Stockton, California
Entered Service At: Seattle, Washington
Place and Date: Phuoc Long Province, Republic of Vietnam, December 2, 1969
Citation: For conspicuous gallantry and intrepidity in action at the risk of his life above and beyond the call of duty. Second Lt. Leisy, Infantry, Company B, distinguished himself while serving as platoon leader during a reconnaissance mission. One of his patrols became heavily engaged by fire from a numerically superior enemy force located in a well-entrenched bunker complex. As 2d. Lt. Leisy deployed the remainder of his platoon to rescue the beleaguered patrol, the platoon also came under intense enemy fire from the front and both flanks. In complete disregard for his safety, 2d Lt. Leisy moved from position to position deploying his men to effectively engage the enemy. Accompanied by his radio operator he moved to the front and spotted an enemy sniper in a tree in the act of firing a rocket propelled grenade at them. Realizing there was neither time to escape the grenade nor shout a warning, 2d Lt. Leisy unhesitatingly, and with full knowledge of the consequences, shielded the radio operator with his body and absorbed the full impact of the explosion. This valorous act saved the life of the radio operator and protected other men of his platoon who were nearby from serious injury. Despite his mortal wounds, 2d Lt. Leisy calmly and confidently continued to direct the platoon's fire. When medical aid arrived, 2d Lt. Leisy valiantly refused attention until the other seriously wounded were treated. His display of extraordinary courage and exemplary devotion to duty provided the inspiration and leadership that enabled his platoon to successfully withdraw without further casualties. Second Lt. Leisy's gallantry at the cost of his life are in keeping with the highest traditions of the military service and reflect great credit on him, his unit, and the U.S. Army.

CHAPTER 7

1970

(† - Indicates Posthumous Award)

Note: The following newspaper article concerning Vietnam appeared on page 7 of *The New York Times* on January 1, 1970:

Agnew Arrives In Vietnam For A One-Day Visit

SAIGON, South Vietnam, Thursday, Jan. 1 - Vice President Agnew flew to Saigon unannounced this morning for a one-day visit to the nation whose lengthy war stimulated the Nixon doctrine of Asian self-reliance.

Mr. Agnew interrupted, as expected, the official schedule of his 23-day diplomatic mission to the 10 Asian and Pacific nations to meet with the South Vietnamese President, Nguyen Van Thieu, and bring New Year's greetings to American troops near Saigon.

The Vice President arrived at Tonsonhut Airport just before noon after a two hour flight from Manila, the first Asian stop on his tour.

His arrival was during an official cease fire. Mr. Agnew was scheduled to leave tomorrow for Taiwan.

The Vice President's helicopter touched down on the lawn of the presidential palace in Saigon a few minutes after noon, Saigon time. With him were the United States Ambassador, Ellsworth Bunker, and the Deputy Ambassador, Samuel Berger, and Gen. William B. Rosson, second in command of American forces here.

Mr. Agnew was greeted by Vice President Nguyen Cao Ky, who led him up the palace steps to a podium where they listened to their countries' national anthems. Armed guards stood on the roof of the palace.

After a ceremonial inspection of the palace honor guard, Vice President Agnew was led inside the palace to meet President Nguyen Van Thieu.

Explains Nixon Doctrine

Mr. Agnew's trip to Asia, which he interrupted for the stop in Saigon, is to explain to United States allies the philosophy behind President Nixon's Asian doctrine.

The nature of Mr. Agnew's message from President nixon emerged yesterday during a private meeting with President Ferdinand E. Marcos that the United States intended to remain a power in the Pacific.

MILLER, FRANKLIN D.

Rank and Organization: Staff Sergeant, U.S. Army, 5th Special Forces Group, 1st Special Forces.
Born: January 27, 1945, Elizabeth City, North Carolina
Entered Service At: Albuquerque, New Mexico
Place and Date: Kontum Province, Republic of Vietnam, January 5, 1970
Citation: For conspicuous gallantry and intrepidity in action at the risk of his life above and beyond the call of duty. S/Sgt. Miller, 5th Special Forces Group, distinguished himself while serving as team leader of an American-Vietnamese long range reconnaissance patrol operating deep within enemy controlled territory. leaving the helicopter insertion point, the patrol moved forward on its mission. Suddenly, one of the team members tripped a hostile boobytrap which wounded four soldiers. S/Sgt. Miller, knowing that the explosion would alert the enemy, quickly administered first aid to the wounded and directed the team into positions across a small stream bed at the base of a steep hill. Within a few minutes, S/Sgt. Miller saw the lead element of what he estimated to be a platoon size enemy force moving toward his location. Concerned for the safety of his men, he directed the small team to move up the hill to a more secure position. He remained alone, separated from the patrol, to meet the attack. S/Sgt. Miller single-handedly repulsed two determined attacks by the numerically superior enemy force and caused them to withdraw in disorder. He rejoined his team, established contact with a forward air controller and arranged the evacuation of his patrol. However, the only suitable extraction location in the heavy jungle was a bomb crater some 150 meters from the team location. S/Sgt. Miller reconnoitered the route to the crater and led his men through the enemy controlled jungle to the extraction site. As the evacuation helicopter hovered over the crater to pick up the patrol, the enemy launched a savage automatic weapon and rocket propelled grenade attack against the beleaguered team, driving off the rescue helicopter. S/Sgt. Miller led the team in a valiant defense which drove back the enemy in its attempt to overrun the small patrol. Although seriously wounded and with every man in his patrol a casualty, S/Sgt. Miller moved forward to again single-handedly meet the hostile attackers. From his forward exposed position, S/Sgt. Miller gallantly repelled two attacks

by the enemy before a friendly relief force reached the patrol location. S/Sgt. Miller's gallantry, intrepidity in action, and selfless devotion to the welfare of his comrades are in keeping with the highest traditions of the military service and reflect great credit on him, his unit, and the U.S. Army.

†**PETERSEN, DANNY J.**
Rank and Organization: Specialist Fourth Class, U.S. Army, Company B, 4th Battalion, 23d Infantry, 25th Infantry Division.
Born: March 11, 1949, Horton, Kansas
Entered Service At: Kansas City, Missouri
Place and Date: Tay Ninh Province, Republic of Vietnam, January 9, 1970
Citation: Sp4c. Petersen distinguished himself while serving as an armored personnel carrier commander with Company B during a combat operation against a North Vietnamese Army Force estimated to be of battalion size. During the initial contact with the enemy, an armored personnel carrier was disabled and the crewmen were pinned down by the heavy onslaught of enemy small arms, automatic weapons and rocket propelled grenade fire. Sp4c. Petersen immediately maneuvered his armored personnel carrier to a position between the disabled vehicle and the enemy. He placed suppressive fire on the enemy's well fortified position, thereby enabling the crewmembers of the disabled personnel carrier to repair their vehicle. He then maneuvered his vehicle, while still under heavy hostile fire to within 10 feet of the enemy's defensive emplacement. After a period of intense fighting, his vehicle received a direct hit and the driver was wounded. With extraordinary courage and selfless disregard for his own safety, Sp4c. Petersen carried his wounded comrade 45 meters across the bullet swept field to a secure area. he then voluntarily returned to his disabled armored personnel carrier to provide covering fire for both the other vehicles and the dismounted personnel of his platoon as they withdrew. Despite heavy fire from three sides, he remained with his disabled vehicle, alone and completely exposed. Sp4c. Petersen was standing on top of his vehicle, firing his weapon, when he was mortally wounded. His heroic and selfless actions prevented further loss of life in his platoon. Sp4c. Petersen's conspicuous gallantry and extraordinary heroism are in the highest traditions of the service and reflect great credit on him, his unit, and the U.S. Army.

Note: The following is a newspaper account of the battle for which Sp4c. Petersen was awarded the Medal of Honor.

U.S. Reports 109 Of Foe Killed In Battle

SAIGON, South Vietnam, Jan. 9 - American infantrymen supported by tanks, artillery and air strikes today reported having killed 109 North Vietnamese and Viet Cong soldiers in two days of fighting on the slopes of a mountain overlooking the sprawling American base at Tay Ninh.

The United States command said Two Americans had been killed and 10 wounded, among them a helicopter crewman injured when his craft was shot down.

The enemy soldiers are reported to have been dug in for months in the caves of the 3,235-Foot mountain, which rises sharply from a plain 55 miles northeast of Saigon. Its name is Nuibaden, but to the Americans it is known as Black Virgin Mountain.

The Americans control the plain around the Tay Ninh base of the 25th Infantry Division and the First Cavalry Division (Airmobile). The Americans also hold the top of the mountain, which serves as a communications relay center. But the enemy forces have controlled the slopes and have used the position to shell the Tay Ninh base periodically.

Enemy Opens Fire

Yesterday three companies of soldiers from the First Brigade of the 25th Infantry Division backed up by tanks were sweeping an area on the north face of the mountain when, the United States command said, enemy forces opened fire with small-arms, automatic weapons and rocket grenades.

The American tanks and heavy machine guns fired back, and helicopter gunships and F-4 and F-104 jets were called in to bomb and strafe the enemy positions. The fighting continued all day yesterday, the United States command reported. After the enemy withdrew at dark, the bodies of 62 enemy soldiers in the mixed force of Viet Cong and North Vietnamese were reported to have been found. The fighting resumed today, according to reports from the field, and 47 more enemy soldiers were reported killed.

CLAUSEN, RAYMOND M.

Rank and Organization: Private First Class, U.S. Marine Corps, Marine Medium Helicopter Squadron 263, Marine Aircraft Group 16, 1st Marine Aircraft Wing.

Born: October 14, 1947, New Orleans, Louisiana

Entered Service At: New Orleans, Louisiana

Place and Date: Republic of Vietnam, January 31, 1970

Citation: For conspicuous gallantry and intrepidity at the risk of his life above and beyond the call of duty while serving with Marine Medium Helicopter Squadron 263 during operations against enemy forces. Participating in a helicopter rescue mission to extract elements of a platoon which had inadvertently entered a minefield while attacking enemy positions, Pfc. Clausen skillfully guided the helicopter pilot to a landing in an area cleared by one of several mine explosions. With 11 marines wounded, one dead, and the remaining eight marines holding their positions for fear of detonating other mines, Pfc. Clausen quickly leaped from the helicopter and, in the face of enemy fire, moved across the extremely hazardous mine laden area to assist in carrying casualties to the waiting helicopter and in placing them aboard. Despite the ever-present threat of further mine explosions, he continued his valiant efforts, leaving the comparatively safe area of the helicopter on six separate occasions to carry out his rescue efforts. On one occasion while he was carrying one of the wounded, another mine detonated, killing a corpsman and wounding three other men. Only when he was certain that all marines were safely aboard did he signal the pilot to lift the helicopter. By the courageous, determined and inspiring efforts in the face of the utmost danger, Pfc. Clausen upheld the highest traditions of the Marine Corps and of the U.S. Naval Service.

PENRY, RICHARD A.

Rank and Organization: Sergeant, U.S. Army, Company C, 4th Battalion, 12th Infantry, 199th Infantry Brigade.
Born: November 18, 1948, Petaluma, California
Entered Service At: Oakland, California
Place and Date: Binh Tuy Province, Republic of Vietnam, January 31, 1970
Citation: For conspicuous gallantry and intrepidity in action at the risk of his life above and beyond the call of duty. Sgt. Penry, Company C, distinguished himself while serving as a rifleman during a night ambush mission. As the platoon was preparing the ambush position, it suddenly came under an intense enemy attack from mortar, rocket, and automatic weapons fire which seriously wounded the company commander and most of the platoon members, leaving small isolated groups of wounded men throughout the area. Sgt. Penry, seeing the extreme seriousness of the situation, worked his way through the deadly enemy fire to the company command post where he administered first aid to the wounded company commander and other personnel. He then moved the command post to a position which provided greater protection and visual communication and control of other platoon elements. Realizing the company radio was damaged and recognizing the urgent necessity to reestablish communications with the battalion headquarters, he ran outside the defensive perimeter through a fusillade of hostile fire to retrieve a radio. Finding it inoperable, Sgt. Penry returned through heavy fire to retrieve two more radios. Turning his attention to the defense of the area, he crawled to the edge of the perimeter, retrieved needed ammunition and weapons and resupplied the wounded men. During a determined assault by over 30 enemy soldiers, Sgt. Penry occupied the most vulnerable forward position placing heavy, accurate fire on the attacking enemy and exposing himself several times to throw hand grenades into the advancing enemy troops. he succeeded virtually single-handedly in stopping the attack. learning that none of the radios were operable, Sgt. Penry again crawled outside the defensive perimeter, retrieved a fourth radio and established communications with higher headquarters. Sgt. Penry then continued to administer first aid to the wounded and repositioned them to better repel further enemy attacks. Despite continuous and deadly sniper fire, he again left the defen-

sive perimeter, moved to within a few feet of enemy positions, located five isolated wounded soldiers, and led them to safety. When evacuation helicopters approached, Sgt. Penry voluntarily left the perimeter, set up a guiding beacon, established the priorities for evacuation and successfully carried 18 wounded men to the extraction site. After all wounded personnel had been evacuated, Sgt. Penry joined another platoon and assisted in the pursuit of the enemy. Sgt. Penry's extraordinary heroism at the risk of his own life are in keeping with the highest traditions of the military service and reflect great credit on him, his unit, and the U.S. Army.

†STEINDAM, RUSSELL A.

Rank and Organization: First Lieutenant, U.S. Army, Troop B, 3d Squadron, 4th Cavalry, 25th Infantry Division.
Born: August 27, 1946, Austin, Texas
Entered Service At: Austin, Texas
Place and Date: Tay Ninh Province, Republic of Vietnam, February 1, 1970
Citation: For conspicuous gallantry and intrepidity in action at the risk of his life above and beyond the call of duty. First Lt. Steindam, Troop B, while serving as a platoon leader, led members of his platoon on a night ambush operation. On the way to the ambush site, suspected enemy movement was detected on one flank and the platoon's temporary position was subjected to intense small arms and automatic weapons fire as well as a fusillade of hand and rocket propelled grenades. After the initial barrage, 1st. Lt. Steindam ordered fire placed on the enemy position and the wounded men to be moved to a shallow bomb crater. As he directed the return fire against the enemy from his exposed position, a fragmentation grenade was thrown into the site occupied by his command group. Instantly realizing the extreme gravity of the situation, 1st Lt. Steindam shouted a warning to alert his fellow soldiers in the immediate vicinity. Then, unhesitatingly and with complete disregard for his safety, 1st. Lt. Steindam deliberately threw himself on the grenade, absorbing the full and fatal force of the explosion as it detonated. By his gallant action and self sacrifice, he was able to save the lives of the nearby members of his command group. The extraordinary courage and selflessness displayed by 1st Lt. Steindam were an inspiration to his comrades and are in the highest traditions of the U.S. Army.

BACA, JOHN P.

Rank and Organization: Specialist Fourth Class, U.S. Army, Company D, 1st Battalion, 12th Cavalry, 1st Cavalry Division.
Born: January 10, 1949, Providence, Rhode Island
Entered Service At: Fort Ord, California
Place and Date: Phuoc Long Province, Republic of Vietnam, February 10, 1970
Citation: For conspicuous gallantry and intrepidity in action at the risk of his life above and beyond the call of duty. Sp4c. Baca, Company D, distinguished himself while serving on a recoilless rifle team during a night ambush mission. A platoon from his company was sent to investigate the detonation of an automatic ambush device forward of his unit's main position and soon came under intense enemy fire from concealed positions along the trail. Hearing the heavy firing from the platoon position and realizing that his recoilless rifle team could assist the members of the besieged patrol, Sp4c. Baca led his team through the hail of enemy fire to a firing position within the patrol's defensive perimeter. As they prepared to engage the enemy, a fragmentation grenade was thrown into the midst of the patrol. Fully aware of the danger to his comrades, Sp4c. Baca unhesitatingly, and with complete disregard for his own safety, covered the grenade with his steel helmet and fell on it as the grenade exploded, thereby absorbing the lethal fragments and concussion with his body. His gallant action and total disregard for his personal well-being directly saved eight men from certain serious injury or death. The extraordinary courage and selflessness displayed by Sp4c. Baca, at the risk of his life, are in the highest traditions of the military service and reflect great credit on him, his unit, and the U.S. Army.

KELLOGG, ALLAN JAY, JR.

Rank and Organization: Gunnery Sergeant, U.S. Marine Corps (then S/Sgt.), Company G, 2d Battalion, 5th Marines, 1st Marine Division.

Born: October 1, 1943, Bethel, Connecticut

Entered Service At: Bridgeport, Connecticut

Place and Date: Quang Nam Province, Republic of Vietnam, March 11, 1970

Citation: For conspicuous gallantry and intrepidity at the risk of his life above and beyond the call of duty while serving as a platoon sergeant with Company G, in connection with combat operations against the enemy on the night of March 11, 1970. Under the leadership of G/Sgt. Kellogg, a small unit from Company G was evacuating a fallen comrade when the unit came under a heavy volume of small arms and automatic weapons fire from a numerically superior enemy force occupying well concealed emplacements in the surrounding jungle. During the ensuing fierce engagement, an enemy soldier managed to maneuver through the dense foliage to a position near the marines, and hurled a hand grenade into their midst which glanced off the chest of G/Sgt. Kellogg. Quick to act, he forced the grenade into the mud in which he was standing, threw himself over the lethal weapon, and absorbed the full effects of its detonation with his body, thereby preventing serious injury or possible death to several of his fellow marines. Although suffering multiple injuries to his chest and his right shoulder and arm, G/Sgt. Kellogg resolutely continued to direct the efforts of his men until all were able to maneuver to the relative safety of the company perimeter. By his heroic and decisive action in risking his life to save the lives of his comrades, G/Sgt. Kellogg reflected the highest credit upon himself and upheld the finest traditions of the marine Corps and the U.S. Naval Service.

†STOUT, MITCHELL W.

Rank and Organization: Sergeant, U.S. Army, Battery C, 1st Battalion, 44th Artillery.

Born: February 24, 1950, Knoxville, Tennessee

Entered Service At: Raleigh, North Carolina

Place and Date: Khe Gio Bridge, Republic of Vietnam, March 12, 1970

Citation: Sgt. Stout distinguished himself during an attack by a North Vietnamese Army sapper company on his unit's firing position at Khe Gio Bridge. Sgt. Stout was in a bunker with members of a searchlight crew when the position came under heavy enemy mortar fire and ground attack. When the intensity of the mortar attack subsided, an enemy grenade was thrown into the bunker. Displaying great courage, Sgt. Stout ran to the grenade, picked it up, and started out of the bunker. As he reached the door, the grenade exploded. By holding the grenade close to his body and shielding its blast, he protected his fellow soldiers in the bunker from further injury or death. Sgt. Stout's conspicuous gallantry and intrepidity in action, at the cost of his own life, are in keeping with the highest traditions of the military service and reflect great credit upon him, his unit and the U.S. Army.

BEIKIRCH, GARY B.

Rank and Organization: Sergeant, U.S. Army, Company B, 5th Special Forces Group, 1st Special Forces.

Born: August 19, 1947, Rochester, New York

Entered Service At: Buffalo, New York

Place and Date: Kontum Province, Republic of Vietnam, April 1, 1970

Citation: For conspicuous gallantry and intrepidity in action at the risk of his life above and beyond the call of duty. Sgt. Beikirch, medical aidman, Detachment B-24, Company B, distinguished himself during the defense of Camp Dak Seang. The allied defenders suffered a number of casualties as a result of an intense, devastating attack launched by the enemy from well-concealed positions surrounding the camp. Sgt. Beikirch, with complete disregard for his personal safety, moved unhesitatingly through the withering enemy fire to his fallen comrades, applied first aid to their wounds and assisted them to the medical aid station. When informed that a seriously injured American officer was lying in an exposed position, Sgt. Beikirch ran immediately through the hail of fire. Although he was wounded seriously by fragments from an exploding enemy mortar shell, Sgt. Beikirch carried the officer to a medical aid station. Ignoring his own serious injuries, Sgt. Beikirch left the relative safety of the medical bunker to search for and evacuate other men who had been injured. He was again wounded as he dragged a critically injured Vietnamese soldier to the medical bunker while simultaneously applying mouth-to-mouth resuscitation to sustain his life. Sgt. Beikirch again refused treatment and continued his search for other casualties until he collapsed. Only then did he permit himself to be treated. Sgt. Beikirch's complete devotion to the welfare of his comrades, at the risk of his life are in keeping with the highest traditions of the military service and reflect great credit on him, his unit, and the U.S. Army.

LEMON, PETER C.

Rank and Organization: Sergeant, U.S. Army, Company E, 2d Battalion, 8th Cavalry, 1st Cavalry Division.
Born: June 5, 1950, Toronto, Canada
Entered Service At: Tawas City, Michigan
Place and Date: Tay Ninh Province, Republic of Vietnam, April 1, 1970
Citation: For conspicuous gallantry and intrepidity in action at the risk of his life above and beyond the call of duty. Sgt. Lemon (then Sp4c.), Company E, distinguished himself while serving as an assistant machine gunner during the defense of Fire Support Base Illingsworth. When the base came under heavy enemy attack, Sgt. Lemon engaged a numerically superior enemy with machine-gun and rifle fire from his defensive position until both weapons malfunctioned. He then used hand grenades to fend off the intensified enemy attack launched in his direction. After eliminating all but one of the enemy soldiers in the immediate vicinity, he pursued and disposed of the remaining soldier in hand-to-hand combat. Despite fragment wounds from an exploding grenade, Sgt. Lemon regained his position, carried a more seriously wounded comrade to an aid station, and, as he returned, was wounded a second time by enemy fire. Disregarding his personal injuries, he moved to his position through a hail of small arms and grenade fire. Sgt. Lemon immediately realized that the defensive sector was in danger of being overrun by the enemy and unhesitatingly assaulted the enemy soldiers by throwing hand grenades and engaging in hand-to-hand combat. He was wounded yet a third time, but his determined efforts successfully drove the enemy from the position. Securing an operable machine-gun Sgt. Lemon stood atop an embankment fully exposed to enemy fire, and placed effective fire upon the enemy until he collapsed from his multiple wounds and exhaustion. After regaining consciousness at the aid station, he refused medical evacuation until his more seriously wounded comrades had been evacuated. Sgt. Lemon's gallantry and extraordinary heroism, are in keeping with the highest traditions of the military service and reflect great credit on him, his unit, and the U.S. Army.

Note: The following is a newspaper account of the battle for which Sgt. Lemon was awarded the Medal of Honor:

Enemy In Vietnam Opens Wide Drive, Ending Long Lull

SAIGON, South Vietnam, April 1 - After six months of relative quiet, the Vietnam War flared up again today with a coordinated series of enemy shelling and ground attacks against American and South Vietnamese targets throughout the country.

A total of 115 shellings and 13 ground assaults were reported by the United States command.

At least 38 Americans were killed, according to official reports. Military spokesmen said they expected that figure to rise as additional reports were received from the field.

[Brig. General William R. Bond, commander of the 199th Light Infantry Brigade, was killed by enemy small-arms fire while inspecting a patrol that had been in contact with Viet Cong forces, The Associated Press reported. He was the fifth American general killed in the war.]

Half the American casualties occurred during a bitter, four-hour enemy attack on a forward artillery base near the Cambodian border.

240 Enemy Killed

A total of 65 South Vietnamese and about 240 enemy soldiers were reported killed, wile 184 Americans and 176 South Vietnamese were listed as wounded in the initial reports.

So far as the allies were concerned, it was the costliest night of fighting in Vietnam in eight months. On August 12, 1969, about 50 Americans and a dozen South Vietnamese died in the last comparable country-wide series of shellings.

"We have been expecting this sort of thing, based on the intelligence that has been coming in," a senior American officer said. "This seems to be the start of the spring-summer campaign that has been mentioned repeatedly by prisoners and in documents we've picked up."

Attacks Began At 1 A.M.

The attacks today began about 1 A.M. when enemy gunners fired mortar shells and rockets into United States and South Vietnamese military installations from northernmost Quang Tri Province to the Mekong Delta.

Of the total of 115 shellings, 40 were against United States units or installations.

The heaviest ground fighting broke out about 2 A.M., when a newly established American artillery base named Illingsworth, about five miles from the Cambodian border in the northwest corner of Tay Ninh Province, came under attack by an estimated battalion of North Vietnamese troops.

The enemy rained more than 200 rounds of mortar and rocket grenades on the base before attacking its lightly defended perimeter in strength.

A soldier who visited the base late this afternoon reported that a group of North Vietnamese had burst the barbed wire surrounding the base and fought hand to hand with the American defenders.

LITTRELL, GARY LEE

Rank and Organization: Sergeant First Class, U.S. Army, Advisory Team 21, II Corps Advisory Group.
Born: October 26, 1944, Henderson, Kentucky
Entered Service At: Los Angeles, California
Place and Date: Kontum Province, Republic of Vietnam, April 4, to 8, 1970.
Citation: For conspicuous gallantry and intrepidity in action at the risk of his life above and beyond the call of duty. Sfc. Littrell, U.S. Military Assistance Command, Vietnam, Advisory Team 21, distinguished himself while serving as a Light Weapons Infantry Advisor with the 23d Battalion, 2d Ranger Group, Republic of Vietnam Army, near Dak Seang. After establishing a defensive perimeter on a hill on April 4, the battalion was subjected to an intense enemy mortar attack which killed the Vietnamese commander, one advisor, and seriously wounded all the advisors except Sfc. Littrell. During the ensuing four days, Sfc. Littrell exhibited near superhuman endurance as he single-handedly bolstered the besieged battalion. Repeatedly abandoning positions of relative safety, he directed artillery and air support by day and marked the unit's location by night, despite the heavy, concentrated enemy fire. His dauntless will instilled in the men of the 23d Battalion a deep desire to resist. Assault after assault was repulsed as he battalion responded to the extraordinary leadership and personal example exhibited by Sfc. Littrell as he continuously moved to those points most seriously threatened by the enemy, redistributed ammunition, strengthened faltering defenses, cared for the wounded and shouted encouragement to the Vietnamese in their own language. When the beleaguered battalion was finally ordered to withdraw, numerous ambushes were encountered. Sfc. Littrell repeatedly prevented widespread disorder by directing air strikes to within 50 meters of their position. Through his indomitable courage and complete disregard for his safety, he averted excessive loss of life and injury to the members of the battalion. The sustained extraordinary courage and selflessness displayed by Sfc. Littrell over an extended period of time were in keeping with the highest traditions of the military service and reflect great credit on him and the U.S. Army.

Note: The following is a newspaper account of the battle for which Sfc. Littrell was awarded the Medal of Honor:

After 6 Days of Intense Fighting; Foe's Upsurge Appears To Be Waning

SAIGON, South Vietnam, April 7 - The enemy's country-wide upsurge on the battlefield appeared to be waning today after six days of intense fighting.

The upsurge, characterized by official military spokesmen as a "high point" rather than as an offensive, is expected to bring the weekly American casualty figure-to be announced on Thursday-near the 200 mark, with South Vietnamese casualties reaching 500 or more.

The fighting has been the heaviest in seven months. In it some enemy units have shown that they are not as under-strength, undersupplied and demoralized as some allied commanders had described them as being.

However, military officials here say that the level of battle-field action is still much lower than it was during similar periods in the first half of last year.

The most concentrated fighting in the last seven days occurred along the Cambodian in the south and central parts of the country and along the edge of the mountains near the coastal lowlands in the five northern provinces.

The heaviest United States build-up was around a tiny outpost manned by a small team of U.S. Special Forces soldiers and several hundred montagnard mercenary at Dak Seang in northern Kontum Province, 10 miles from the Laotian border and 12 miles north of the Benhet Special Forces outpost, which was besieged last summer.

Several thousand North Vietnamese soldiers surrounded the camp and several anti-aircraft batteries harassed Air Force cargo planes attempting to fly in supplies. According to Air Force spokesmen, nearly every plane during the first three days of the airlift was struck by ground fire. Three planes were shot down, resulting in the death of nine crewmen, it was reported.

U.S. BC-25 bombers flew concentrated missions around the camp for several days, and several South Vietnamese ranger battalions and montagnard mercenary companies were air-lifted in to reinforce the camp. More than 2,000 enemy mortar shells were reported to have hit the camp in the last seven days.

South Vietnamese military spokesmen said today that more than 900 enemy soldiers had been killed around the camp since April 1. South Vietnamese casualties were put at nine killed and 18 wounded. No American casualties have been reported.

Most of the enemy casualties occurred yesterday when South Vietnamese rangers were reported to have killed 196 enemy soldiers in a day-long battle, and artillery men and pilots reported killing about 270 more. The bodies of 330 more enemy soldiers were reported to have been found today.

No new fighting was reported around the camp today.

†BUKER, BRIAN L.

Rank and Organization: Sergeant, U.S. Army, Detachment B-55, 5th Special Forces Group, 1st Special Forces.
Born: November 3, 1949, Benton, Maine
Entered Service At: Bangor, Maine
Place and Date: Chau Doc Province, Republic of Vietnam, April 5, 1970
Citation: For conspicuous gallantry and intrepidity in action at the risk of life above and beyond the call of duty. Sgt. Buker, Detachment B-55, distinguished himself while serving as a platoon advisor of a Vietnamese mobile strike force company during an offensive mission. Sgt. Buker personally led the platoon, cleared a strategically located well guarded pass, and established the first foothold at the top of what had been an impenetrable mountain fortress. When the platoon came under the intense fire from a determined enemy located in two heavily fortified bunkers, and realizing that withdrawal would result in heavy casualties, Sgt. Buker unhesitatingly, and with complete disregard for his personal safety, charged through the hail of enemy fire and destroyed the first bunker with hand grenades. While reorganizing his men for the attack on the second bunker, Sgt. Buker was seriously wounded. Despite his wounds and the deadly enemy fire, he crawled forward and destroyed the second bunker. Sgt. Buker refused medical attention and was reorganizing his men to continue the attack when he was mortally wounded. As a direct result of his heroic actions, many casualties were averted, and the assault of the enemy position was successful. Sgt. Buker's extraordinary heroism at the cost of his life are in the highest traditions of the military service and reflect great credit on him, his unit, and the U.S. Army.

†DE LA GARZA, EMILIO A., JR.

Rank and Organization: Lance Corporal, U.S. Marine Corps, Company E, 2d Battalion, 1st Marines, 1st Marine Division.
Born: June 23, 1949, East Chicago, Indiana
Entered Service At: Chicago, Illinois
Place and Date: Near Da Nang, Republic of Vietnam, April 11, 1970
Citation: For conspicuous gallantry and intrepidity at the risk of his life above and beyond the call of duty while serving as a machine gunner with Company E. Returning with his squad from a night ambush operation, L/Cpl. De La Garza joined his platoon commander and another marine in searching for two enemy soldiers who had been observed fleeing for cover toward a small pond. Moments later, he located one of the enemy soldiers hiding among the reeds and brush. As the three marines attempted to remove the resisting soldier from the pond, L/Cpl. De La Garza observed him pull the pin on a grenade. Shouting a warning, L/Cpl. De La Garza placed himself between the other two marines and the ensuing blast from the grenade, thereby saving the lives of his comrades at the sacrifice of his life. By his prompt and decisive action, and his great personal valor in the face of almost certain death, L/Cpl. De La Garza upheld and further enhanced the finest traditions of the Marine Corps and the U.S. Naval Service.

†HOWE, JAMES D.

Rank and Organization: Lance Corporal, U.S. Marine Corps, Company I, 3d Battalion, 7th Marines, 1st Marine Division.
Born: December 17, 1948, Six Mile, Pickens, South Carolina
Entered Service At: Fort Jackson, South Carolina
Place and Date: Republic of Vietnam, May 6, 1970
Citation: For conspicuous gallantry and intrepidity at the risk of his life above and beyond the call of duty while serving as a rifleman with Company I, during operations against enemy forces. In the early morning hours L/Cpl. Howe and two other marines were occupying a defensive position in a sandy beach area fronted by bamboo thickets. Enemy sappers suddenly launched a grenade attack against the position, utilizing the cover of darkness to carry out their assault. Following the initial explosions of the grenades, L/Cpl. Howe and his two comrades moved to a more advantageous position in order to return suppressive fire. When an enemy grenade landed in their midst, L/Cpl. Howe immediately shouted a warning and then threw himself upon the deadly missile, thereby protecting the lives of the fellow marines. His heroic and selfless action was in keeping with the finest traditions of the Marine Corps and of the U.S. Naval Service. He valiantly gave his life in the service of his country.

KAYS, KENNETH MICHAEL

Rank and Organization: Private First Class, U.S. Army, Headquarters and Headquarters Company, 1st Battalion, 506th Infantry, 101st Airborne Division.
Born: September 22, 1949, Mount Vernon, Illinois
Entered Service At: Fairfield, Illinois
Place and Date: Thua Thien Province, Republic of Vietnam, May 7, 1970
Citation: For conspicuous gallantry intrepidity in action at the risk of his life above and beyond the call of duty. Pfc. (then Pvt.) Kays distinguished himself while serving as a medical aidman with Company D, 1st Battalion, 101st Airborne Division near Fire Support Base Maureen. A heavily armed force of enemy sappers and infantrymen assaulted Company D's night defensive position, wounding and killing a number of its members. Disregarding the intense enemy fire and ground assault, Pfc. Kays began moving toward the perimeter to assist his fallen comrades. In doing so he became the target of concentrated enemy fire and explosive charges, one of which severed the lower portion of his left leg. After applying a tourniquet to his leg, Pfc. Kays moved to the fire swept perimeter, administered medical aid to one of the wounded, and helped move him to an area of relative safety. Despite his severe wound and excruciating pain, Pfc. Kays returned to the perimeter in search of other wounded men. He treated another wounded comrade, and, using his own body as a shield against enemy bullets and fragments, moved him to safety. Although weakened from a great loss of blood, Pfc. Kays resumed his heroic lifesaving efforts by moving beyond the company's perimeter into enemy held territory to treat a wounded American lying there. Only after his fellow wounded soldiers had been treated and evacuated did Pfc. Kays allow his own wounds to be treated. These courageous acts by Pfc. Kays resulted in the saving of numerous lives and inspired others in his company to repel the enemy. Pfc. Kays' heroism at the risk of his life are in keeping with the highest traditions of the service and reflect great credit on him, his unit, and the U.S. Army.

†KEITH, MIGUEL

Rank and Organization: Lance Corporal, U.S. Marine Corps, Combined Action Platoon 1-3-2, III Marine Amphibious Force.
Born: June 2, 1951, San Antonio, Texas
Entered Service At: Omaha, Nebraska
Place and Date: Quang Ngai Province, Republic of Vietnam, May 8, 1970
Citation: For conspicuous gallantry and intrepidity at the risk of his life above and beyond the call of duty while serving as a machine gunner with Combined Action Platoon 1-3-2. During the early morning L/Cpl. Keith was seriously wounded when his platoon was subjected to a heavy ground attack by a greatly outnumbering enemy force. Despite his painful wounds, he ran across the fire swept terrain to check the security of vital defensive positions and then, while completely exposed to view, proceeded to deliver a hail of devastating machine-gun fire against the enemy. Determined to stop five of the enemy soldiers approaching the command post, he rushed forward, firing as he advanced. He succeeded in disposing of three of the attackers and in dispersing the remaining two. At this point, a grenade detonated near L/Cpl. Keith, knocking him to the ground and inflicting further severe wounds. Fighting pain and weakness from loss of blood, he again braved the concentrated hostile fire to charge an estimated 25 enemy soldiers who were massing to attack. The vigor of his assault and his well placed fire eliminated four of the enemy soldiers while the remainder fled for cover. During this valiant effort, he was mortally wounded by an enemy soldier. By his courageous and inspiring performance in the face of almost overwhelming odds, L/Cpl. Keith contributed in large measure to the success of his platoon in routing a numerically superior enemy force, and upheld the finest traditions of the Marine Corps and of the U.S. Naval Service.

†WINDER, DAVID F.

Rank and Organization: Private First Class, U.S. Army, Headquarters and Headquarters Company, 3d Battalion, 1st Infantry, 11th Infantry Brigade, Americal Division.
Born: August 10, 1946, Edinboro, Pennsylvania
Entered Service At: Columbus, Ohio
Place and Date: Republic of Vietnam, May 13, 1970
Citation: Pfc. Winder distinguished himself while serving in the Republic of Vietnam as a senior medical aidman with Company A. After moving through freshly cut rice paddies in search of a suspected company size enemy force, the unit started a thorough search of the area. Suddenly they were engaged with intense automatic weapons and rocket propelled grenade fire by a well entrenched enemy force. Several friendly soldiers fell wounded in the initial contact and the unit was pinned down. Responding instantly to the cries of his wounded comrades, Pfc. Winder began maneuvering across approximately 100 meters of open, bullet swept terrain toward the nearest casualty. Unarmed and crawling most of the distance, he was wounded by enemy fire before reaching his comrades. Despite his wounds and with great effort, Pfc. Winder reached the first casualty and administered medica laid. As he continued to crawl across the open terrain toward a second wounded soldier he was forced to stop when wounded a second time. Aroused by the cries of an injured comrade for aid, Pfc. Winder's great determination and sense of duty impelled him to move forward once again, despite his wounds, in a courageous attempt to reach and assist the injured man. After struggling to within 10 meters of the man, Pfc. Winder was mortally wounded. His dedication and sacrifice inspired his unit to initiate an aggressive counterassault which led to the defeat of the enemy. Pfc. Winder's conspicuous gallantry and intrepidity in action at the cost of his life were in keeping with the highest traditions of the military service and reflect great credit on him, his unit and the U.S. Army.

ROCCO, LOUIS R.

Rank and Organization: Warrant Officer (then Sergeant First Class), U.S. Army, Advisory Team 162, U.S. Military Assistance Command.
Born: November 19, 1938, Albuquerque, New Mexico
Entered Service At: Los Angeles, California
Place and Date: Northeast of Katum, Republic of Vietnam, May 24, 1970
Citation: WO Rocco distinguished himself when he volunteered to accompany a medical evacuation team on an urgent mission to evacuate eight critically wounded Army of the Republic of Vietnam personnel. As the helicopter approached the landing zone, it became the target for intense enemy automatic weapons fire. Disregarding his own safety, WO Rocco identified and placed accurate suppressive fire on the enemy positions as the aircraft descended toward the landing zone. Sustaining major damage from the enemy fire, the aircraft was forced to crash land, causing WO Rocco to sustain a fractured wrist and hip and a severely bruised back. Ignoring his injuries, he extracted the survivors from the burning wreckage, sustaining burns to his own body. Despite intense enemy fire, WO Rocco carried each unconscious man across approximately 20 meters of exposed terrain to the Army of the Republic of Vietnam perimeter. On each trip, his severely burned hands and broken wrist caused excruciating pain, but the lives of the unconscious crash survivors were more important than his personal discomfort, and he continued his rescue efforts. Once inside the friendly position, WO Rocco helped administer first aid to his wounded comrades until his wounds and burns caused him to collapse and lose consciousness. His bravery under fire and intense devotion to duty were directly responsible for saving three of his fellow soldiers from certain death. His unparalleled bravery in the face of enemy fire, his complete disregard for his own pain and injuries, and his performance were far above and beyond the call of duty and were in keeping with the highest traditions of self-sacrifice and courage of the military service.

†MURRAY, ROBERT C.

Rank and Organization: Staff Sergeant, U.S. Army, Company B, 4th Battalion, 31st Infantry, 196th Infantry Brigade, 23d Infantry Division.

Born: December 10, 1946, Bronx, New York

Entered Service At: New York, New York

Place and Date: Near the village of Hiep Duc, Republic of Vietnam, June 7, 1970

Citation: S/Sgt. Murray distinguished himself while serving as a squad leader with Company B. S/Sgt. Murray's squad was searching for an enemy mortar that had been threatening friendly positions when a member of the squad tripped an enemy grenade rigged as a boobytrap. Realizing that he had activated the enemy boobytrap, the soldier shouted for everybody to take cover. Instantly assessing the danger to the men of his squad, S/Sgt. Murray unhesitatingly and with complete disregard for his own safety, threw himself on the grenade absorbing the full and fatal impact of the explosion. By his gallant action and self sacrifice, he prevented the death or injury of the other members of his squad. S/Sgt. Murray's extraordinary courage and gallantry, at the cost of his life above and beyond the call of duty, are in keeping with the highest traditions of the military service and reflect great credit on him, his unit, and the U.S. Army.

†LUCAS, ANDRE C.

Rank and Organization: Lieutenant Colonel, U.S. Army, 2d Battalion, 506th Infantry, 101st Airborne Division.
Born: October 2, 1930, Washington D.C.
Entered Service At: West Point, New York
Place and Date: Fire Support Base Ripcord, Republic of Vietnam, July 1, to 23, 1970
Citation: Lt. Col. Lucas distinguished himself by extraordinary heroism while serving as the commanding officer of the 2d Battalion. Although the fire base was constantly subjected to heavy attacks by a numerically superior enemy force throughout this period, Lt. Col. Lucas, forsaking his own safety, performed numerous acts of extraordinary valor in directing the defense of the allied position. On one occasion, he flew in a helicopter at treetop level above an entrenched enemy directing the fire of one of his companies for over three hours. Even though his helicopter was heavily damaged by enemy fire, he remained in an exposed position until the company expended its supply of grenades. he then transferred to another helicopter, dropped critically needed grenades to the troops, and resumed his perilous mission of directing fire on the enemy. These courageous actions by Lt. Col. Lucas prevented the company from being encircled and destroyed by a larger enemy force. On another occasion, Lt. Col. Lucas attempted to rescue a crewman trapped in a burning helicopter. As the flames in the aircraft spread, and enemy fire became intense, Lt. Col. Lucas ordered all members of the rescue party to safety. Then, at great personal risk, he continued the rescue effort amid concentrated enemy mortar fire, intense heat, and exploding ammunition until the aircraft was completely engulfed in flames. Lt. Col. Lucas was mortally wounded while directing the successful withdrawal of his battalion from the fire base. His actions throughout this extended period inspired his men to heroic efforts, and were instrumental in saving the lives of many of his fellow soldiers while inflicting heavy casualties on the enemy. Lt. Col. Lucas' conspicuous gallantry and intrepidity in action, at the cost of his own life, were in keeping with the highest traditions of the military service and reflect great credit on him, his unit and the U.S. Army.

†FRATELLENICO, FRANK R.

Rank and Organization: Corporal, U.S. Army, Company B, 2d Battalion, 502d Infantry, 1st Brigade, 101st Airborne Division.
Born: July 14, 1951, Sharon, Connecticut
Entered Service At: Albany, New York
Place and Date: Quang Tri Province, Republic of Vietnam, August 19, 1970
Citation: Cpl. Fratellenico distinguished himself while serving as a rifleman with Company B. Cpl. Fratellenico's squad was pinned down by intensive fire from two well fortified enemy bunkers. At great personal risk Cpl. Fratellenico maneuvered forward and, using hand grenades, neutralized the first bunker which was occupied by a number of enemy soldiers. While attacking the second bunker, enemy fire struck Cpl. Fratellenico, causing him to fall to the ground and drop a grenade which he was preparing to throw. Alert to the imminent danger to his comrades, Cpl. Fratellenico retrieved the grenade and fell upon it an instant before it exploded. His heroic actions prevented death or serious injury to four of his comrades nearby and inspired his unit which subsequently overran the enemy position. Cpl. Fratellenico's conspicuous gallantry, extraordinary heroism, and intrepidity at the cost of his life, above and beyond the call of duty, are in keeping with the highest traditions of the military service and reflect great credit on him, his unit, and the U.S. Army.

†ENGLISH, GLENN H., JR.

Rank and Organization: Staff Sergeant, U.S. Army, Company E, 3d Battalion, 503 Infantry, 173d Airborne Brigade.

Born: April 23, 1940, Altoona, Pennsylvania

Entered Service At: Philadelphia, Pennsylvania

Place and Date: Phu My District, Republic of Vietnam, September 7, 1970

Citation: S/Sgt. English was riding in the lead armored personnel carrier in a four vehicle column when an enemy mine exploded in front of his vehicle. As the vehicle swerved from the road, a concealed enemy force waiting in ambush opened fire with automatic weapons and anti-tank grenades, striking the vehicle several times and setting it on fire. S/Sgt. English escaped from the disabled vehicle and, without pausing to extinguish the flames on his clothing, rallied his stunned unit. He then led it in a vigorous assault, in the face of heavy enemy automatic weapons fire, on the entrenched enemy position. This prompt and courageous action routed the enemy and saved his unit from destruction. Following the assault, S/Sgt. English heard the cries of three men still trapped inside the vehicle. Paying no heed to warnings that the ammunition and fuel in the burning personnel carrier might explode at any moment, S/Sgt. English raced to the vehicle and climbed inside to rescue his wounded comrades. As he was lifting one of the men to safety, the vehicle exploded, mortally wounding him and the man he was attempting to save. By his extraordinary devotion to duty, indomitable courage, and utter disregard for his own safety, S/Sgt. English saved his unit from destruction and selflessly sacrificed his life in a brave attempt to save three comrades. S/Sgt. English's conspicuous gallantry and intrepidity in action at the cost of his life were an inspiration to his comrades and are in the highest traditions of the U.S. Army.

CHAPTER 8

1971

(† - Indicates Posthumous Award)

Note: The following newspaper article concerning Vietnam appeared on page 3 of *The New York Times* on January 1, 1971:

U.S. Combat Deaths Rise By 15 To 41 In Week Despite Truce

SAIGON, South Vietnam, Dec. 31 - The United States command announced today a sharp rise in American combat deaths last week despite the Christmas cease-fire.

Forty-one Americans were said to have died in action in Indochina in the week ended Saturday, compared with 26 the week before. Both the enemy and the allies had proclaimed truces over Christmas, the enemy for three days and the allies for one.

United States Army spokesmen also announced today that for the fourth week in a row the number of American soldiers who died as a result of noncombat causes exceeded the number of battle deaths. Forty-two men died of such causes as accidents, disease and drugs last week.

Since Jan. 1, 1961, which the United States command takes as the statistical beginning of American involvement in the war, 44,208 Americans are listed as having died in action, and 9,035 to noncombat causes.

†DAHL, LARRY G.

Rank and Organization: Specialist Fourth Class, U.S. Army, 359th Transportation Company, 27th Transportation Battalion, U.S. Army Support Command.

Born: October 6, 1949, Oregon City, Oregon

Entered Service At: Portland, Oregon

Place and Date: An Khe, Binh Dinh Province, Republic of Vietnam, February 23, 1971

Citation: Sp4c. Dahl distinguished himself by conspicuous gallantry and intrepidity while serving as a machine gunner on a gun truck near An Khe, Binh Dinh Province. The gun truck in which Sp4c. Dahl was riding was sent with two other gun trucks to assist in the defense of a convoy that had been ambushed by an enemy force. The gun trucks entered the battle zone and engaged the attacking enemy troops with a heavy volume of machine-gun fire, causing a large number of casualties. After a brief period of intense fighting the attack subsided. As the gun trucks were preparing to return to their normal escort duties, an enemy hand grenade was thrown into the truck in which Sp4c. Dahl was riding. Instantly realizing the great danger, Sp4c. Dahl called a warning to his companions and threw himself directly onto the grenade. Through his indomitable courage, complete disregard for his safety, and profound concern for his fellow soldiers, Sp4c. Dahl saved the lives of the other members of the truck crew while sacrificing his own. Sp4c. Dahl's conspicuous gallantry, extraordinary heroism, and intrepidity at the cost of his life, above and beyond the call of duty, are in keeping with the highest traditions of the military service and reflect great credit on himself, his unit and the U.S. Army.

FITZMAURICE, MICHAEL JOHN

Rank and Organization: Specialist Fourth Class, U.S. Army, Troop D, 2d Squadron, 17th Cavalry, 101st Airborne Division.
Born: March 9, 1950, Jamestown, North Dakota
Entered Service At: Jamestown, North Dakota
Place and Date: Khesanh, Republic of Vietnam, March 23, 1971
Citation: For conspicuous gallantry and intrepidity in action at the risk of his life above and beyond the call of duty. Sp4c. Fitzmaurice, 3d Platoon, Troop D, distinguished himself at Khesanh. Sp4c. Fitzmaurice and three fellow soldiers were occupying a bunker when a company of North Vietnamese sappers infiltrated the area. At the onset of the attack Sp4c. Fitzmaurice observed three explosive charges which had been thrown into the bunker by the enemy. Realizing the imminent danger to his comrades, and with complete disregard for his personal safety, he hurled two of the charges out of the bunker. He then threw his flak vest and himself over the remaining charge. By this courageous act he absorbed the blast and shielded his fellow soldiers. Although suffering from serious multiple wounds and partial loss of sight, he charged out of the bunker, and engaged the enemy until his rifle was damaged by the blast of an enemy hand grenade. While in search of another weapon, Sp4c. Fitzmaurice encountered and overcame an enemy sapper in hand-to-hand combat. Having obtained another weapon, he returned to his original fighting position and inflicted additional casualties on the attacking enemy. Although seriously wounded, Sp4c. Fitzmaurice refused to be medically evacuated, preferring to remain at his post. Sp4c. Fitzmaurice's extraordinary heroism in action at the risk of his life contributed significantly to the successful defense of the position and resulted in saving the lives of a number of his fellow soldiers. These acts of heroism go above and beyond the call of duty, are in keeping with the highest traditions of the military service, and reflect great credit on Sp4c. Fitzmaurice and the U.S. Army.

Note: The following is a newspaper account of the battle for which Sp4c. Fitzmaurice was awarded the Medal of Honor.

Enemy Troops Repulsed After Assault On Khesanh

SAIGON, South Vietnam, Tue. March 23 - North Vietnamese soldiers carrying satchel charges broke in to Khesanh today behind a heavy artillery barrage, but were driven out with heavy losses, the United States command said.

Reports from the field said that several helicopters had been destroyed by shells or satchel charges planted by sappers. Less than a dozen Americans were reported killed or wounded.

The report said that North Vietnamese gunners had fired 200 artillery rounds into Khesanh and about 40 sappers had attacked the major support base for the push into Laos. A spokesman said that some got inside the base and 20 were killed.

Khesanh, near the border with Laos in the northwest part of South Vietnam, has been shelled for nine consecutive days, but today's attack was the first ground assault against it since it reopened. Hundreds of United States helicopters have used it as a base for flights into Laos since the Saigon Government drive began Feb. 8.

United States field officers said the shelling came from Soviet-made 122mm guns dug in about half a mile inside Laos.

THACKER, BRIAN MILES

Rank and Organization: First Lieutenant, U.S. Army, Battery A, 1st Battalion, 92d Artillery.
Born: April 25, 1945, Columbus, Ohio
Entered Service At: Salt Lake City, Utah
Place and Date: Kontum Province, Republic of Vietnam, March 31, 1971
Citation: For conspicuous gallantry and intrepidity in action at the risk of his life above and beyond the call of duty. First Lt. Thacker, Field Artillery, Battery A, distinguished himself while serving as the team leader of an Integrated Observation System collocated with elements of two Army of the Republic of Vietnam units at Fire Base 6. A numerically superior North Vietnamese Army force launched a well planned, dawn attack on the small, isolated, hilltop fire base. Employing rockets, grenades, flamethrowers, and automatic weapons, the enemy forces penetrated the perimeter defenses and engaged the defenders in hand-to-hand combat. Throughout the morning and early afternoon, 1st. Lt. Thacker rallied and encouraged the U.S. and Republic of Vietnam soldiers in heroic efforts to repulse the enemy. He occupied a dangerously exposed observation position for a period of four hours while directing friendly air strikes and artillery fire against the assaulting enemy forces. His personal bravery and inspired leadership enabled the out-numbered friendly forces to inflict a maximum of casualties on the attacking enemy forces and prevented the base from being overrun. By late afternoon, the situation had become untenable. First Lt. Thacker organized and directed the withdrawal of the remaining friendly forces. With complete disregard for his personal safety, he remained inside the perimeter alone to provide covering fire with his M-16 rifle until all other friendly forces had escaped from the besieged fire base. Then, in an act of supreme courage, he called for friendly artillery fire on his own position to allow his comrades more time to withdraw safely from the area and, at the same time, inflict even greater casualties on the enemy forces. Although wounded and unable to escape from the area himself, he successfully eluded the enemy forces for eight days until friendly forces regained control of the fire base. The extraordinary courage and selflessness displayed by 1st. Lt. Thacker were an inspiration to his comrades and are in the highest traditions of the military service.

†ADAMS, WILLIAM E.

Rank and Organization: Major, U.S. Army, A/227th Assault Helicopter Company, 52d Aviation Battalion, 1st Aviation Brigade.
Born: June 16, 1939, Casper, Wyoming
Entered Service At: Kansas City, Missouri
Place and Date: Kontum Province, Republic of Vietnam, May 25, 1971
Citation: Maj. Adams distinguished himself on May 25, 1971, while serving as a helicopter pilot in Kontum Province in the Republic of Vietnam. On that date, Maj. Adams volunteered to fly a lightly armed helicopter in an attempt to evacuate three seriously wounded soldiers from a small fire base which was under attack by a large enemy force. He made the decision with full knowledge that numerous anti-aircraft weapons were positioned around the base and that the clear weather would afford the enemy gunners unobstructed view of all routes into the base. As he approached the base, the enemy gunners opened fire with heavy machine-guns, rocket-propelled grenades and small arms. Undaunted by the fusillade, he continued his approach determined to accomplish the mission. Displaying tremendous courage under fire, he calmly directed the attacks of supporting gunships while maintaining absolute control of the helicopter he was flying. He landed the aircraft at the fire base despite the ever increasing enemy fire and calmly waited until the wounded soldiers were placed on board. As his aircraft departed from the fire base, it was struck and seriously damaged by enemy anti-aircraft fire and began descending. Flying with exceptional skill, he immediately regained control of the crippled aircraft and attempted a controlled landing. Despite his valiant efforts, the helicopter exploded, overturned, and plummeted to earth amid the hail of enemy fire. Maj. Adams' conspicuous gallantry, intrepidity, and humanitarian regard for his fellow man were in keeping with the most cherished traditions of the military service and reflect utmost credit on him and the U.S. Army.

CAVAIANI, JON R.

Rank and Organization: Staff Sergeant, U.S. Army, Vietnam Training Advisory Group, Republic of Vietnam.
Born: August 2, 1943, Royston, England
Entered Service At: Fresno, California
Place and Date: Republic of Vietnam, June 4, and 5, 1971 *✗ not June 6—July 9*
Citation: S/Sgt. Cavaiani distinguished himself by conspicuous gallantry and intrepidity at the risk of his life above and beyond the call of duty in action in the Republic of Vietnam on June 4, and 5, 1971, while serving as a platoon leader to a security platoon providing security for an isolated radio relay site located within enemy held territory. On the morning of June 4, 1971, the entire camp came under an intense barrage of enemy small arms, automatic weapons, rocket propelled grenade and mortar fire from a superior size enemy force. S/Sgt. Cavaiani acted with complete disregard for his personal safety as he repeatedly exposed himself to heavy enemy fire in order to move about the camp's perimeter directing the platoon's fire and rallying the platoon in a desperate fight for survival. S/Sgt. Cavaiani also returned heavy suppressive fire upon the assaulting enemy force during this period with a variety of weapons. When the entire platoon was to be evacuated, S/Sgt. Cavaiani unhesitatingly volunteered to remain on the ground and direct the helicopters into the landing zone. S/Sgt. Cavaiani was able to direct the first three helicopters in evacuating a major portion of the platoon. Due to intense increase in enemy fire, S/Sgt. Cavaiani was forced to remain at the camp overnight where he calmly directed the remaining platoon members in strengthening their defenses. On the morning of June 5, a heavy ground fog restricted visibility. The superior size enemy force launched a major ground attack in an attempt to completely annihilate the remaining small force. The enemy force advanced in two ranks, first firing a heavy volume of small arms automatic weapons and rocket propelled grenade fire while the second rank continuously threw a steady barrage of hand grenades at the beleaguered force. S/Sgt. Cavaiani returned a heavy barrage of small arms and hand grenade fire on the assaulting enemy force but was unable to slow them down. He ordered the remaining platoon members to attempt to escape while he provided them with cover fire. With one last courageous exertion, S/Sgt. Cavaiani recovered a machine-gun, stood up,

completely exposing himself to the heavy enemy fire directed at him, and began firing the machine-gun in a sweeping motion along the two ranks of advancing enemy soldiers. Through S/Sgt. Cavaiani's valiant efforts with complete disregard for his safety, the majority of the remaining platoon members were able to escape. While inflicting severe losses on the advancing enemy force, S/Sgt. Cavaiani was wounded numerous times. S/Sgt. Cavaiani's conspicuous gallantry, extraordinary heroism and intrepidity at the risk of his life, above and beyond the call of duty, were in keeping with the highest traditions of the military service and reflect great credit upon himself and the U.S. Army.

†HAGEN, LOREN D.

Rank and Organization: First Lieutenant, U.S. Army, Infantry, U.S. Army Training Advisory Group.
Born: February 25, 1946, Fargo, North Dakota
Entered Service At: Fargo, North Dakota
Place and Date: Republic of Vietnam, August 7, 1971
Citation: First Lt. Hagen distinguished himself in action while serving as the team leader of a small reconnaissance team operating deep within enemy held territory. At approximately 0630 hours on the morning of August 7, 1971, the small team came under a fierce assault by a superior sized enemy force using heavy small arms, automatic weapons, mortar, and rocket fire. First Lt. Hagen immediately began returning small arms fire upon the attackers and successfully led this team in repelling the first enemy onslaught. he then quickly deployed his men into more strategic defense locations before the enemy struck again in an attempt to overrun and annihilate the beleaguered team's members. Firs Lt. Hagen repeatedly exposed himself to the enemy fire directed at him as he constantly moved about the team's perimeter, directing fire, rallying the members, and resupplying the team with ammunition, while courageously returning small arms and hand grenade fire in a valorous attempt to repel the advancing enemy force. The courageous actions and expert leadership abilities of 1st Lt. Hagen were a great source of inspiration and instilled confidence in the team members. After observing an enemy rocket make a direct hit on and destroy one of the team's bunkers, 1st Lt. Hagen moved toward the wrecked bunker in search for team members despite the fact that the enemy force now controlled the bunker area. With total disregard for his own personal safety, he crawled through the enemy fire while returning small arms fire upon the enemy force. Undaunted by the enemy rockets and grenades impacting all around him, 1st Lt. Hagen desperately advanced upon the destroyed bunker until he was fatally wounded by enemy small arms and automatic weapons fire. With complete disregard for his personal safety, 1st Lt. Hagen's courageous gallantry, extraordinary heroism, and intrepidity above and beyond the call of duty, at the cost of his own life, were in keeping with the highest traditions of the military service and reflect great credit upon him and the U.S. Army.

CHAPTER 9
1972

(† - Indicates Posthumous Award)

Note; The following newspaper article concerning Vietnam appeared on the front page of *The New York Times* on January 1, 1972:

Saigon Charges Truce Violations

SAIGON, South Vietnam, Jan. 1 - The Saigon military command said today that the New Year's cease-fire in South Vietnam had been shattered by a score of Viet Cong attacks that killed nine South Vietnamese and wounded 20.

A Communique from the South Vietnamese headquarters said that there had been 20 "enemy-initiated incidents" since the start of the 72-hour Viet Cong cease-fire at 1 A.M. yesterday. A 24-hour allied cease-fire began at 6 P.M. yesterday.

The Saigon command said that 16 enemy soldiers had been killed.

The United States command reported one attack against American forces on New Year's Eve. Nine mortar rounds were fired at a United States convoy en route from Danang to Hue, but they caused no casualties or damage the command said.

Meanwhile, B-52 bombers and scores of smaller planes flew over Laos and Cambodia to attack North Vietnamese supply routes. United States reconnaissance jets swept over North Vietnam to assess damage caused by five successive days of bombing there that ended Thursday.

The raids on the north, the longest, heaviest and deepest in more than three years, destroyed 11 air defense sites, according to the American command's preliminary reports.

Preliminary official reports indicated that United States planes had encountered at least 30 surface-to-air missiles and one MIG interceptor. Other reports suggested that the number of SAM's had been considerably higher than 30.

Two of three American jets lost were navy planes downed by SAMs Thursday, a United States command spokesman said. An Air Force jet was lost Sunday, reportedly from unknown causes.

The United States command reported that one of the six downed crewmen had been rescued, and it listed five others as missing. The Hanoi radio has named one Air Force crew and has said two Americans were killed. The North Vietnamese have also claimed to have captured two of the Navy fliers.

The United States command reported that on Thursday the Viet Cong attacked an armored personnel carrier 20 miles northeast of Saigon, wounding four Americans.

The crews of rocket-firing United States helicopters reported killing five North Vietnamese soldiers and destroying a truck in a convoy moving from Laos into northwestern Ashau Valley in South Vietnam.

A search was underway in northwestern Laos for a United States Central Intelligence Agency supply plane, missing since Monday with three Americans and one Laotian aboard.

A source at Air America, a United States-supported airline, there was "a very remote possibility" that the plane, a C-123, had been shot down by Chinese antiaircraft fire.

The plane was reported headed from Vientiane to western Sayaboury Province near the Thai border where guerrillas backed by the C.I.A. are operating.

Just north of the province is the terminus of a road that the Chinese are building out of Yunan Province in China to the Mekong River in Laos. The Chinese forbid anyone approaching the road by air to get closer than 25 miles and have stationed antiaircraft guns along it.

NORRIS, THOMAS R.

Rank and Organization: Lieutenant, U.S. Navy, SEAL Advisor, Strategic Technical Directorate Assistance Team, Headquarters, U.S. Military Assistance Command.
Born: January 14, 1944, Jacksonville, Florida
Entered Service At: Silver Spring, Maryland
Place and Date: Quang Tri Province, Republic of Vietnam, April 10, to 13, 1972
Citation: Lt. Norris completed an unprecedented ground rescue of two downed pilots deep within heavily controlled enemy territory in Quang Tri Province. Lt. Norris, on the night of April 10, led a five man patrol through 2,000 meters of heavily controlled enemy territory, located one of the downed pilots at daybreak, and returned to the Forward Operating Base (FOB). On April 11, after a devastating mortar and rocket attack on the small FOB, Lt. Norris led a three man team on two unsuccessful rescue attempts for the second pilot. On the afternoon of the 12th, a forward air controller located the pilot and notified Lt. Norris. Dressed in fishermen disguises and using a sampan, Lt. Norris and one Vietnamese traveled throughout that night and found the injured pilot at dawn. Covering the pilot with bamboo and vegetation, they began the return journey, successfully evading a North Vietnamese patrol. Approaching the FOB, they came under heavy machine-gun fire. Lt. Norris called in an air strike which provided suppression fire and a smokescreen, allowing the rescue party to reach the FOB. By his outstanding display of decisive leadership, undaunted courage, and selfless dedication in the face of extreme danger, Lt. Norris enhanced the finest traditions of the U.S. Naval Service.

†BENNETT, STEVEN L.

Rank and Organization: Captain, U.S. Air Force, 20th Tactical Air Support Squadron, Pacific Air Forces.
Born: April 22, 1946, Palestine, Texas
Entered Service At: Lafayette, Louisiana
Place and Date: Quang Tri, Republic of Vietnam, June 19, 1972
Citation: Capt. Bennett was the pilot of a light aircraft flying an artillery adjustment mission along a heavily defended segment of route structure. A large concentration of enemy troops was massing for an attack on a friendly unit. Capt. Bennett requested tactical air support but was advised that none was available. He also requested artillery support but this too was denied due to the close proximity of friendly troops to the target. Capt. Bennett was determined to aid the endangered unit and elected to strafe the hostile positions. After four such passes, the enemy force began to retreat. Capt. Bennett continued the attack, but, as he completed his fifth strafing pass, his aircraft was struck by a surface-to-air missile, which severely damaged the left engine and the left main landing gear. As fire spread in the left engine, Capt. Bennett realized that recovery at a friendly airfield was impossible. He instructed his observer to prepare for an ejection, but was informed by the observer that his parachute had been shredded by the force of the impacting missile. Although Capt. Bennett had a good parachute, he knew that if he ejected, the observer would have no chance of survival. With complete disregard for his own life, Capt. Bennett elected to ditch the aircraft into the Gulf of Tonkin, even though he realized that a pilot of this type aircraft had never survived a ditching. The ensuing impact upon the water caused the aircraft to cartwheel and severely damaged the front cockpit, making escape for Capt. Bennett impossible. The observer successfully made his way out of the aircraft and was rescued. Capt. Bennett's unparalleled concern for his companion, extraordinary heroism and intrepidity above and beyond the call of duty, at the cost of his life, were in keeping with the highest traditions of the military service and reflect great credit upon himself and the U.S. Air Force.

THORNTON, MICHAEL EDWIN

Rank and Organization: Petty Officer, U.S. Navy, Navy Advisory Group.

Born: March 23, 1949, Greenville, South Carolina

Entered Service At: Spartanburg, South Carolina

Place and Date: Republic of Vietnam, October 31, 1972

Citation: For conspicuous gallantry and intrepidity at the risk of his life above and beyond the call of duty while participating in a daring operation against enemy forces. PO Thornton, as Assistant U.S. Navy Advisor, along with a U.S. Navy Lieutenant serving a Senior Advisor, accompanied a three man Vietnamese Navy SEAL patrol on an intelligence gathering and prisoner capture operation against an enemy occupied naval river base. Launched from a Vietnamese Navy junk in a rubber boat, the patrol reached land and was continuing on foot toward its objective when it suddenly came under heavy fire from a numerically superior force. The patrol called in naval gunfire support and then engaged the enemy in a fierce firefight, accounting for many enemy casualties before moving back to the waterline to prevent encirclement. Upon learning that the Senior Advisor had been hit by enemy fire and was believed to be dead, PO Thornton returned through a hail of fire to the lieutenant's last position; quickly disposed of two enemy soldiers about to overrun the position, and succeeded in removing the seriously wounded and unconscious Senior Naval Advisor to the water's edge. He then inflated the lieutenant's lifejacket and towed him seaward for approximately two hours until picked up by support craft. By his extraordinary courage and perseverance, PO Thornton was directly responsible for saving the life of his superior officer and enabling the safe extraction of all patrol members, thereby upholding the highest traditions of the U.S. Naval Service.

Note: The Navy Lt. that Petty Officer Thornton saved was Lt. Norris who also was awarded the Medal of Honor for a previous action.

SUMMARY

p. 4 – "Bibliography"

Medals of Honor By Service

Army	155
Navy	15
Marines	57
Air Force	12

151 Medals of Honor were awarded posthumously

It was a genuine pleasure, and I might add quite emotional at times, reading the citations of these men, but there are no words that could adequately describe these 239 individuals' heroism; their actions speak for themselves.

It would also be impossible to put into words the courage that it took for the millions of men and women to go to Vietnam, so I'll just close by saying that I'm very proud of all of you, I salute you and something that should have been said many years ago, **Thank You**.

INDEX

Adams, William E., 339
Albanese, Lewis, 69
Anderson, James Jr., 80
Anderson, Richard A., 294
Anderson, Webster, 127
Ashley, Eugene, Jr., 167
Austin, Oscar P., 256

Baca, John P., 313
Bacon, Nicky Daniel, 223
Baker, John F., Jr., 60
Ballard, Donald E., 202
Barker, Jedh Colby, 123
Barnes, John Andrew III, 135
Barnum, Harvey C., Jr., 32
Beikirch, Gary B., 316
Belcher, Ted, 68
Bellrichard, Leslie Allen, 107
Benavidez, Roy P., 191
Bennett, Steven L., 346
Bennett, Thomas W., 247
Blanchfield, Michael R., 287
Bobo, John P., 93
Bondsteel, James Leroy, 281
Bowen, Hammett L., Jr., 286
Brady, Patrick Henry, 149
Bruce, Daniel D., 264
Bryant, William Maud, 275
Bucha, Paul William, 179
Buker, Brian L., 323
Burke, Robert C., 205

Capodanno, Vincent R., 119
Caron, Wayne Maurice, 214
Carter, Bruce W., 292
Cavaiani, Jon R., 340
Clausen, Raymond M., 309
Coker, Ronald L., 277

Connor, Peter S., 38
Cook, Donald Gilbert, 12
Creek, Thomas E., 250
Crescenz, Michael J., 230
Cutinha, Nicholas J., 176

Dahl, Larry G., 335
Davis, Rodney Maxwell, 122
Davis, Sammy L., 138
Day, George E., 118
De La Garza, Emilio Jr., 324
Dethlefsen, Merlyn H., 83
DeVore, Edward A., Jr., 181
Dias, Ralph E., 300
Dickey, Douglas E., 92
Dix, Drew Dennis, 159
Doane, Stephen Holden, 278
Dolby, David Charles, 44
Donlon, Roger Hugh C., 10
Dunagan, Kern W., 279
Durham, Harold Bascom, Jr., 128

English, Glenn H., Jr., 333
Estocin, Michael J., 97
Evans, Donald W., Jr., 73
Evans, Rodney J., 291

Ferguson, Frederick Edgar, 158
Fernandez, Daniel, 37
Fisher, Bernard Francis, 40
Fitzmaurice, Michael John, 336
Fleek, Charles Clinton, 109
Fleming, James P., 231
Foley, Robert F., 61
Folland, Michael Fleming, 288
Foster, Paul Hellstrom, 125
Fournet, Douglas B., 194
Fous, James W., 200

Fox, Wesley L., 253
Fratellenico, Frank R., 332
Fritz, Harold A., 241

Gardner, James A., 35
Gertsch, John G., 290
Gonzalez, Alfredo, 161
Graham, James A., 110
Grandstaff, Bruce Alan, 104
Grant, Joseph Xavier, 66
Graves, Terrence C., 170
Guenette, Peter M., 206

Hagemeister, Charles C., 86
Hagen, Loren D., 342
Hartsock, Robert W., 257
Harvey, Carmel B., Jr., 112
Herda, Frank A., 213
Hibbs, Robert John, 39
Holcomb, John Nobel, 232
Hooper, Joe R., 173
Hosking, Charles E., Jr., 87
Howard, Jimmie E., 46
Howard, Robert L., 237
Howe, James D., 325

Ingalls, George Alan, 95

Jackson, Joe M., 197
Jacobs, Jack H., 178
Jenkins, Don J., 240
Jenkins, Robert H., Jr., 268
Jennings, Delbert O., 70
Jimenez, Jose Francisco, 295
Joel, Lawrence, 27
Johnson, Dwight H., 155
Johnson, Ralph H., 177
Johnston, Donald R., 273
Jones, William A., III, 224

Karopczyc, Stephen Edward, 84
Kawamura, Terry Teruo, 272
Kays, Kenneth Michael, 326
Kedenburg, John J., 208
Keith, Miguel, 327
Keller, Leonard B., 101

Kelley, Thomas G., 285
Kellogg, Allan Jay, Jr., 314
Kerrey, Joseph R., 269
Kinsman, Thomas James, 169

Lambers, Paul Ronald, 216
Lang, George C., 254
Langhorn, Garfield M., 245
LaPointe, Joseph G., Jr., 283
Lassen, Clyde Everett, 210
Lauffer, Billy Lane, 57
Law, Robert D., 255
Lee, Howard V., 56
Lee, Milton A., 186
Leisy, Robert Ronald, 302
Lemon, Peter C., 317
Leonard, Matthew, 81
Levitow, John L., 260
Liteky, Angelo J., 143
Littrell, Gary Lee, 320
Livingston, James E., 193
Long, Donald Russell, 51
Lozada, Carlos James, 141
Lucas, Andre C., 331
Lynch, Allen James, 145

Marm, Walter Joseph, Jr., 29
Martini, Gary W., 98
Maxam, Larry Leonard, 160
McCleery, Finnis D., 199
McDonald, Phill G., 207
McGinty, John J. III, 54
McGonagle, William L., 111
McKibben, Ray, 233
McMahon, Thomas J., 270
McNerney, David H., 88
McWethy, Edgar Lee, Jr., 113
Michael, Don Leslie, 94
Miller, Franklin D., 305
Miller, Gary L., 252
Modrzejewski, Robert J., 52
Molnar, Frankie Zoly, 108
Monroe, James H., 76
Morgan, William D., 261
Morris, Charles B., 49
Murray, Robert C., 330

Nash, David P., 236
Newlin, Melvin Earl, 115
Noonan, Thomas P., Jr., 246
Norris, Thomas R., 345
Novosel, Michael J., 299

Olive, Milton L. III, 26
Olson, Kenneth L., 198
O'Malley, Robert E., 20
Ouellet, David G., 82

Patterson, Robert Martin, 196
Paul, Joe C., 21
Penry, Richard A., 310
Perkins, William Thomas, Jr., 124
Peters, Lawrence David, 120
Petersen, Danny J., 307
Phipps, Jimmy W., 282
Pierce, Larry S., 25
Pittman, Richard A., 55
Pitts, Riley L., 129
Pless, Stephen W., 117
Port, William D., 154
Poxon, Robert Leslie, 284
Prom, William R., 249
Pruden, Robert J., 301

Rabel, Laszlo, 229
Ray, David Robert, 271
Ray, Ronald Eric, 48
Reasoner, Frank S., 19
Roark, Anund C., 203
Roberts, Gordon R., 289
Robinson, James W., Jr., 41
Rocco, Louis R., 329
Rogers, Charles Calvin, 227
Rubio, Euripides, 63

Santiago-Colon, Hector, 211
Sargent, Ruppert L., 85
Sasser, Clarence Eugene, 153
Seay, William W., 221
Shea, Daniel John, 280
Shields, Marvin G., 17
Sijan, Lance P., 132
Sims, Clifford Chester, 175

Singleton, Walter K., 91
Sisler, George K., 74
Skidgel, Donald Sidney, 298
Smedley, Larry E., 146
Smith Elmelindo R., 77
Sprayberry, James M., 184
Steindam, Russell A., 312
Stewart, Jimmy G., 43
Stockdale, James B., 297
Stone, Lester R., Jr., 265
Stout, Mitchell W., 315
Stryker, Robert F., 130
Stumpf, Kenneth E., 100

Taylor, James Allen, 133
Taylor, Karl G., Sr., 235
Thacker, Brian Miles, 338
Thornton, Michael Edwin, 347
Thorsness, Leo K., 96

Vargas, M. Sando, Jr., 188

Warren, John E., Jr., 243
Watters, Charles Joseph, 140
Wayrynen, Dale Eugene, 106
Weber, Lester W., 259
Wetzel, Gary George, 152
Wheat, Roy M., 116
Wickam, Jerry Wayne, 151
Wilbanks, Hilliard A., 78
Willett, Louis E., 75
Williams, Charles Q., 15
Williams, Dewayne T., 226
Williams, James E., 58
Wilson, Alfred M., 266
Winder, David F., 328
Worley, Kenneth L., 215
Wright, Raymond R., 102

Yabes, Maximo, 79
Yano, Rodney J.T., 239
Yntema, Gordon Douglas, 157
Young, Gerald O., 134
Young, Marvin R., 218

Zabitosky, Fred William, 172